JAGUAR

The definitive history
of a great British car

1980 winner of
The Guild of Motoring Writers' Montagu Trophy
for the year's best example of
'historical writing and research' in the motoring field

JAG

The history o

Andrev

Foreword by S

 Patrick Stephens, Wellingborough

Title pages *The Newcomers: First effort as a works team—*
baptism of fire for the virtually-untried SS1 tourer in the 1933
Alpine Trial. The three factory-loaned cars were painted red,
white and blue. Seen here is the most successful of them, the
white car of Charles Needham. Its eighth in class hardly fore-
told the marque's great success in this tough event, only three
years later, to mark the start of the great Jaguar sports-car era.
(This picture was painted by former Daimler apprentice
draughtsman and SS user, F. Gordon Crosby, an all-time great
among motoring artists).

First published October 1980
Reprinted October 1981
Reprinted November 1981
Reprinted March 1982
Second edition June 1985
Reprinted August 1985
Reprinted May 1986

British Library Cataloguing in Publication Data

Whyte, Andrew
    Jaguar: the history of a great British car.
    —2nd ed.
    1. Jaguar Cars Ltd.—History
    I. Title
    338.7′6292′0941   HD9710.G74J3

ISBN 0-85059-746-3

Patrick Stephens Limited is part of the
Thorsons Publishing Group.

Text Photoset in 10 on 11 Plantin by Manuset Limited,
Baldock, Herts. Printed in Great Britain on 115 gsm
Clandon Matt coated cartridge, and bound, by The Garden
City Press, Letchworth, Herts, for the publishers Patrick
Stephens Limited, Denington Estate, Wellingborough,
Northants, NN8 2QD, England.

Contents

Above *Sir William Lyons, Chairman and Managing Director of Jaguar Cars Ltd until 1972, photographed for* The Autocar *at the Swallow Road works in 1948, at the start of the first export drive. (He was knighted in 1956.)* **Below** *John Egan, Chairman and Managing Director of Jaguar since spring 1985, who led the company back to independence in 1984—a year of record production and sales.*

Foreword by Sir William Lyons

RDI, D Tech, FRSA, Hon FI Mech E
Honorary President, Jaguar plc

It is not very often that I am persuaded to write forewords for books, but this author has been persuasive. In any case, and much as it always pleases me to think there is something new to be written on the subject, I was beginning to feel that there could hardly be a place for yet another book on Jaguar. There are so many already, and I consider some of them to be excellent.

Then I realised, everything that has been written so far has tended to concentrate upon the motor cars themselves, and their achievements. With a few notable exceptions, the people of the company are generally unknown. I am glad that the author of this book is someone who spent more than 20 years with my company, and came to know many of the people he writes about. Although he has left Jaguar to become a full-time author and journalist, I know he still takes an active part in various projects related to the continuity of the *marque* name we created back in 1935—a name more a part of the English language now, it seems, than that of the graceful animal which helped to inspire it.

As well as combining the people with the events of Jaguar's history, Andrew Whyte has made the first serious attempt at piecing together the very earliest days, before SS or Jaguar, when we were making Swallow sidecars and special coachwork for Austin and Morris motor cars. We did not look upon our activities as being history-making at the time, and I believe that most of the old printed material and other non-essential items were left to be scrapped when we took the plunge and left Blackpool for Coventry in 1928.

Until just before we introduced the first Jaguars, the business was a partnership. I must admit that I never found it particularly easy to work with someone else, for we had very different views about how the business should be run!

Making a success of a business venture—*that* was my original aim in life. Jaguar has been an *ad*venture too, and I have derived a great deal of pleasure from my work. The product itself has always been designed to give its owner pleasure; I heard a story of one owner who found the most peaceful way of gathering his thoughts and taking important decisions was to go out and sit in the cockpit of his Jaguar, without even having to drive it! I think that was one of the nicest compliments. The pleasure of living with a Jaguar car is, I know, rather different from the pleasure of working *for* Jaguar—the Company. Times have changed, but I still see each of these states continuing to provide contentment for many people.

If today's Jaguar people can continue to put in the effort and generate the enthusiasm that my colleagues did on my behalf, the name 'Jaguar' can go on being 'British and proud of it' indefinitely.

Foreword to the second edition

Nearly five years have passed since I wrote the foreword to the first edition of this definitive history of Jaguar. The hopes I expressed in my last paragraph then, which I wrote in the spring of 1980 just after John Egan's appointment, have been fulfilled. The effort *has* been put in; the enthusiasm *has* been generated.

In the 1985 Jaguars I see the development of just the sort of motor car I would have wished to develop myself. I have been only too pleased to provide advice and comment to today's Jaguar management and stylists and engineers, but hasten to place the credit with them—for the cars are their work entirely.

Progress never happens automatically. It must be earned. Jaguar is earning its return to the forefront of the industry; and, with vigilance and dedication from all concerned, it will surely maintain its position at the top.

I'm very proud of the whole Jaguar team. It's so rewarding to see one's life's work being continued by others so vigorously. I wish John Egan and his directors, and everyone involved, every success in their further endeavours. This wish includes the loyal and enthusiastic customer, who makes all business possible in the first place.

W Lyons

Author's note—Sir William Lyons, September 4 1901—February 8 1985: *Soon after his new Foreword was written (and as this edition was about to be printed) Sir William died peacefully at Wappenbury Hall, in Warwickshire, his home for close on half a century. When I spoke to him for the last time in January he was very much 'on form', wanting quick answers to his questions—as always—and expressing his satisfaction that, at last, his own record for a year's deliveries of new cars had been exceeded. Taken for the* Coventry Evening Telegraph, *this picture captures the relaxed mood of Jaguar's founder and Honorary President on August 3 1984, the opening day for the sale of shares in the new Jaguar company. A service of thanksgiving for the life of Sir William Lyons was to be held in St Michael's Cathedral, Coventry, on February 27 1985. One era of Jaguar was over. Another had begun.* **AW, 2/85.**

Preface

When, a long time ago, I decided to write this book I thought that the research would stop at a certain point, then the writing would begin—and that would be that. Since then, not only have other Jaguar books been published but I have made the pretty obvious discovery that there is *no* natural ending to any research. The simplest artificial one is The Time Limit. The deeper one delves, the more one tries to 'stretch' time and the more difficult it becomes to edit-out hard-won snippets of information. I must therefore express gratitude to my publishers who have co-operated so readily in letting me present the story very much in the way I wanted, yet making sure it remained a single volume of reasonable proportions.

The encouragement I have had, particularly from past and present Jaguar people, has been tremendous and I am only sorry that space is far too scarce for everyone to be mentioned. My unbounded thanks go to Sir William and Lady Lyons for the many hours they spent re-living the Swallow, SS and Jaguar days, sorting-out photographs, and reading the manuscript of Part One. In addition, I am especially grateful to Sir William for the Foreword. Bill Heynes, Harry Teather and their wives likewise provided the kind of help without which this book simply would not carry authenticity. They gave me the true feeling of what it was like to work for the company before I joined it, and read and commented upon many of the chapters.

Other former Jaguar directors went out of their way to provide anecdotes to add to our many conversations, particularly Jack Beardsley, Walter Hassan, my sometime chief F.R.W. 'Lofty' England, Harry Mundy, Alan Newsome, John Silver, and Arthur Thurstans. The research facilities provided by MD Bob Knight, now retired, technical chief Jim Randle and their staffs are greatly appreciated; the same goes for Mike Beasley (manufacturing) and Neville Neal (service and market supply) whose records have been most useful in compiling the tables. In referring to works assistance, Eric Barnes, Alan Hodge and their colleagues must receive special mention, as must chief photographer Roger Clinkscales. As well as Jaguar's, the photographic departments of Canley, Cowley and Longbridge could not have been more helpful. Elsewhere in BL, Bob Berry (who became involved specifically with Jaguar once again in 1980), John Morgan in Japan, Michel Cognet in France, Hans Reif in Switzerland, and John Dugdale and Fred Horner in the USA have contributed useful background material. Fred was secretary of the association of North American Jaguar clubs; so many members of these and other Jaguar and Daimler clubs worldwide have encouraged and helped me that my gratitude to them all must be collective. I have to single-out David Harvey and Paul Skilleter in the UK, however. There cannot be two more dedicated Jaguar enthusiasts. Paul went out of his way to help me trace photographs; Michael Sedgwick, researcher of the original definitive Jaguar history, was similarly generous—although even *he* was stumped in the search for a real live FIAT-Swallow! Bob Currie was my excellent guide on motorcycling matters.

Miss Nancy Fenton and Mrs Mary Whittaker found splendid photographs for me, as did Mrs Winnifred Walmsley who kindly met me in Blackpool. There, I was also fortunate enough to meet W.H. Axon, F. Glover, George Kellie, Fred Pryar, W.H. Scott and others who recalled, or were employed at, Swallow. Harry Teather's conducted tour of the various Swallow premises, all of which are still standing, was a highlight of that trip, and I am grateful to the various proprietors, especially Mr Ismail Gibrail, for letting us explore. Thanks are due to Wilfred Webb and Owen Ashmore for similar assistance when I went to Stockport. Additional material from Mrs W. Bransby, Sidney Robbins and Mr and Mrs Norman Robbins helped me greatly. At Henlys, Gordon Chandler and Maurice Bayliss gave up much of their time to read and comment, while Norman Redfern (formerly of Parkers of Bolton), Mrs G.R. Hughes and Ken Rawlings of P.J. Evans Ltd, James and Sally Ritchie (Ritchies of Glasgow), Ian Appleyard of Leeds and Ole Sommer of Copenhagen are just a few of the other members of the motor trade who aided me.

The conversations I have had with Harry Adey, Ted Brookes, Bob Blake, Ron Beaty, Jack Cox, Trevor Crisp, 'Jock' Blain, George Buck, Tony Cartwright, Wilf Chamberlain, Keith Cambage, Tony Cochrane, Norman Dewis, Ted Gough, George Hind, Digby Larque, George Lee, Percy Leeson, Bill Norbury, Jack Randle, Wal Turner, Phil Weaver, John and Les Witherall and many more have been of great value. I was delighted to track down Harry Gill and Cyril Holland, two of the absolutely key men of Swallow days, and they were kind enough to supply photographs—as were Lyndon Smith and Rex Huckvale. I was fortunate to obtain the services of one of my own contemporaries, Tim Loakes, who prepared two excellent illustrations and here I must give due acknowledgment to other suppliers of pictures, especially to Michael Bowler, Tony Curtis, and Ray Hutton, respective editors of *Thoroughbred and Classic Cars, Motor,* and *Autocar,* where Warren Allport unearthed hidden treasure.

I also thank the many people at the *Blackpool Gazette,* the *Coventry Evening Telegraph,* the *Stockport Express,* the *Palm Beach Post,* and *Daily Express* and other publications for seeking-out important 'quotes' from the past. Bill Boddy (who first suggested I write a book), Robert Braunschweig, Paul Frère, Guy Griffiths, and Cyril Posthumus (my earlier 'boss' at *Motoring News*) all gave me inspiration at times when the project seemed least likely to get 'off the ground'. When it finally did so, my own family showed great patience and restraint and, of course, I thank them most of all.

Andrew Whyte
Ettington, June 1980

Author's note for the 1985 edition

In 1975 the Ryder Report brought an end to Lord Stokes' dreams for BL. That report spelled doom for many individual parts of British Leyland, and nearly did so for Jaguar. The immediate danger had been averted just before the 1980 edition of this book was published. Now, five years on, Jaguar has achieved its independence in a dramatic fashion, and (having seen a dream of my own fulfilled) I have had to be very careful not to get too eulogistic in bringing the story up to date. After all, the story of 'Jaguar Reborn' is only just beginning.

Particular thanks are due to John Egan and the 1985 Jaguar Cars Ltd board, each member of which took the time and trouble to co-operate with me in bringing the story up to date, thereby deviating from his task of making further Jaguar history. Special gratitude is owed to the Jaguar Cars Inc team in Leonia, New Jersey—notably Graham Whitehead, Michael Dale (Vice-President, sales and service), and press chief Michael Cook. Among

Jaguar Cars Ltd Board of Directors, 1985; John Egan MSc(Econ), BSc, aged 45, Chairman since 1980, flanked by Graham Whitehead, CBE (nearest camera), 56, President of Jaguar Cars Inc and Chairman of Jaguar Canada Inc; and Michael Beasley, C Eng, MI Prod E, 42, Manufacturing Director (seated left). Behind them, from left to right, are David Boole, 38, Communications & Public Affairs; James Randle, C Eng, FI Mech E, 47, Product Engineering; Neil Johnson, FIMI, MI Mktg, 36, Sales & Marketing; David Fielden, 47, Product Quality; John Edwards BSc, FCMA, 36, Group Finance; Patrick Audrain, 44, Purchasing; and Kenneth Edwards, C Eng, FI Prod E, MI Mech E, 60, Personnel Director & Company Secretary. The Jaguar plc Board as at spring 1985 consisted of John Egan as Chairman with Michael Beasley, John and Ken Edwards and Graham Whitehead plus (non-executive directors) Edward Bond, Raymond Horrocks and Hamish Orr-Ewing.

many UK Jaguar people to have provided help for the second edition were Richard Chillingsworth for production/despatch statistics, and Roger Clinkscales, Michael Cann, and James Callaghan of the photographic unit—plus, naturally, a good proportion of those who helped before.

Since writing the original foreword, I have lost some good friends and colleagues without whose presence this history of a great British car would not have been comprehensive. Cyril Holland, the man who created the first Swallow bodies and who undoubtedly saved the company in 1929, died in 1983 at a ripe old age; he no longer felt bitter towards the company, and many Jaguar enthusiasts had the pleasure of sharing his enthusiasm for the marque in the last few years of his life. Sadly, too, Harry Teather died last year after barely a decade of retirement, much of it spent in ill-health. More than anyone, he and his widow Connie put the Blackpool and early Coventry days into perspective for me.

Most untimely of all was the sudden death of Michael Sedgwick at his typewriter in 1983. Of all motoring historians he was the best—and the readiest to share his knowledge. He did the first-ever serious research on Jaguar, and he should be credited with that.

Andrew Whyte

Above *Photographed in London's West End, on return from yet another Alpine Rally victory for Jaguar, is William Lyons' second great sporting masterpiece, the XK 120. Sir William's daughter Pat (then Mrs Ian Appleyard), her husband's regular co-driver, is seen with him and their famous and battle-scarred car in 1950.* **Below** *William Lyons' first high-performance two-seater—the SS Jaguar 100, announced in autumn 1935. This picture of the famous works car (which later raced at Brooklands) was taken by Tommy Wisdom in an idyllic French setting. He was en route with his wife 'Bill' (Elsie) to take part in the 1936 Alpine Trial, in which they would make the best performance overall.*

PART 1, THE PEOPLE

1: Le Mans landmark

It was midnight. William Lyons and his men listened carefully each time the familiar drone rose to a crescendo, burst past them, and receded—giving way once again to the *musette* sounds of the fairground behind them. To anyone looking-in on the situation at quarter-distance in the 1951 Le Mans 24-hour race, everything looked set for a British victory at last; yet William Lyons was less than happy, as he peered out through the darkness from the pit-counter. In the first 50 laps, from four o'clock in the afternoon, he had watched his brand new Jaguar XK 120C models build-up a solid 1-2-3 formation in the world's most famous motor race, looking impregnable despite strong competition. This was a new experience for the 49-year old Lancastrian; on the other hand it was no more than he had expected of his embryo team. Then the craggy Italian veteran, Clemente Biondetti—four times a Mille Miglia winner, twice the Targa Florio—had brought in Car No 23, pointed to the oil-pressure gauge, and raised his palms in resignation. The gauge had been found to work and there was plenty of oil in the sump. Now Jaguar's technical chief, Bill Heynes, and his engine test king, Jack Emerson, were in solemn conclave, while racing manager 'Lofty' England kept a tighter-than-ever rein on the two remaining C-types.

Peter Whitehead (Jaguar XK120C) acknowledges Charles Faroux's chequered flag; this was the Coventry firm's first victory at Le Mans. The year—1951.

Above left *Bertie Henly and William Lyons, touring the USA in the 1950s.* **Above right** *Two great works drivers—Stirling Moss and Mike Hawthorn.* **Right** *Racing was very different when Jaguar returned to it in the 1980s and independent teams were contracted to bring the name back to the world's famous circuits. Both Bob Tullius and Tom Walkinshaw, based in the USA and UK respectively, combined the jobs of the team boss and race driver, in technical collaboration with Jaguar's engineers.*

As midnight passed, No 22—the new lap record-holder thanks to Stirling Moss!—roared through once again, sounding healthy enough as it disappeared into the long curve under the Dunlop bridge for the 93rd time. The bagpipe-cum-organ music of the sideshows swelled, only to be interrupted by the blast of another passing car. Those who listened with practised ear could tell who was driving carefully and who was really trying; there was the momentary crackle as a driver would lift his right foot, 'trailing' the throttle as rain began to fall or simply startled by some shadow he could not recall from the previous lap. Smaller cars would buzz away towards the Esses without a change of note, but occasionally even one of *them* would spin wildly, maybe on oil, its driver's heart-beat shooting momentarily into his head until he collected himself and his car and tiptoed back into the race. How many men and women have gone through the drizzle of a Le Mans night in June asking themselves: What on earth am I doing here? At least the Jaguar pit-team could keep reasonably dry, except for the duty signaller. Suddenly Lofty England tensed, and checked the stop-watch. No 22—where was No 22?

Stirling Moss was accelerating out of Arnage, one of the few sharp corners at Le Mans, when No 22's oil pressure dropped to zero. Overheating metal began welding itself together and, in a trice, a connecting rod broke. For Moss it was all over, too. This second Jaguar retirement confirmed what was happening; the oil piping in the sump, recently rerouted because of changes to the oil pump itself, was proving to be inadequately supported. Vibration was causing fracture—and, when this happened, no oil was being picked up and delivered. This was hardly a foreseeable cause of failure in engines that had been meticulously prepared (to give over 200 bhp for the first time) and fully tested with the appropriate 80-octane fuel.

Preventive maintenance could not be contemplated. There is no race in which one can expect to start removing sumps *and* retain the chance of winning. Phil Weaver, Jack Lea and Joe Sutton, who were looking after the cars, suddenly felt weary; no one could contemplate sleep. Now Lofty England could only slow the remaining C-type down as much as possible while ensuring it kept the lead it had inherited, instructing the drivers to keep the engine running in its smoothest range. Peter Walker and Peter Whitehead had been selected for the experience; they responded magnificently to the challenge of nursing Jaguar No 20 home. So superior had the new cars proved in the early stages that their main opponents—the 5.4 Cunninghams, the 4.5 Talbots, and the 4.1 Ferraris—were either not fast enough to do anything about the 3.4-litre C-type's huge advantage or in worse trouble than the British team themselves. The cool, quiet Peter Whitehead cruised over the finishing line to give the Jaguar one of the greatest victory margins ever seen in the history of Le Mans; only then, after what had seemed more like an eternity, did William Lyons and his men permit themselves smiles of relief. As 'God Save the King' was heard around the circuit to Gallic acclaim for the first time in 16 years, it was a proud Jaguar team that stood to attention.

This was a truly great moment for Britain in the history of motor racing and indeed all sports. In the top echelons of racing, as in the motor industry itself, Britain's emergence from the effects of the war had been slow. Another six years would pass before British cars and British drivers dominated Grand Prix racing simultaneously, and in the meantime Jaguar cars would be victorious at Le Mans four more times! Nowadays, when it sometimes seems as if there are few worthy or pioneering heights still to be scaled, it is not only nostalgia that makes people want to re-live great moments of the past. In the case of Jaguar Cars it has proved a useful and morale-boosting exercise in the difficult times.

Above Three great Jaguar men—Harry Teather (later Purchase Director), Ben Mason (Export) and John Silver (Production) in 1953. **Below** Happiness is a great racing car! Lofty England and Norman Dewis shake hands over it (D-type, 1954). Behind them (left to right): Malcolm Sayer, Phil Weaver, Bob Knight, Joe Sutton, Keith Cambage, Gordon Gardner, Arthur Ramsey and Len Hayden. **Above right** Top men: Bill Heynes and Arthur Whittaker—respectively Vice Chairman (engineering) and Deputy Chairman—in the USA together (Mrs M. Whittaker).

In five years (1975 to 1980) without a true leader—that is to say, a chief executive with powers of delelgation to a full management board—Jaguar survived largely through the knowledge that the great days *could* be repeated, and great things achieved, if only the Jaguar car, the people who made it, and the customer were identified and treated as something special. There is, after all, no market for an ordinary Jaguar.

From 1980 to 1985, recognition of that simple fact was translated into action by John Egan, whom Jaguar plc's chairman—Hamish Orr-Ewing, appointed in 1984—described to *Sunday Times* feature-writer John Huxley as, in many ways, 'a reincarnation of Sir William Lyons'.

Sir William (he was knighted back in 1956) and John Egan do, indeed, share a Lancashire upbringing and a singleness of purpose which each man has recognised in the other—for they have come to know one another well. The admiration is mutual. Not only did Jaguar return, in triumph, to the private sector in 1984. It proved itself, once again, a marque capable of winning a 24-hour race. . . . Jaguar has scaled the heights once more.

In 1951, William Lyons was undoubtedly thinking ahead—if not as far as the 1980s—as he congratulated his Le Mans-winning team before hurrying back to Coventry and his self-imposed task of running Britain's fastest-growing motor firm. The Mark Seven saloon had just been announced; but the firm was about to start a move, within Coventry, to bigger premises—today's Browns Lane factory, then being run by Daimler (not yet part of the Jaguar saga). It was not all plain sailing then, any more than it would be later. What was different in 1951 was that Jaguar was beginning to win the big races and rallies around the world bringing prestige, *and* large quantities of dollars, to Britain. The North American market made Jaguar what it was—*and* it is responsible for the record-breaking business achievements of the revived company in the mid-1980s.

To Lyons in 1951 and Egan thirty years later, racing was purely a business adjunct. Thirty years earlier, though, William Lyons had been an enthusiast *and* a racer himself, albeit at club level. One particular day in 1921 had been more significant than all the others—the day a new neighbour had sold him a rather unusual home-made sidecar for his motor-cycle. . . .

2: Beside the seaside (1920 to 1926)

Between Fleetwood on the Wyre estuary to the north, and Lytham St Anne's with its world-famous golf course where the Ribble merges with the Irish Sea, there lies a rather featureless peninsula called the Fylde. Most of the Fylde coast is taken up by the North Shore and the South Shore which together form Britain's most-visited holiday resort, Blackpool, in the county of Lancashire.

To taste Blackpool's unmistakable flavour, the visitor only needs to travel the seven-mile length of promenade—preferably riding in, or on, one of England's last regular-service trams. On the one side, a profusion of red brick, brashly postered; rows of bright lights and fruit machines, punctuated by a miniature Eiffel Tower . . . miniature, yet still over 500 feet high. On the other side, broad stretches of sand and the bracing sea air breathed by around eight million visitors each year.

The holiday and conference businesses still thrive, as does the small TVR motor company. Here, too began one of the *biggest* success stories of the British motor industry.

Towards the close of the 19th century a musician named Lyons was visiting Blackpool. The orchestra he played in was from Ireland, his home country, but on this particular tour he met his bride-to-be, Minnie Barcroft, and decided to make Blackpool his home. Both had strong personalities, and they were a devoted couple. William Lyons set up a small music business and gave it the title: Lyons's Music and Pianoforte Warehouse. The young Irishman continued to play in and sometimes conduct the orchestras that came to the concert halls in Blackpool town, or on one of the piers. He enjoyed writing songs too.

William and Minnie Lyons had two children, Carol and (the younger) William. William Junior was born on September 4 1901 and educated locally, first at Poulton-le-Fylde Grammar School where he found he had an aptitude for sports generally, excepting cricket. Running was his particular *forte*. Schoolwork did not appeal to him and he did it neither well nor badly. Then he went to Arnold House, later called Arnold School, at South Shore, Blackpool. There his academic career continued to be what he calls 'undistinguished', but he did come to admire the 'formidable' headmaster, F.T. Pennington. He stayed on until he was 17, by which time his enthusiasm for motorcycles was well advanced.

Lyons applied for an apprenticeship at Vickers's Barrow yards, and passed the 'tough' entrance examination. He was on the point of entering the shipbuilding world when his father, by now a prominent member of the Blackpool community, told him of another opening that might suit him better. Although not personally interested in the motor industry, William Lyons Senior knew A.W. Hubble, Managing Director of Crossley Motors Ltd, and it was decided that William Lyons Junior should go there as a trainee, studying engineering in the evenings at Manchester 'Tech'.

Crossley was then a highly-respected name in vehicle-making, the pioneer racing motorist, Charles Jarrott, having done much of the reputation-gathering. With his part-

Above *High tide at Blackpool, home of the Swallow* (Blackpool Gazette). **Below** *Billy Lyons, aged nine, collects his running prize at Poulton Grammar.*

Bill Lyons, aged 18, on a Sunbeam with characteristic oil-bath chain chase. The year—1919.

ner, William Letts, Jarrott ran a car-sales business in London; in their firm's earliest days they had concentrated upon selling mainly foreign makes, Letts being the specialist in American cars, Jarrott in European ones. Unsuccessful in their search for a high-quality British product to sell, Jarrott and Letts had persuaded Crossley to make one specially for them to the design of former Daimler engineer J.S. Critchley. The Crossley-Critchley had been large and orthodox and solid; it had performed quite well too, and was first seen in public at the 1904 Crystal Palace show. Up to that time the Crossley name had been associated chiefly with gas engines.

The great war was in its final throes when Lyons started work at Crossley's Gorton, Manchester, works. Crossley were then riding on the crest of a wave that had picked up only a few other companies, the very solidity of Crossley chassis having ensured their suitability for military purposes as staff cars, ambulances, tenders and even small lorries. The company had kept going right through the war, making, in effect, civilian chassis for military uses by a number of governments.

It was not until several years later that the decisions which set Crossley on the slippery slope to extinction were taken. It might seem strange, therefore, that after only a very short period at Gorton, Lyons made his way back to Blackpool—to his parents' considerable displeasure! It was not to be a small-cog-in-a-large-wheel life for young Lyons, whose particular brands of resourcefulness and individuality were emerging rapidly.

For a while he fulminated in his father's piano repair and renovation workshops, dreaming of having his own business; but what should he do to start it? . . . and what should he make? He even looked seriously at the idea of making gramophones, for he now had plenty of opportunity to compare what was on the market. In his spare time he was able to keep up his motorcycling hobby, and among his closest friends who shared it were

Arnold Breakell (who was to join Courtaulds) and Geoffrey Nabb who had done daring deeds as Earl Haig's despatch rider in the war just ended. These three enthusiasts were instrumental in re-forming the Blackpool, Fylde and District Motor Club, and at one stage Lyons was its vice-captain.

Another acquaintance of the younger William Lyons was Jack Mallalieu, manager of Jackson Brothers, holders of the local Sunbeam franchise. When Mallalieu invited Lyons to join him, the answer was an immediate affirmative. Shortly after this initiation into the retail motor trade, Mallalieu left Jackson's to form Brown and Mallalieu (Brown being a textile magnate from Bolton), and Lyons went with him. Brown and Mallalieu had acquired the Metropole Garage from one Jos Street—a bus operator who had moved to new premises in Cocker Street, slightly to the north of the centre of Blackpool. (These premises were to play an important part in Lyons' business life some years later.)

Lyons did all sorts of jobs for Brown and Mallalieu, and sometimes drove the charabanc. Officially he was a junior salesman, a job he was apparently good at, for Mallalieu sent him to London in November 1919 to work at the first post-war motor show. This was a very happy time for Lyons, and it was while working for Brown and Mallalieu that he bought his first car. He could not afford a Rover or a Morris of the type he was selling, and it was another salesman—a 'rep' for Bovril!—who persuaded Lyons that he ought to buy his Buckingham.

J.F. Buckingham, whose main claim to fame was the design of a particularly unpleasant, incendiary-type, bullet had made several types of light car in Coventry in the immediate pre-war period. His early models were called 'Chota' (Hindustani for 'small'), but were then re-named after their maker. Buckinghams were quite successful in competitions, but the *marque* was to die in the early 1920s—after brief resuscitation in T.G. John's Holyhead Road works, and prior to Alvis 12/50 production starting there.

Lyons' pre-war Buckingham was attractive to look at, but from the time he collected it—when it would not start—it was never satisfactory. That car was soon sold, and Lyons returned to two wheels and the motorcycle events which peacetime had restored to sports-starved enthusiasts. In his youth he bought and sold a variety of motorcycles, among them several well-known British makes. He had a *penchant* for American machines too; his favourite was a Harley-Davidson—one of three 'Daytona Specials' in Britain, he recalls. Lyons bought it from Bert Houlding of the Matador company in nearby Preston, and rode it successfully in speed hill-climbs. He was especially pleased when he won at Waddington Fells, in the Forest of Bowland. Another favourite was his Indian.

During Lyons' childhood, the family lived in Newton Drive, due inland from the town centre and close to Blackpool's biggest recreation ground, Stanley Park. Now their home was a corner house on the north side of King Edward Avenue, North Shore. At right-angles to the sea-front, King Edward Avenue is approached (not inappropriately) via Queens Promenade. For the younger Willilam Lyons it was just over a mile to work, at the Brown and Mallalieu showrooms in General Street. His father had to travel several blocks further, to his shop in Bank Hey Street in the shadow of Blackpool Tower.

His appetite whetted, William Lyons Junior was beginning to need an outlet for his latent business talents when, in the middle of 1921, another house in King Edward Avenue (No 23, on the south side) changed hands. The new occupiers seemed a jolly lot. They also seemed to have an exceptional amount of paraphernalia with them, much of it being delivered down the alley that ran parallel to King Edward Avenue and into the double garage at the end of their garden. Looking across the intersection of King Edward Avenue with Holmfield Road from the Lyons' house, it took very little time to learn what was going on, especially when smart young men on their motorcycles would stop at No

23, only to be directed round the corner and down the alley. *Very* occasionally, one of the visitors would leave—weaving shakily towards the sea —with a shining Zeppelin-shaped sidecar attached. William Lyons became more and more interested, and soon he was to find out that the new neighbours were called Walmsley.

★   ★   ★

Thomas Matley Walmsley was a prosperous coal merchant in Stockport, an industrial town south-east of Manchester and very close to the Gorton district already familiar to Lyons. Walmsley and his brother had inherited the business from their father. So good was trade that the Walmsley family were able to move from their home in Beech Road, Davenport, to a new detached house built for them in a pleasantly quiet cul-de-sac near open country to the south of Stockport. Situated off Woods Moor Lane, the cul-de-sac was called Flowery Field. Nowadays the house is called, simply, 'No 5, Flowery Field' but in 1904, when they moved in, the Walmsleys gave it the name 'Fairhaven'.

It was a happy household, or so it would appear from the parties that are still remembered by a relative, W.H. Axon, then apprenticed to a Stockport garage. Tom Walmsley's son, William, was an easy-going lad, but he had the makings of a craftsman about him and was inventive. When he left school he took an interest in the business, and one of his services to the company was to make a device, using a revolving drum, that mechanically polished the horse brasses to save the men who worked for him doing them by hand. The Walmsleys made their own railway wagon bodies and high-sided coal-carts, and this is how William became interested in coach-building.

Then came the 1914-1918 war in which William Walmsley served in the Cheshire yeomanry, a 'prestige' regiment for which, apparently, he had had to provide his own horse! Afterwards he returned to 'Fairhaven' with a gratuity, a not-too-badly-injured leg, and an ex-War Department Triumph motorcycle; but he did not stay in the army or rejoin the coal business, which carried on for a while but was later wound-up for auction by his cousins. Instead Bill stayed at home and refurbished ex-WD 'bikes for his friends. The young man with the bluff and forceful manner and the ready smile was popular with

'Fairhaven', Flowery Field, Stockport—a cheerful family home today as it was in the early days of the century, when the Walmsleys lived there. The shed where the first of Bill Walmsley's sidecars was made no longer exists; it was near the bottom of the garden, almost directly behind the garage in this photograph.

Registered in January 1921, the 'Ot-as-ell' combination had been running untaxed for much of 1920. This was the picture printed by the Stockport Express *as Walmsley's original publicity postcard* (Stockport Express).

the girls and it may well have been with them in mind that the idea of making a sidecar came to him.

Today the garden of 'No 5' is split in two, a bungalow having been built behind 'Fairhaven'. In the Walmsleys' time, a path led through that part of the garden and out behind the property, into Moorland Road near the corner of Woods Moor Road. On this path was a shed (no longer there) about the size of a small garage and here it was that Bill Walmsley started work on the design of a modern sidecar.

In 1920 a few commercial manufacturers were already trying to make their outfits seem more up-to-date than the usual wicker work and other plain-jane sidecars. Particularly *avant garde* that year was a sporty Harley-Davidson combination, the 'chair' being shaped like a chubby cigar. Generally, however, the sidecar had made little aesthetic progress since the very first one had appeared, some 18 years earlier.

With the help of Fred Gibson, who lived at nearby Heaton Moor, Walmsley found a flair for working in ash and alloy, and built the first of his dashing creations. One of his sisters, Blanche—who was married to Fred—gave some assistance with the furnishings, as did his other two sisters, Molly and Winifred. Walmsley ran the 'prototype'—to which he gave the name 'Ot-as-Ell'. Fred had Sidecar Number Two, and an un-named pal from Bramhall, bought the third. In a letter (signed 'Jaguar Cars' second client' and published many years later in *The Autocar*) this person gave his version of the Walmsley story, not mentioning 'Swallow' although there is little doubt that the name had already been coined, but including the comment that 'Bill soon tumbled to the idea that there was money in his hobby and within a few months he had a real selling agent in Deansgate, Manchester'. The same enthusiast suggested that demand had been such that the 'garden shed became inadequate' and that Walmsley had employed 'two or three' men, and made sidecars in a local garage for a few months.

Edwin Webb at the door of his shop in the early 1920s, as Shell's Albion delivers petrol by the canload. The motorcycle combination is an Armis-Watsonian. (The Armis was so-called because it was introduced immediately after the war.) This was where Fred Gibson bought his new Triumph. The teenager on the right, with the Levis two-stroke, is Wilfred Webb who helped Walmsley make his first sidecar at nearby Flowery Field (W. Webb).

The first statement is certainly wrong, and the address probably refers to the Manchester premises of Stanley Parker, who is not due to join this narrative until a little later. It is also believed that any help Walmsley had was 'casual labour'. The additional premises are more of a mystery; Bill Walmsley's first wife, then his fiancée, now living in Dorset, does not think there *were* any—and not at the spot I was shown when I visited Stockport in 1979 to try to picture the 'geography' for myself. The person who conducted me around was Wilfred Webb, a former president of the Stockport Motor Club, who lives in retirement in Stockport Great Moor. Just round the corner from his home, where Lake Street meets the A6 (Buxton Road) is a motorcycle centre. He has sold-out now but this was where he had spent his working life; his father Edwin, started the business there as a cycle shop and took Wilfred on when he left school in his early teens.

Edwin Webb had been a great cyclist in his day. In 1913, riding tandem with C.H. Turner, he had covered 381¾ miles in 24 hours. To make this run 'official', no pacing was allowed—and, since public roads were being used, the riders had to wear tights to protect passers-by from the sight of flailing knees. With such impositions, their 16 mph average was some achievement. His son, Wilfred, was a sportsman too, but more keen on motorcycles and cars, and pressed his father to service and sell motorcycles as well as bikes. Among the Webb's customers was Fred Gibson who bought a new all-chain-drive Triumph, more powerful than the old despatch-rider machines which his 'partner' (and brother-in-law) was putting together at Flowery Field, only a few hundred yards away across the railway line. Wilfred's curiosity was aroused when he heard that another motorcycle 'business' was starting-up so near to Webb's cycle shop.

Webb was still a teenager when he met Walmsley and began assisting him in the shed at 'Fairhaven', which he could enter and leave by way of the path from Moorland Road. Wilfred Webb often worked there as a spare time hobby and helped build the first Walmsley sidecar there in 1920. It was an original design, and Wilfred Webb is sure that its maker was not at that time aware of any remotely similar-looking 'chair'. He remembers the template, and cutting aluminium sheet with 'tinsnips' along scribed lines. The eight aluminium panels were all similar, so the 'chair' had a symmetrical cross-section, forward of the 'cut-out' for the passenger. He also remembers the first Walmsley sidecar as having a chassis supplied by Watsonian, not Hadens' as has been recorded previously (*they* supplied Walmsley later). He showed me the place where he recalled visiting one of two lock-up garages in the grounds of the Bamford Arms Hotel opposite St George's Church, about a mile away on the main road into Stockport. It had been a bigger garage, apparently, and here (he told me) several sidecars were made—although exactly *how* many may never be known—verifying the statement of *The Autocar* letter-writer.

The ex-WD Triumphs arrived in component form and were, of course, unregistered. Walmsley did not bother to register his own, and the first of his Swallow combinations ran around with the fictitious Irish-looking number T1 291 for 'a long time' before being registered DB 1238 at Stockport Town Hall on January 28 1921. The *Stockport Express* printed a photographic postcard with such information as the price of the sidecar—£28, plus £4 for hood, screen, lamp and wheel disc—and the claim that this 'chair' was 'made to sit *in*, not on'.

Gibson and Webb should be put on record as the first people to take part in competitions with a Swallow outfit. Wilfred Webb told me how they went in for the 1921 East Cheshire Trial which started and finished at the 'Angel' in Knutsford. Webb went as ballast and navigator in the sidecar, and their great feat of that day was to get to the top of the notorious trials hill, Litton Slack, unaided. Theirs was the only single-cylinder combination to do so, and thus the only such outfit to complete the whole course of the trial.

Fred Gibson was not quite the help he might have been to Bill Walmsley, and their partnership soon ended—'amicably'. After that, it was usually Bill's sister, Winifred, who sewed the hoods and side-curtains. Mrs Bransby (as she later became) has told me that 'quite a few' sidecars were made in the garage at Flowery Field.

Tom Walmsley decided to retire to the seaside, and on June 17 1921 he handed over the keys of 'Fairhaven' to its new owner. The Walmsleys then set off for Blackpool. Now this has got to be a coincidence—'Fairhaven's' purchaser was called George William Swallow.

⋆   ⋆   ⋆

When the Walmsley family arrived at King Edward Avenue, Blackpool, in the summer of 1921, Bill Walmsley commandeered the garage. With his wife, Emily, now doing most of the trimming, Swallow output continued at an increased but still leisurely pace (one a week is thought to have been the general aim). Then William Lyons came across the road to buy a Swallow sidecar. He shared Walmsley's youthful enthusiasm; more particularly, he possessed commercial awareness of a high order.

No serious attempt was being made to create a money-making business, although the possibilities seemed endless. There was no advertising, and sales were to friends or just a matter of luck. For example, the Blackpool violinist, W.H. Scott, who performed with Geraldo's and other famous orchestras when he came touring locally, was a very keen motorcyclist. When he saw Walmsley's eyecatching combination parked outside the

Carlton Hotel, he waited for the owner's return to find out about the exotic-looking 'chair'—there and then ordering one to match his AJS. (He believes his Swallow to have been the third to come from King Edward Avenue).

It was Lyons' big chance! Here was a product to challenge his skill in starting a business from scratch! Bill Walmsley shrugged the idea aside, but Lyons was determined. Emily, who remembers the late night discussions in father-in-law's kitchen, wanted to see her husband's business increase too; after all, there was now a baby on the way.

It did not take long for Tom Walmsley to visualise what his new neighbour's son could do to place his own son's business-cum-hobby on the road to providing a proper career for the support of his family. William Walmsley was now approaching the age of 30. William Lyons, on the other hand, was still only 20 when his father went with Tom Walmsley to Williams Deacon's Bank in Blackpool's Talbot Square and agreed to guarantee an over-draft of £1,000 for the embryo Swallow Sidecar Company. Having accepted that it was the right thing to do, young Walmsley at last became the somewhat reluctant partner; Lyons had reservations, too, for he knew already that although the Swallow's creator made a good product, success in a big business was not among his ambitions.

Lyons left Brown & Mallalieu early in 1922, having found somewhere to begin trading. Only a very short distance from Blackpool's 'Golden Mile', a bright new light was about to be switched on.

*   *   *

As the plan began to take shape, the elder William Lyons' friends (and friends of friends)—in particular Messrs Haworth, Jessop and Francis—played their part in encouraging the new business. Haworth was an accountant, and it was he who introduced young Lyons to a Mr Outhwaite, the owner of a tiny factory producing electrical equipment on the ground floor, but not fully utilising the two upper floors. One of the features of the first floor was a pair of doors that opened straight out 'into space' thus providing direct access for loading or unloading, which would otherwise have had to be done by using the very steep staircase at the east end of the building. Outhwaite's was a tall narrow edifice at the Lytham Road end of Bloomfield Road, just across the railway from Blackpool football ground, and south of the town centre.

Lyons' first port of call on the road to success was Jessop's, the solicitors. Jessop drew up the lease agreement quite early in 1922, but it was a frustrating time for William Lyons, because he was still only 20 and too young to sign company documents. Although the partnership was not yet ratified, Lyons and Walmsley were allowed to move in to Bloomfield Road before the lease became official, as there was a great deal of clearing-up after previous tenants to be done before the real work could begin. Mr Francis, the manager of Williams Deacon's Bank in Talbot Square with the guarantees of the two fathers, did all he could to encourage this unusual new industry to thrive in Blackpool.

In a corner of the first floor at Bloomfield Road they put up a small office which Sir William now recalls as measuring about eight feet by six feet. While Walmsley was bringing in his equipment, Lyons started on the paperwork, the first thing being to adver-

Above far left *William Walmsley (in cap) at Blackpool. With him is his friend, also from Stockport, Charlie Waterhouse, who often competed in motorcycling events with a Swallow combination* (Mrs E.L. Robbins). **Above left** *William Lyons, at about the time he went into partnership with William Walmsley.* **Left** *Partners! Walmsley on a Brough Superior; Lyons in the sidecar that was to lead to the formation of one of the world's most famous car companies. The picture was taken in King Edward Avenue, Blackpool.*

Left *Built on the slope up to a railway bridge, the original Bloomfield Road premises were not exactly ideal. Goods went in and out through the double doorway on the first floor. This picture was taken some years after Swallow moved out. The building is used in much the same way today, with different small companies on each floor.*

Right *Looking north up Lytham Road in the 1920s, towards the Blackpool Tower. Bloomfield Road is off to the right, Woodfield Road to the left. A stone's throw from the beach, this is the heart of boarding-house country* (Blackpool Gazette).

tise for labour. First to be signed-on was Richard Binns, who became 'foreman'. Dick Binns was a pattern-maker by trade, his first job when he arrived at Swallow being to make the work-benches! Two tinsmiths, Jim Greenwood and Joe Yates, had the job of making sidecar production a reality on a regular basis. Greenwood in particular was to be instrumental in simplifying the sidecar panelling for 1924. Binns was responsible for making the wooden nose-cone, and the block for the ex-War Department 'Auster' laminated aero-screens fitted to all early Swallow 'chairs'. Cyril Marshall was the coach-painter. ('I can't get my tongue round that', said Walmsley. 'You'll be called Sam!')

There was no full-time trimmer. The first regular upholsterer and hood-fitter was Arnold Hollis who initially was able to do the work in one or two days a week, despite such interruptions as covering the company's first office desk (which Walmsley himself had made, but not before producing the bill for his tools, and asking Lyons to go '50-50').

'Mucking-in' was to become a feature of the growth of the company, for Lyons' success came largely from keeping his labour force to an absolute minimum. This did not always work. (Later, in Coventry, there was the time when stones needed clearing from the site for a playing field. He did not proceed with his original idea on that occasion, and brought in a contractor instead. The idea *had* been to issue employees with empty buckets to be filled as they tramped their way home at the end of the day!) Another reason for adaptability among Swallow employees was the seasonal nature of the business. The less adaptable you were in those days, the greater the likelihood of being laid-off when trade was slack. You had to be able to turn your hand to almost any job.

Swallow's first general factotum came in response to an advertisement for an apprentice coachbuilder. Harry Leslie Gill, a butcher's son, was only 15 when he joined the embryo Swallow company, but he had already gained some engineering experience in his family's home town of Leeds where he had left school at the age of 13. Other than the partners themselves, Harry Gill was the first Swallow employee who would stay on and become a key member of the company when it moved to Coventry. Meantime, he would do anything and everything asked of him—from turning the wooden tail-blocks to slipping

along Lytham Road and up the 'prom' to the music shop in Bank Hey Street where William Lyons Senior, would countersign the cheques or other papers. From September 4 1922, however, this was a job he would not have to do again. That day was his son's 21st birthday; from then on, *his* signature became 'official'. Young Lyons felt as if a great weight had been lifted off him and the world was opening out before him. At last, the Swallow Sidecar Company became his own real live business—or, at any rate, half of it did! Although Lyons and Walmsley were not always in accord they did agree on two things: that each would take home a weekly salary of £6, and that they would aim to make ten sidecars a week. Lyons was to be the one to make sure the shots were on target and then proceed to build on that achievement.

Soon extra premises were needed, but Francis at the bank remained as receptive as ever, despite big bites into the overdraft, as two extra buildings were rented. The first was in Back Woodfield Road a *cul-de-sac* behind private and boarding houses, several hundred yards away across the Lytham Road. At first, this location was used largely for packing and despatching. The other building, on the corner of John Street and Moon Avenue came a little later; it was nearer to Bloomfield Road and had the best access of all three in terms of delivery and collection of goods. Here, completed sidecar bodies, stored on racks, awaited chassis-fitting. This extra space made it possible to go on using the cramped confines of Bloomfield Road as Swallow's headquarters, for bodies could now be taken to Back Woodfield Road for mounting, and so chassis no longer had to be lifted up into the awkward Bloomfield Road workshop.

Haworth, who had originally helped Lyons obtain the premises, became Swallow's first accountant. Then when Lyons needed a shorthand typist, Haworth again came to the rescue, and so the company gained its first female employee, Dorothy Atkinson. 'Dolly' Atkinson was a quiet girl and not particularly well-suited to working for the 'go-getting' leader of the small firm she had joined. However, she came to enjoy being part of the team and was very disappointed when, a few years later, she was not invited to move with the company to Coventry.

Next to join Swallow was Henry Teather's son, Harry. Henry Teather had been a sand-moulder in the industrial north, but had moved to Blackpool for the fresh air and a but-cher's life (as Harry Gill's father did!) After a brief look at his father's shop, Harry Teather began his working life at the *Blackpool Gazette* offices in Temple Street, and it was in the paper's composing room that he saw a Swallow advertisement being put together for the 'Sits Vac' column. He applied, was accepted, and started work at Bloomfield Road in April 1923. Like Gill, Teather was only 15 when he joined, working as a jack-of-all trades and in particular with 'Sam' Marshall on the paintwork. Harry and Sam shared an interest in photography and music. Sam was a pianist. 'He could get through Chopin's Minute Waltz in forty-five seconds', recalled Harry Teather who, as a wage-earner, was able to take violin lessons by then.

Teather's own views on the audacity of the Swallow project were to be recorded 35 years later in the *Jaguar Apprentices' Magazine:*

'In retrospect it would not appear to have been a propitious time to launch a venture for the manufacture of luxury sidecars, as the boom which had persisted since the armistice was beginning to tail off and the pattern of declining trade and mass unemployment, culminating in the General Strike of 1926, was already becoming evident.

'In addition, Morris was manufacturing the old Bullnose in quantity and at a price which brought all-weather motoring practically within reach of all who could afford to motor at all. It was thought by many that the advent of the cheap small car would ring the death knell for the motorcycle side-car business, just as it was confidently predicted that radio would kill the gramophone stone dead. Just how wrong expert predictions *can* be may be gathered from the fact that sidecar sales were to prosper right up to the outbreak of war in 1939.'

As Harry Teather pointed out later, the gramophone record continues to flourish despite television and tape decks, cassettes and the rest—fascinating to think that William Lyons, had *he* been musical, *might* have made a fortune from gramophones.

The motorcycle press picked up the story of the new sidecar *marque* in the Autumn of 1922, and it was at about this time that Lyons first began buying advertising, usually taking an eighth of a page at a time. The first Swallow catalogue was a disaster and, on ad-vice from Jessop, was withdrawn. The reason for this was because of the likelihood of legal action by the Swift company, in whose last days the Swallow company would later make coachwork to fit their car chassis. At this particular time, Swift were implying that Swallow's style of 'bird' was too near their own for their liking. However, as the catalogue had been badly printed anyway, its withdrawal was not such a bad thing.

Lyons worked long hours and would often arrive late at Francis' door in Talbot Square when he went for the wages on a Saturday morning, thus (by his own admission) keeping his employees late, too. With his dedication to the business side, Lyons was not a party to the first, and quite unofficial 'Swallow' body to be fitted to a motor car. When one day Walmsley obtained from his brother-in-law, Fred Gibson in Stockport, the burnt-out remains of an Austro-Daimler car, and had it taken to Back Woodfield Road, Harry Gill helped make a new body while Arthur Whittaker refurbished the chassis and engine.

Arthur Whittaker, a former apprentice at the Imperial Garage, Blackpool, had joined Swallow as salesman at the age of 17. It was largely a summer job, driving around the country visiting retail traders on a Preston-built Matador (powered by the locally-made Granville Bradshaw-designed oil-cooled engine) with a Swallow sidecar. He put in huge mileages in all weathers, but did not really enjoy being a salesman; his days as deputy-chairman of Jaguar were yet to come. When the opportunity arose at a quiet selling

Above *William Lyons and his fiancée Greta Brown in Scotland in 1923 with their Model 1 Swallow outfit.* **Below** *On the same holiday, they meet up with the rest of the Brown family. Greta perches on the Studebaker; her sister Gladys sits on the running-board.*

Above *Bill and Emily Letitia Walmsley on Blackpool's 'golden mile', 1923.* **Above right** *Bill Lyons and his fiancée, Greta Brown (right) and her sister.* **Above far right** *Sidecar bodies in the John Street store; most are Model 4s, but there is a 'Scrapper' on the floor. Cyril Marshall reads the* Amateur Photographer *over Harry Teather's shoulder, circa 1924* (H. Teather).

period, it suited him very well to get back to some activity where he could use his hands such as working on the Austro-Daimler. Walmsley paid Gill and Whittaker for this work as it amounted to an extra-mural activity. That Austro-Daimler, which Walmsley ran for a short while before selling it, was the only car to be bodied by Swallow during the company's time in South Blackpool. 'It was a very smart-looking car', the former Mrs Walmsley told me, 'but I'm sure my pushing caused the wheels to turn more often than the engine did!'

Lyons and Walmsley rode combinations themselves, of course. Together they had been to Nottingham where young George Brough—who had recently left his father W.E. Brough's motorcycle works to start one of his own—was building the machines that were to be known as 'the Rolls-Royce of motorcycles'. The partners returned to Blackpool with a Brough-Superior V-twin 'SS80' apiece.

By 1923, Lyons was engaged to Greta Brown, who came from Cuddington, near Thame, where her father, Albert Jenner Brown, was a schoolmaster. Her grandfather had been headmaster of St John's Church-of-England School in Blackpool and her first memory of a visit there (when she was three or four years old) is of being in disgrace for burying the front door key on the beach. When grandfather died, her father took over his job and brought the family to Blackpool permanently. As a teenager she had known of the serious young man called Billy Lyons who had a fine-looking Buckingham car, and who lived not far away in King Edward Avenue. However, in 1921 when they had begun to see each other regularly, he was back on two wheels after his brief venture with four. At

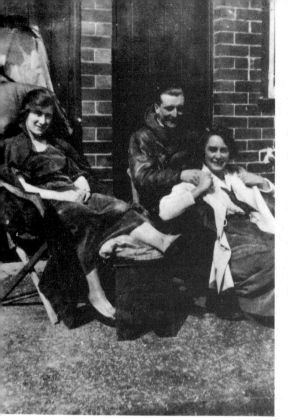

first the Browns used to wonder why the fellow did not call for Greta at their house in Holly Road. However this was easily explained for, by meeting at the corner of the road, use could be made of the slope to get Billy's motorcycle started.

The first Swallow presence at the Motorcycle Show happened by luck, for the company was not eligible according to 'the rules'. However, Lyons and Walmsley went to London with their Broughs, knowing that one exhibitor had pulled out. They booked in to Mrs Shirley's 'digs' in Russell Square, then went along to Olympia, where they had arranged to take over the vacant space. Thus, the 1922 Show saw Swallow on a small corner site. By the following year, however, Swallow sidecars were being shown by several motorcycle makers too, including DOT, Matador and Brough.

.Arthur Whittaker was Swallow's first regular Olympia duty salesman where occasionally he was helped by William Docking, who was to marry Greta Brown's sister, Gladys, and become a Blackpool councillor. During the 1923 Show, several Swallow dealers were appointed. (Lyons knew Iliffe Press' northern manager, Raymond Bailey, who was a great help in introducing this newcomer to the trade.) The three display sidecars were sold, thus saving the expense of packing them up again and getting them sent back to Blackpool by rail. From about this time, for a short period, Swallow boasted a 'London Office'—a rented room in Coomer Road, Fulham.

It was probably at the 1923 Show that William Lyons and George Brough—similarly demanding men—nearly fell out. Brough was the customer, and he wanted his special show sidecar trimmed in cloth and finished in cream. This was the first attempt to paint the shining alloy panels of a Swallow sidecar and it took much patience by all concerned before the job was done to Brough's satisfaction.

I interviewed George Brough, still jaunty, flat cap akimbo, for *Jaguar Journal* in 1963. His admiration for Sir William Lyons was unstinting. He was full of praise for Jaguars and had just bought his seventh! He described his new E-type as 'the best car I have ever

Gynn Square, Blackpool, June 12 1924 (not far from King Edward Avenue). A Swallow Super Sports Model 4 (right) looks 'official' rather than competitive, as does the Hispano Suiza lurking behind the timekeepers' hut. Setting off up Queen's Promenade (to share a class win with Mays' Bugatti) in this one-kilometre sprint organised by the York MC is Eddie Hall in the Aston-Martin, 'Bunny', nearest camera. Racing him is N.T. Beardsall in the Hodgson, a brand-new Anzani-engined marque from Leeds. Standing just behind the hut is Lyons' brother-in-law, William Docking; maybe he had brought the combination along? (N. Murray/F.E. Ellis collection).

driven'—without as much as referring to the fine cars he himself had made for a while! Of the early Swallow sidecars he told me they had 'a flair that the others just hadn't got'. That the admiration was mutual is evident from the fact that Lyons and Walmsley replace their side-valve JAP-engined SS80 models for the even more powerful ohv Matchless-powered Brough-Superior SS100.

It was from the Olympia show that Lyons, Docking and Whittaker were returning in Lyons' father's car (used in order to save the three railfares!) when the engine gave out at Stoney Stratford; they had to remove a broken piston in the dark before they could chug home on the three remaining 'pots'. The car in question was a Talbot 10/23 tourer which Lyons, who much admired it for its smooth running and good performance, had advised his father to buy. It was an 1,100 cc ohv four-cylinder car developed by Georges Roesch from the small Darracq that had been known in Britain as the 'Talbot 8/18' after the takeover by the Paris-based company. It was quite 'French' in character, and modern for its day. Apart from this incident, that particular car seems to have been trouble-free and, when Lyons was otherwise engaged on Sundays, working or competing in club events, he would get Harry Gill to take his parents out in it for drives—inland to the Trough of Bowland or north to the Lake District—at a strict 30 mph.

William and Greta Lyons—having become man and wife at St Stephen-on-the-Cliffs, North Shore, Blackpool, on September 15 1924—took the Talbot on their honeymoon. For the second year running they made for the Highlands. In 1923 Lyons had accompanied the Browns to Scotland on their family holiday—Gladys driving her parents in their Studebaker and Lyons following on his Swallow outfit, with Greta in the sidecar.

Near Carlisle, Lyons, normally a wise decision-maker, turned off at a 'puppies for sale' sign and bought one. The puppy, however, so threatened to wreck the honeymoon, leaving soaked carpets and sleepless guests at every hotel, that arrangements had to be made to pack it off home by rail. Despite this episode, dogs were to become a feature of the Lyons household, and are to this day. Thereafter they had a more peaceful stay, mainly at the Invermoriston Hotel, before setting off for their Blackpool flat. Later they moved into a bungalow called 'Westbourne' in Blackpool's Bispham Road. Incidentally, Bill and Emily Walmsley, and their son, Bobby, were to move out (from Handley Road) to Bispham Road, too—taking their house name, 'Swallowdene', with them.

Lyons and Walmsley were both active motor club members, Walmsley was more the 'social' member whereas Lyons was always the keen competitor. He was also anxious that Swallow should compete with Hughes of Birmingham in the big event of which he was so fond—the Isle of Man TT. Hughes had a virtual monopoly in the supply of racing side-cars, and Lyons wanted to break in; so he spoke to Lewis of Matador.

Lewis was entering a Matador-Blackburne for the 1924 Sidecar TT and said he would be pleased to buy a prototype racing Swallow. The Matador-Swallow combination ran quite well in practice, so Lyons later 'saw red' when he found that Lewis' racing manager had fitted a Hughes 'chair' in place of the Swallow. However before the actual race, the Swallow was refitted and ridden to third place by Almond Tinkler. Lyons had learned a lesson which was to make him for ever circumspect in his approach to competitions as a manufacturer.

A much better bet was Lyons' alliance with Harry Reed who had founded the DOT motorcycle company back in 1903. Reed's 348 cc Bradshaw-engined machine lived up to the initials he had given it ('Devoid Of Trouble') and finished second overall in the same race which actually admitted combinations of up to 600 cc. Another Swallow outfit was fourth. The Sidecar TT was held only in 1923, 1924, and 1925, incidentally.

The biggest single contribution to Swallow's progress in 1924 was the introduction of

William Lyons with his father's Talbot and infamous puppy—a 1924 Scottish honeymoon photograph.

the simpler and much lighter pentagonal 'Model 2', though the octagonal 'Model 1', based upon Walmsley's original, continued to be popular for several years. Production increased, and a development of the 'Model 2'—the long-tailed 'Model 4—became *the* most popular Blackpool Swallow. Walmsley often had design ideas at night and kept a pad and pen by the bed so he could make notes or sketches. One of these ideas was a fascinating 'Walmsley Special', a four-wheeled 'push-car' he made for his baby son Bobby, based on the 'Model 4' style! Later he made him a 'Swallow' pedal car.

Chassis manufacturers often made complete sidecars, too, so Swallow had the underlying problem of the 'opposition' being a major supplier. Several different chassis-makers supplied Swallow over the years. Earlier, when he was still on his own, Walmsley bought chassis from A.H. Haden of Birmingham but, when the partnership began, Swallow's chassis were ordered from Montgomery's of Coventry. As the business built up in the mid-1920s, however, the closest Midland ally became C.W. Hayward and Company, who provided two types of chassis—a twin-axle model and a lightweight known as the Universal because it could be fitted to either side of a motorcycle. Hayward's do not seem to have minded complete illustrations, descriptions and parts prices being shown in Lyons' catalogues without any indication that these chassis were not Swallow's own.

A task that soon became an essential part of Swallow's business was that of creating a 'service' department, not only to fit sidecars to dashingly-ridden motorcycles as they arrived, two-wheeled, in the alley of Back Woodfield Road, but to provide help and solace when they roared out again, three-wheeled, only to hit the nearest kerb or wall! To ride a motorcycle combination was usually a totally new experience, as many a motorcyclist learned the hard way so, on the back page of the Swallow catalogue was set-out the sidecar guarantee, and some careful phrasing related to the term 'misuse'.

William Lyons has always declared himself a firm believer in publishing customer testimonials, and in the Swallow catalogue he included extracts from letters received from

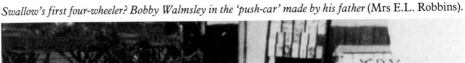

Swallow's first four-wheeler? Bobby Walmsley in the 'push-car' made by his father (Mrs E.L. Robbins).

owners who had been happy with their treatment at the works, the prompt delivery of parts, or the behaviour of their machine as a whole. Perhaps the earliest Swallow sidecar to receive a testimonial was the one bought in 1923 by George Williams of Blackpool and fitted to his John Osborn-built OEC-Blackburne in time for his honeymoon in North Wales. 'I still recall with gratitude the generous treatment I received from (Sir) William when the sidecar chassis fractured and he gave me a full replacement', said Mr Williams nearly 50 years later.

While the Swallow name was destined never to grace an Isle of Man winner, there were successes in other spheres of competition. Among the great riders to use Swallows was George Dance, the Sunbeam works rider who later became a smallholder at Penn near Wolverhampton; he was the first regular user of a sidecar listed as 'Model 6' and nicknamed 'The Scrapper' at Swallows. Others using this type incuded Bert Le Vack (who was also twice holder of the two-wheel world speed record on Brough-Superiors), Tony Worters, and Jack Emerson. Emerson, who rode ABC, Norton, and Zenith machines, later came to Jaguar Cars as a key member of the XK engine development team! J.A. Prestwich (of JAP engine fame) and Joe Wright (another world record man) rode with Swallows attached; George Patchett, Michael McEvoy's competition manager at the McEvoy motorcycle works in Derby, raced a 'Model 4' Swallow before becoming involved in designs for FN in Belgium and Jawa in Czechoslovakia; Ivan Riddoch (Zenith-Blackburne) and Dougal Marchant (Chater-Lea) used Swallow 'Scrappers' for record breaking. In 1926 Marchant—who developed an engine for the Chater-Lea company, to replace the proprietary Blackburne—took all 16 available world records in one particular sidecar class! Amongst the speeds reached by his Chater-Lea-Swallow were 86.35 mph for the 'flying' kilometre and 73.72 mph for 100 km from a standing start. Later Marchant and Le Vack became designers for the Swiss Motosacoche company.

Also a regular sprinter was Charlie Waterhouse, a friend of the Walmsleys from Stockport, and on two occasions (a sprint meeting on Queens Promenade, Blackpool, and another at Ainsdale Sands near Southport) he carried Eric Brooks in the Swallow sidecar of his 500 cc Sunbeam outfit. Eric Brooks had been chosen because of his light weight—about six stones! He was then employed at Swallows to mount bodies (mostly the 'Model 4') on to Hayward chassis. He was with Swallow for only a year when he moved with his family to Manchester in 1926. Among his colleagues then were Ronald Gledhill (known as 'Ginger'), Bill Vardy (who came from Nottingham) and Harry Teather, all of whom *were* to stay on, and move with Swallow to Coventry. Brooks, who returned to live in Blackpool later in life, used to write consignment notes for sidecars and parts leaving the shop. He remembers the usual means of delivery and collection as being 'Jim the carter' with a railway-company dray and a 'real handful of horse that had large teeth and wicked eyes'.

Another vehicle to visit the Swallow works regularly was, of course, Hayward's pantechnicon and its consignments of sidecar chassis. Charles Hayward, a Wolverhampton pattern-maker by trade, manufactured sidecars early on in a career during which he became *Sir* Charles Hayward, chairman of Firth Cleveland the steel company, before retiring to the tiny Channel Island of Jethou to enjoy a ripe old age. His only son Jack is another larger-than-life character. From his Bahamas base, millionaire Hayward, familiarly known as 'Union Jack', has become world-famous for the financial backing he gives to projects promoting Britain—from women's cricket and ocean rowing to recovering Brunel's *SS Great Britain* and buying Lundy Island for the National Trust. He ploughed nearly a quarter-of-a-million pounds into the Liberal Party out of his belief in effective opposition—and pure patriotism. It seems that his father was similarly philanthropic one Friday in 1926 when, with his characteristic brilliance in economic planning,

Just as stylish as the original, the five-sided Swallow 'Model 4' (seen here with Emily Walmsley aboard, with her husband on the Brough) was easier and cheaper to make.

William Lyons persuaded Charles Hayward's driver to stay on in Blackpool for the weekend.

Out of the blue (as Sir William puts it) Thomas Walmsley— knowing the desperate muddle his son and partner were in, trying to run a rapidly-expanding business in three places at once—had purchased a large building on the north side of town; then he had leased it to what was about to be called The Swallow Sidecar and Coach Building Company. There were several more Swallow employees by now and, with their help and that of Hayward's lorry, the complete removal from the three old sites to the one new one in Cocker Street was accomplished during Saturday and Sunday with virtually no loss of sidecar production.

What Charles Hayward said when his wagon re-appeared on Monday morning is not on record. Many years later Harry Teather was to meet Sir Charles and tell him of the unwitting contribution he had made to the progress of the small company as it struggled for a foothold, in the year of the General Strike. Sir Charles Hayward smiled benevolently, as if he had known about it all along.

3: Swallow's first four-wheelers
(1926 to 1928)

Before his 'escape' from Bloomfield Road, after more than four years in the old premises, William Lyons had nursed a dream. Not long after his marriage, he had acquired a two-year-old Austin Seven, one of the earliest. Much as he admired 'Herbert Austin's master-piece', he began to try to imagine how it might be improved. Specialists were already beginning to make their own 'improvements' to the car, and one day a visitor to Bloomfield Road showed Lyons his Austin Seven open two-seater with skimpy fabric Gordon England bodywork. This particular car was interesting if only to demonstrate how much further the theme *could* be taken, how much more style and luxury *could* be added. Here was Lyons, nearly five years into a venture that was to be his life's work, and he was still only making sidecars. He must do something. The acquisition of the Cocker Street works made that 'something' possible.

While still at Bloomfield Road, Lyons had been fretting inwardly upon another problem. He needed a 'right hand', and 'Dolly' Atkinson ('who wouldn't say boo to a goose') could not provide it. He could not risk getting someone less than 'good'—preferably 'extra special'. It was Lyons' mother who set the wheels in motion, as she thought of the girl who worked in her husband's shop—a girl who could be bettering herself. Alice Fenton was vivacious and something of an extrovert, as witness her piano-playing which attracted crowds at the open doorway (much as they might gather around a television shop window now) when she was not doing other work for William Lyons Senior. She had left school early, for she needed to earn a living early in life both for herself *and* for her family! Her father had been blinded in an accident at the Thornton-le-Fylde chemical works (now part of ICI) and lived at home with his wife (formerly a lady's maid) and their two daughters Alice and Nancy. Their small house was in Hawes-side Lane, not very far from Bloomfield Road.

Her great chum, Doris (now Mrs Turner), remembers that they both took the 'commercial' (rather than the 'domestic') course at the Palatine Central School in their early teens, so her shorthand and typing meant that when Alice went job-hunting she stood a better chance than most of picking and choosing. But jobs were hard to come by, and it was partly her ability to play the piano that got her one in the Lyons music shop. Like anyone else remotely interested in Blackpool, however, she knew that, for all its Heath Robinson qualities, the Swallow Sidecar Company had grown at great speed and was still growing. Alice Fenton handed in her notice at Bank Hey Street and became young Lyons' secretary at Bloomfield Road. So, having settled cheerfully into the Swallow environment in its original form, Alice Fenton took the news of the move to Cocker Street in her stride. She had thought this little company was on its way somewhere but now it was taking an express train. This was living and, as Doris Turner remembers to this day, Alice loved life with a capital 'L'.

The Blackpool businessman Jos Street does not seem to have been very successful. He

SWALLOW SIDECAR & COACH BUILDING CO.

Above *Proper premises at last—something to shout about. This advertisement is from the* Blackpool Gazette *dated November 6 1926. The notice above the main door reads: 'Proprietors, W. Walmsley & W. Lyons'.* **Below** *Bobby Walmsley soon grew out of his 'push-car', and father made the boy one he could pedal, proudly calling it 'Swallow'.*

had moved from the Metropole Garage when Brown and Mallalieu had acquired it. Then he had moved out of his big garage on the corner of Cocker and Exchange Streets, and Jackson Brothers (for whom Lyons had once worked) used it for a short period. Street had had a huge lift put in (for buses) on the Exchange Street side of the building, and there was another door facing Cocker Street itself, above which was soon to be painted the simple but proud statement. 'Proprietors: W. Walmsley and W. Lyons'. Access to the new 'Swallow's nest' was excellent, both floors being designed to take heavy vehicles. The sidecar operation did not occupy anything like the space available, and quieter periods of 1926 were spent preparing to justify the company's new title—The Swallow Sidecar *and Coach Building* Company. A coachpainting bay was constructed in the south-west ground floor corner, with panelled walls, dampened curtains and polished floor. A large portion of the upper floor was fitted-out for making new hoods and sidecurtains for motor cars as well as the traditional Swallow product.

Whilst these preparations were in hand, Lyons was occupied in the most vital part of his master plan—to recruit skilled labour. On November 6 1926 an advertisement, in the name of both partners, was placed in the *Blackpool Gazette and Herald* (incorporating the *Fylde News and Advertiser*). It was by far the largest space the company had ever taken, and announced that 'the commodious Coach Building and Coach Painting Works in Cocker Street' had been acquired. 'Alterations are now completed and enquiries are solicited . . . all classes of Bodywork will be undertaken . . . a Highly Skilled Staff is employed in each department, Coach-painers, Finishers, and Trimmers having been engaged from Midland Car Factories. Clients are assured of the original Factory finish being restored to their cars, at the lowest possible cost. To find experienced labour in the Blackpool area, where there was little or no coachbuilding, was virtually impossible so Lyons had also advertised in the Birmingham, Coventry and Wolverhampton newspapers. The response was good. Of the Midlanders who came north, it was Cyril Holland who would prove to be the company's greatest 'find'.

At this stage there was no specific Swallow body, but some car trimming *was* being done as the illustrated advertisement had shown. One newcomer to Cocker Street, shortly after Swallow moved in, was Lyndon Smith whose father (a Whitehaven tailor) had brought his family from Cumberland to the Fylde Coast in 1919, as a teacher of his craft at the local post-war rehabilitation centre. Lyndon Smith used to look in on Bloomfield Road as an enthusiast, and wonder at Swallow's activity, before passing on his way to the football ground. In view of his later financial attainments it is worth noting that he started at Cocker Street, aged 15, at five shillings a week, and much resented its immediate reduction to four-and-eightpence because of the insurance stamp. He walked to work from Clevedon Street, and was sometimes given a lift for the last few blocks by Arthur Whittaker whose sister had taught Smith at school, and who had graduated to a nine hp Belsize-Bradshaw, with an oil-cooled two-cylinder engine of the same ilk as his old motor cycle. When Lyndon Smith had first arrived he was put to work with the brightest of Lyons' bright new stars. Much of the 'new blood' at Swallow had learned body-making at the Mead and Deakin factory in Birmingham (where Rhode cars were still being made, though that would not be the case for very much longer). Holland had worked at several Birmingham and Coventry factories, including Morris; his apprenticeship, however, had been at the Lanchester works. He had not been looking for a move north but, when he realised how little coachbuilding knowledge there was at Swallow, he decided to take his own to Blackpool.

Standing in the Cocker Street works one day was a very sorry-looking Talbot Darracq special that had rolled over in a race on Southport Sands, and been brought to Blackpool by Abingdon Street Motors, round the corner. Cyril Holland's craftsmanship was a revelation to Lyndon Smith, who was able to see the special being re-bodied as a professionally-made 'one-off' sports-racer. One of Smith's jobs was to cut-out new floor-boards from timber selected by Holland. What Holland had brought with him was creativity. He could be given an idea and interpret it as a drawing, then mark it out and form it in wood and metal.

One day Cyril Holland found himself drawing a two-seater with a rounded nose, a rounded, drooping tail, and a frowning countenance which was the result of imposing a wide-angle 'vee' on a near-vertical windscreen. It was not so much a drawing as a very rough sketch. 'I want that drawn-up properly, to suit the dimensions of an Austin Seven chassis', said Lyons, and went back into his office to think about where to get one. He considered several of his sidecar dealers before asking Alice Fenton to telephone Bolton 1348 and ask for Stanley Parker. 'Quite out of the question', was Parker's prompt reply. 'As an Austin dealer I'd be ruled out-of-order if I supplied you with a chassis.' Lyons was persuasive, reminding Parker of the Swallow sidecar's success so far and telling him how determined he was to go ahead and make motor cars. 'I shall do it somehow', he said 'so why not help me with the first one? I'll give you the first dealership.'

Parkers, 'Automobile Factors and Engineers', had their main offices and garage in Bradshawgate, Bolton, with further premises in Deansgate, Manchester. They were also known to Walmsley from his Stockport days. Although they were to retain their distinc-tion of being Jaguars longest-established dealership for many years, the connection was to cease in the days of British Leyland's most restrictive policies which led to so many distributors and dealers losing their franchise or interest or both. Later Parkers would sell Lancias and Talbots, perpetuating an interesting combination of agencies dating from the 1920s when (besides Austin, Morris, and locally-made Crossley) Parker was a distributor for Talbot Darracq and Chrysler. Stanley Parker had another think. He, too, knew what starting from scratch was like. He had begun his own motorcycle business some 12 years earlier. He already knew the appeal of the Swallow sidecar.

On January 21 1927, Parker advised Lyons that he had been able to obtain what he wanted, and sent him an invoice to his home address:

	£ s d
One special seven hp Austin Chassis *only*. Complete with maker's chassis equipment.	£112.0.0
Rail and delivery charges, Birmingham-Manchester	2.5.0
	£114.5.0

That price excluded an 'introductory commission' of 12½ per cent, £14 having been repaid to Lyons by Parker. There were still several years to go before declaration of the £100 car price war.

The Austin Seven was already in its fifth year of production. Like so many motoring ideas, it had been French-inspired (by the Bugatti-designed Bébé Peugeot, the original modern small car). Herbert Austin and William Lyons were similar in that what training they lacked they made up for by an instinct for what *looked* right. Austin, too, could get people to interpret his 'thumbnail' sketches and make what he wanted.

There were several special-bodied Austin Sevens on the market before the Swallow, notably those made at Wembley by glider-pilot turned racing-driver E.C. Gordon England. Rarer, but interesting in the present context, was an ultra-light Austin Seven two-seater, with a pointed tail not unlike that of a racy sidecar. It looked ungainly with the hood overhanging a shallow vee-windscreen and headlamps mounted on top of the wings where they must have vibrated like anything; but the simple body was neatly finished in polished aluminium. Its builder was in the same line of business as Lyons—none other than Hughes, the Birmingham sidecar makers! Swallow were not going to let *their* coachwork look like a sidecar though.

Sir Herbert Austin was not a noted respector of persons. He had kept E.C. Gordon England waiting after inviting him to the Austin Works for the first time; or perhaps England arrived early, thus explaining one account that he had an opportunity to meet several Austin employees before he saw Austin? Lyons was very put-out later on, when Austin failed to keep an appointment with him to discuss delivery of chassis when this was becoming something of a problem. He marched away from Austin's office, not just because he had not been able to talk about the unpredictable supply situation, but furious at the older man's discourtesy. Sir William Lyons says the experience was a major reason for his decision to market several other makes of chassis with Swallow coachwork.

Back in 1927, while preparations were being made to clothe the first Austin Seven Swallow, Cocker Street was also throbbing with industry as the sidecar business expanded. 1926 had seen the start of regular sales of Swallows abroad. The first overseas agent for Swallow sidecars was Emil Frey of Zürich. Frey was a young man, though not quite as young as Lyons, when he started his small motorcycle agency in 1924. He was a sportsman, too, and introduced grass-track racing into Switzerland. Two years after he had

The prototype Austin-Swallow of early 1927, shown without its hinge-back hard-top. Note spindly struts for the cycle-type wings in this illustration, carefully re-drawn by former Jaguar technical artist, Tim Loakes. Only the word 'Austin' appeared on the front at this stage.

Right *Fixed mudguards and running-boards soon became standard, as can be seen from this early batch of open two-seaters (and one with hard-top) parked along the Exchange Street side of the Swallow premises which the partners rented for two years from Thomas Walmsley before moving from Blackpool to Coventry.*

Left *Behind the simple back-cloth to this 'Model 4' picture can be seen the first Austin-Swallow saloon, nearing completion at the Cocker Street works.*

begun, Frey opened Zürich's first big motorcycle showroom and took on several franchises among them Swallow sidecars.

Frey's racing successes included a Swiss Grand Prix win on a Sunbeam and victory in the Klausen Pass mountain-climb on a 500 cc HRD-JAP—the machine created by Howard Davies who was to join the Swallow company himself. When Frey won the 1927 Solitude sidecar event in Germany, he provided the little Blackpool company with its first overseas race victory. It was not long before Frey became sole BSA distributor for Switzerland, and soon after that he was selling motor cars, too. Known and respected throughout Switzerland, the large *Emil Frey Aktiengesellschaft*, now controlled by his son, Walter, has offshoots in a variety of industries. The connection is still there, however, and *Emil Frey AG* is therefore the longest-established distributor in the world for Jaguar, including Swallow and SS of course. In autumn 1984, a youthful Emil Frey celebrated 60 years in the motor business—and his family firm's continuing association with Jaguar.

As with any enterprise, Swallow would get itself into difficulty with its agents and owners from time to time, perhaps through late delivery. The earliest recorded complaint was from the Netherlands, and amused Lyons enough to pass it on to the local paper. The whole story bears repeating:

'Cradle of Sadness

Dutch Firm and a Blackpool Sidecar.

Illuminating shafts of humour have a happy knack of penetrating even the walls of official and commercial life. They shed their light at unexpected moments and in unlikely quarters, as was revealed this week when a richly diverting letter was received in connection with a normally prosaic piece of business by the Swallow Sidecar and Coach-building Company of Blackpool.

Remembering that "language is given us that we might say kind things to one another," in the words of the philosopher, imagine the mixed feelings of the recipient, who is justifiably proud of the world-wide fame achieved by his firm's commodities, upon reading the appended epistle from a Dutch customer. The un-

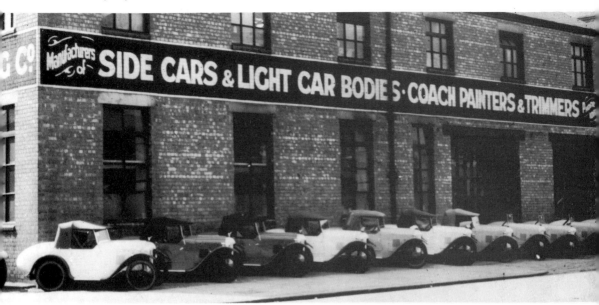

consciously humorous mutilation of colloquial English, lends a quaint twist to the context:

"Gentlemen,—It will be about 10 days ago that I telegraphed (send you a wire), that this blooming side car frame was released by the Custom officers, who have kept this frame apparently for about two months under guard. Can it be worse? How on earth will it ever be possible for us Continental people to do quick and sound business with you? So you will have by this time the side car frame some days in Blackpool.

We beseech and implore you to repair this damned frame soonest possible and despatch it quickest possible back. My customer is simply furious, and we are getting it on our nerves if this 'casus belli' is not coming back in due course.

"Please do write us how it works down there at Blackpool, and write me the time within I can re-expect this 'cradle of sadness.'

"Awaiting your news soon, we remain, dear Sirs, yours truly,

V. UTHAND."

The contents, though at first sight they appear to be unkind, are nothing of the sort. The criticism is directed against the Customs and against the accepted business policy of British firms who demand cash against pro forma invoices when dealing with foreign firms with which they have not had previous experience.

The business deal concerned, it should be added, has been satisfactorily completed. And a complete and sound Swallow sidecar is by now doubtless a pretext for vast pride on the part of some sporting young flying Dutchman, whose fury is happily appeased!'

In the spring of 1927, Swallow were ready to announce their first car, the Austin-Swallow two-seater. It was registered FR 7995; the chassis number was CHAI/2203. The car was photographed with and without a hard-top. This like the rest of the body was made of aluminium. The top—which caused *The Autocar* to describe the little machine as a 'miniature convertible saloon-coupé'—was mounted to the rear of the body via a hinge.

The idea was to pivot the roof when getting in or out, then bring it forward after completing the athletic manoeuvre and secure it by spring-loaded catches to the windscreen. On one test-drive along the 'prom' in a stiffish breeze, William Lyons experienced the sudden shock of having the roof detach itself from the catches and snap open, damaging itself and the neatly-rounded tail. The hinged-top idea was not kept for long. Another poor feature of that very first car, as described in *The Autocar* of May 20 1927, was its domed aluminium wings, the front ones being of the cycle type that 'steered' with the front wheels. Their spindly mountings failed in use, and either got caught up in the wheel-spokes or let a wing drop on the tyre and rotate with it—very dangerous either way! Good features were far more numerous than bad ones, however, although the means of achieving the desired effect were not always the most professional. The most widely-quoted example is that of 'dinging' the radiator filler neck down into the header tank so that Swallow's curved cowl would fit over it.

During 1927 the Austin Swallow was not made in great numbers because the varnishing shop was a limiting factor, where there was room for only two cars to dry-off at a time. As that took so long, it boiled down to the fact that, while still at Blackpool, Swallow could 'process' only two cars a day. In other words, the maximum car output in any one week was 14 if working continued on Saturday and Sunday. Often it did. Sidecar production was brought up to nearly 100 a week in the Cocker Street premises which had seemed large to begin with but, in a very short time, were to prove inadequate.

Arthur Whittaker had been taken 'off the road', to become chief assistant to Lyons on the business and service side and was to prove far more outstanding in business than as a salesman! A third girl, Constance Dickson, bright, quick and petite, joined the staff as Whittaker's secretary. There was little space for offices, and theirs was in a corner of the stores, with a skylight as the only window.

Through the latter part of 1927, the little Austin Swallow was developed, and another idea introduced, this time Morris-based. At about the time Lyons and Walmsley first met, 33 year-old Cecil Kimber—with several years experience at Sheffield-Simplex, AC, and

Prototype 'pen-nib' Austin Swallow, with sliding windows, photographed on the Fylde in 1928.

Alice Fenton 'modelling' the Morris Cowley-Swallow at the gates of Stanley Park, Blackpool, in 1927
(Miss N. Fenton).

Wrigley's (component suppliers) behind him—had landed himself the job of general manager at William Morris' retail business in Oxford called The Morris Garages. The story of Kimber and the MG car he created is legendary, and is well documented in several books, notably those of Wilson McComb who worked for the MG company and car club for ten years. Kimber's first sporting cars had the familiar 'bull nose' and special coachwork; the 'MG' octagon advertised them, although the marque name was still 'Morris'. By 1927 the MG had become square-nosed and virtually a marque in its own right. Kimber was a man who, like Lyons, appreciated what made a car look harmonious as an entity. His early saloons, or 'salonette' models, as he preferred to call them, had V-windscreens, rounded roofs, oval windows and two-tone paintwork. His open cars were stylish, too, and featured matching or contrasting bright colours, and machine-turned surfaces.

Another Morris-modifier was Swallow's old TT rival of the sidecar trade, Hughes of Birmingham, who had made an aluminium body for Reg Brown of Sunbeam motorcycles in the mid-20s. Based on the style of Brown's own 30/98 Vauxhall coachwork, Hughes' open four-seater was built on a Morris 14/28 'Oxford' chassis, and given the 'low look' by spring-flattening and increasing the rake of the steering column. McComb has recorded that Morris Garages had a Sunbeam agency and that Kimber knew Brown's car through this connection. There is nothing to suggest that Lyons or Walmsley were familiar with Hughes' Morris conversion which was almost-cerainly a 'one-off'. Swallow's look at the Morris market was to be a very brief one, anyway. The chassis they chose was not the 'Oxford' upon which the contemporary 'MG' was based, but the less powerful 1½-litre Morris 'Cowley'.

The Morris Cowley-Swallow sports two-seater was announced in mid-August 1927 and, like the first Austin-Swallow, was painted in cream and Crimson Lake. On the latest car, however, the two-toning was emphasised by a curling, tapering tail that hid a dickey seat. Lyons' 'old firm' Brown and Mallalieu, were the first to put one on show, and it was probably this car that Lyndon Smith remembers seeing as a prize in a glass case by Blackpool's pleasure beach fairground. Swallow's Cowley was much cheaper than the 'MG' models of 1927 and 1928, the list price being £210 with Ace discs to hide the artillery wheels which helped to make so many cars of the period look more old-fashioned than perhaps they were. For an extra £10 wire wheels were offered, but I have found no photographic record illustrating them. This was the only Swallow model not to have wire wheels as standard. In Coventry Lyons was forced to accept some FIAT chassis on artillery wheels which had to be scrapped as no-one wanted them.

William Lyons took very little time off, but there was one event in 1927 which resulted in his allowing himself some free hours—the birth of a daughter, Patricia. Already, however, Lyons' mind was concentrated upon the future of his company and he could see that his ambitions for it would mean another big move before long. The car business could not be expanded appreciably at the Cocker Street site, and bills for long-distance transportation of supplies were becoming astronomical. One way of reducing costs was to tow Austin Seven chassis six at a time round the corner from the railway station. On the other hand, the cost to Swallow of leaving chassis in the railway yard during peak periods was becoming impossible, too; yet there was severe limitation on storage space at the works, where jobs were sometimes done out on the pavement in fine weather—an added entertainment for holidaymakers en route from their boarding houses to the beach.

Having made his local car distribution arrangements, with Parker's in Manchester and Bolton, and Brown and Mallalieu in Blackpool, Lyons had set off for Birmingham with an appointment to see a potential agent called Frank Hallam. For some reason Hallam failed to turn up, thereby losing what might have been the opportunity of a lifetime. Lyons went straight on to the John Bright Street premises of P.J. Evans Ltd, who had been Standard's main Birmingham distributors since 1912. Percy J. Evans, winner of the 1911 Junior TT on a lightweight Humber and a keen motorist too, had been to Strasbourg in 1922 to see Henri Rougier's streamlined Voisin win the first French Touring Car Grand Prix. Tragically, he had been killed at Saverne afterwards, when his Paris-bound aeroplane crashed. His business now had two managing directors, Stanley Rodway and Norman Steeley. They met Lyons and examined his brightly-coloured little Austin, looked at each other and, with the same kind of impulse that had brought William Lyons to their showroom, offered to buy 50. It was the start of a long and fruitful collaboration, and P.J. Evans Ltd remains one of Jaguar's most prosperous distributors.

By far the most important selling move for Lyons came as a result of a meeting with Brown and Mallalieu's rather sharp ex-sales manager, Charlie Hayes, who had joined Henlys Ltd in London. Hayes saw that Lyons was 'going places' and tried to discuss a private business transaction but, having got so near, Lyons persuaded Hayes to introduce him to Henlys' top men—Frank Hough and Herbert Henly himself. There, in Henlys' Great Portland Street offices, to Lyons acknowledged amazement, an order for 500 chassis was placed with the Austin company, to be delivered to Talbot Street Station, later called Blackpool North. Thus was born the big storage problem. Henlys' required delivery rate—20 cars a week—together with the other orders he had in hand, meant not that Lyons *should* but that he *must* now expand the business very quickly indeed. To him, there was no alternative. He was not discouraged one little bit when he arrived back in Blackpool, flushed with the excitement of the prospects that now lay ahead, to be told by the blunt Bill Walmsley that he 'must be mad'.

Swallow's final year in Blackpool was one of hectic activity. First, the early problems of the Austin-Swallow two-seater had to be sorted out, and this included re-designing the wings and the hard-top. At the same time, as a result of the new deal with Henlys, an Austin-Swallow saloon had to be created, too. Cyril Holland worked with a will—first drawing a full scale side-elevation of the car on the workshop wall, then organising the jigs for the body frame and the panelling. Although some panel work was done locally, the main contract for the curved panelling was placed with the small Birmingham firm of Musgrove and Green.

Swallow's little Austin saloon was even more distinctive than the open two-seater. The accent was again on curves, for the need to be different from 'everyday' cars remained paramount. There were cerain similarities to Kimber's MG 'Salonette' and T.G. John's 12/50 Alvis saloon as clothed by 'Bobby' Jones of Carbodies—with rounded peak over a V-windscreen and oval rear window. The 'two-tone' treatment was *certainly* similar to that of the Alvis with the colour-dividing rib running forward along the waistline of the car, then curving up over the bonnet-top to give a dashing 'pen-nib' effect at the radiator—a style that had actually been started in America a few years earlier, but was virtually untried in Britain. At Austin Seven scale, nothing like this had ever been seen before, and there was simply no other saloon as luxurious as the Austin-Swallow on the market for under £200.

While the Austin saloon was being developed, so were other ideas. Several new makes of chassis were considered, but none became a series-production job in Blackpool. Harry Gill remembers being sent off late one day to Wolverhampton for a Clyno chassis, and having to stop at Warrington on the way back for a pair of bicycle lamps to tie on as darkness fell. The motor industry generally was having a hard time, and Clyno were among those unfortunate firms already on the slippery slope—not helped by the defection of their highly professional car-sellers, the Rooteses, to Hillman. A Swallow body *was* put on to that Clyno; it was an open tourer, and the Walmsleys ran it. The rear springs were flattened too much for use laden, as Walmsley found on looking at the car's reflection in a shop window one day. This car was replaced by an Alvis 12/50, purchased in chassis form via Henlys. *It* was given the Swallow pen-nib treatment by Cyril Holland, who built its two-door saloon body. Sir William Lyons recalls T.G. John's displeasure; no more Alvis

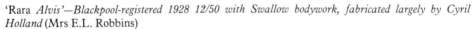

'Rara *Alvis*'—Blackpool-registered 1928 12/50 with Swallow bodywork, fabricated largely by Cyril Holland (Mrs E.L. Robbins)

chassis were supplied, but the partners ran a 'production model' Alvis for a while. Methods were still rather primitive. Harry Gill would find himself cutting out Austin-Swallow radiator badges with a fretsaw one day and hacking at a Morris clutch housing the next! The Austins and the Morrises had their steering columns lowered considerably in order to achieve the 'Swallow effect'. Quite what Herbert Austin or William Morris would have said or done about how that effect was achieved can only be imagined. By cutting away that housing, it was found that the Cowley's driving position could be lowered even more, and that was what mattered most.

Among the significant additions to the Swallow payroll in the Cocker Street days was another teenage apprentice, George Lee, who came as an apprentice coachmaker and stayed with the company until his retirement in 1976, very nearly completing 50 years service. There were the Thacker brothers, and the Marsh brothers (Arthur and Harold from the Black Country), Arthur Maddox, and Fred Perry—all Midlanders. Norman Holt and Charlie Atkinson are also remembered from this period, when the number of Swallow employees was rising towards the 50 mark.

It was Bernard Hartshorn who knew of Lyons' urgent need to find a trained blacksmith, and he advised his friend Jack Beardsley about the vacancy. Hartshorn, formerly a milk roundsman, came to Swallow as a wing-fitter. Beardsley was in fact a 'whitesmith'—the trade's terminology for a man trained mainly in the working of tinned metal. His seven years of training at Peter Bromley's small business near Blackpool had certainly made a very superior tinsmith of him. Jack Beardsley's first job at Swallow—to flatten the leaves of Morris Cowley springs in the interests of ride-height.—definitely brought a professional touch to this distinctly unprofessional but popular modification, which had gone wrong on Walmsley's Clyno. Funnily enough, Beardsley's job on the Austin Sevens was just the opposite—to *bend* the seven-leaf rear springs, thus increasing wheel-arch clearance to accommodate the extra weight of Swallow's bodywork without the danger of fouling. Like Alice Fenton, Arthur Whittaker, and Harry Teather, Jack Beardsley was to progress to senior management level at Jaguar in the years that followed. For the time being he was like Cyril Holland and Harry Gill—adept at the craft of making silk purses from sow's ears—as was Percy Birch, the first full-time trimmer.

Harry Teather had already spent five years with Swallow. He had worked in every department, and his experience included trimming, frame-making, panelling, wood-turning, fitting and painting. He seemed to have 'stuck' in the paint department when, early in 1928, he found himself feeling sick at the smell of peardrops during a cellulose spraying demonstration—so he changed jobs yet again! In fact he was badly needed upstairs to look after the stores (including packing spares orders, and their despatch), for Arthur Whittaker's duties were now so extensive that he could not cope, even with Connie Dickson's help.

At about this time, because he was diminutive and athletic, it was Harry Teather who was called in when the huge bus lift descending became wedged against the roof of one of the prototype saloons and tipped it up, after the careless operator had failed to look underneath. Teather had to crawl around in the latticework to free the mechanism. The car bounced up again, repairably squashed. That lift must have been unique in the district, for Harry Teather also remembered it being used to unload Sir Henry Segrave's V12 Sunbeam after its 152.33 mph world record run at Southport. The reason for its presence in Blackpool was probably that Jackson Brothers, the Sunbeam agents, were to display it. (The present occupiers of Cocker Street, Blackpool, remember having to call in specialists from Fleetwood docks to dismantle the lift when they wanted it out of the way some years ago.) Segrave was young Bobby Walmsley's great hero, especially after he had paused for a chat during a Blackpool sprint meeting.

As the evenings began to draw in, in that autumn of 1928, William Lyons' trips to the Midlands became more frequent. He had considered a further move on the Fylde peninsula but decided against it. Swallow *must* have a permanent home and he found it in Coventry. When the notices went up around the works, inviting employees to stay with the company but leave Blackpool, about 50 people were working for the Swallow Sidecar and Coach Building Company. Harry Teather once calculated that 32 of them made the move to Coventry. He himself agreed to come only after the promise of a substantial increase in wages—from one to three pounds a week. For some enthusiastic yet practical people like himself it was the start of a new way of life, while for the Midlanders it was like going home. Those who did not move south went to Burlingham (later Duple) bus and coach works, or changed their trade to stay in the north.

Some people went to Coventry as an 'advance party'. Because of his responsibility for the factory's contents, Harry Teather had to stay behind and ensure that everything was packed and despatched in sequence. To ensure minimum production losses, the first major items to go were boxed sets of parts, just ahead of the main party. Teather was very nearly the last of the team to leave the empty Cocker Street works; but he did not leave sadly for he knew from the miracles Swallow had performed already that he was a member of a winning team—and there were not many of those around the industry on November 7 1928. The very last person to leave was probably the newly-recruited company secretary, Jack Lee. He was not going to Coventry, and he stayed on to 'fill in the blanks' and sign the stereotype letters that Alice Fenton had prepared for those who requested introductions to new jobs.

Among the piles of unwanted material left behind were several boxes of glass plate negatives and printers blocks. History, to William Lyons as to Henry Ford, was 'bunk'—at least it was then. With so much to look forward to, so many ambitions to be fulfilled, and so much hard work to be done on the way, who would want to remember what had been achieved by Swallow in those funny little Blackpool factories? It is fortunate that some negatives *were* still to be found in a photographer's collection in Blackpool in the late 1970s. Judging from the quality, they may well have been rejects that William Lyons was never shown at the time—but they did include several interesting 'new' shots of Swallow's Blackpool products.

It would not be long before the bank and the two fathers were paid off by Lyons and Walmsley. Tom Walmsley re-let the Cocker Street works to a road haulage firm, Tichenor and Brown. Today the premises are occupied by the Ismail company, as they have been for many years. The proprietor, Ismail Gibrail, came from British Somaliland as a youth, and was in the district in the Swallow days, so he knows that his tea and coffee blending machines are standing where trimmers' hammers once clicked and one of the world's great car manufacturing companies was born.

4: Coventry, and first contact with Standard (1928 to 1931)

Some people took the move from Lancashire in their stride; others took a while to adjust. Even William Lyons found only the immediate vicinity of Coventry Cathedral attractive after his first walk around the Midland city centre where he and Walmsley lived, for their first few weeks, at the Queen's Hotel in Hertford Street which now forms part of Coventry's 'pedestrian only' shopping precinct. Lyons had used this hotel during his earlier visits, when he had made his first significant Coventry 'contact' a Mr Aylesbury, who ran The Midland Bent Timber Company and who had introduced him to Charles Odell, the estate agent. There had been numerous business premises for sale in Coventry, but none available on lease-hold—and that was all Lyons and Walmsley could afford.

To the north of Coventry, in the triangle formed by the industrial suburbs of Radford and Holbrooks (part of Foleshill), and the coal-mining one of Keresley, there was a large area of parkland, some of which still exists. Most of it, however, has been developed for housing and as an industrial estate. The park known as Whitmore Park has lent its name to this whole district. Through Odell, Lyons met Harry Noel Gillitt, secretary of the syndicate that controlled businesses on the Whitmore Park estate. A son-in-law of Starley of Rover as well as a solicitor, Gillitt knew the 'Coventry scene' well and was to prove a staunch ally to Lyons. Gillitt told Lyons about a factory, already quite old, and only partly in use. It consisted of four separate blocks each on a different level, situated at the end of a rutted and often muddy 'unadopted' main estate road. The sloping ground meant that there was plenty of potential storage space under the floors. Designed and used for the packing of shells with explosives, the factory had floors that were wooden and fixed with copper nails to help limit the possibility of a spark. There may well have been no explosions, but the two empty blocks were certainly in dire need of attention after some ten years of disuse. All the same, there was plenty of room in just one block to accommodate Swallow for the immediate future and, with the possibility of expansion on site, Lyons knew he must try and obtain these premises somehow.

Fortunately, on their initial tour of inspection Gillitt and Lyons developed a strong respect for one another, and Gillitt was able to return to the Whitmore Park syndicate chairman, George Gray, with a plan to let one block to Swallow at £1,200 per year for three years, with an option to purchase *both* empty blocks freehold for £12,000 after that time. The syndicate agreed, to Lyons' delight. The deed was done. Bernard Gray, son of the syndicate chairman, had offered to clean up the premises—but (thought Lyons) Bill

Above left *Broadgate, Coventry, shortly after Lyons and Walmsley moved from Blackpool. Only the bank building still stands. Beyond it, in Hertford Street (now part of the pedestrian shopping precinct), was the Queen's Hotel where they stayed for a time* (Coventry City Collection). **Left** *Fred Gardner's sawmill in the old shell-filling factory, which the company was to occupy for more than 20 years. (Fred stands white-collared, hands on hips, without the hat upon which it was said he used to jump.)*

Cyril Holland (in cow-gown) stands on one of the old rails that ran through the works. Body framework nearest camera is for the FIAT chassis which were obsolete and therefore available as a batch for Swallow during the company's first year in Coventry. Sir William Lyons acknowledges the great debt owed to Cyril Holland for returning to the company in Coventry, and overcoming Swallow's body-production crisis in the winter of 1928-1929.

Walmsley was an NCO once; he would love to supervise that part of the operation. So the offer was turned down!

The many facets of moving between factories 140 miles apart meant that Lyons and Walmsley would spend most weekdays in Coventry, returning to Blackpool at weekends leaving Jack Chandler—who was to become the general works contractor—in charge of tidying up premises. This did not prevent the newly-laid electric cable from being stolen and having to be replaced quickly and at great cost, much to Lyons' chagrin. Harry Teather remembered his own arrival in Coventry on November 7 1928 only too well. 'I took the tram from Broadgate, along the Foleshill Road to Courtaulds. Coventry must have been the only city anywhere to have trams with square wheels! It was nearly another mile from there along Lockhurst Lane, across the level crossing, into Holbrook Lane and finally, on foot, up that track through the estate. Our works seemed a long way up it, too! That year it seemed to rain and rain for weeks, and my first impression on that murky afternoon was that this must be one of the most depressing places on earth. The vision of the coke braziers and dim temporary lighting which first greeted me at the works is one that lives with me still.'

That rough track through Whitmore Park (which had a 'Foleshill' postal address) was to become known as 'Swallow Road', and is marked as such on current Coventry street plans, even though Dunlop have obliterated its junction with Holbrook Lane in making today's access arrangements. One can, however, still see the blocked-up doors of the factories whose tenants would not contribute to the resurfacing work which Swallow eventually had to organise, when estate road conditions became virtually impossible for suppliers or employees to live with. (There would even come a time when goods would be dumped at the bottom of that drive.)

In the winter of 1928 enthusiasm and necessity quickly overcame depression. As Harry Teather's account in the *Jaguar Apprentices' Magazine* explains: 'One did not have time to

The Coventry works in 1929, with the wooden floor which Glikstens would have loved to acquire had the factory ever been demolished. (Dunlop still use the old factory, as offices.) The distinctive Austin-Swallow tail and hard-top are clearly seen in this 1929 shot.

ponder the respective merits of the town we had left and the city of our adoption; a working day of at least 12 hours saw to that. Every member of the company, staff included, worked these extended hours for months . . . In fact the next two years were so busy that I, at any rate, was not aware that another depression had crept up on the country.'

Swallow's forward trend was against all industrial portents and those unaware of his single-mindedness might have been forgiven for thinking that Lyons stood no chance. As it was, the shell-filling works proved readily adaptable to the separation of departments, and the 'flow' through them soon went up towards the 50-cars-a-week target. The main set-back to Swallow's early progress in Coventry was in the 'productionising' of the wooden framework to permit higher output, easier assembly, and cheapness. Having been offered no removal expenses to return to the Midlands, Cyril Holland had stayed on in Blackpool to work for Burlingham. Aylesbury provided another introduction for Lyons, however, in Frank Etches. Etches had (claimed Aylesbury) developed steam-bending methods in body frame manufacture when working for Triumph cars; so Lyons had brought him in at the start, to organise body assembly in Coventry. Unfortunately, the steam-bent timber tended to bend back! Etches had made himself ill from overwork and finally resigned with the worry of it. He never came back. At least the 50 sets of car parts, packed up and sent from Blackpool by Harry Teather, could be assembled!

Apart from the partners, Arthur Whittaker, and Alice Fenton, the first senior superintendents in Coventry were Harry Gill (mounting department), Arthur Marsh (paint shop), Harry Teather (stores), Ned Carey (trim shop), Jack Beardsley (metalwork and finishing), Dick Cronkshaw (sidecar shop), and Fred Gardner (sawmill); and—after a few months and new inducements—Cyril Holland returned to run the bodyframe and panelling department. Fred Gardner was one of the first 'newcomers' to join Swallow after the move, and formed a rather one-sided 'bond' with Lyons. He was an extrovert, and more 'familiar' than Lyons usually liked. He stayed on with Jaguar until well into his 70s, when he was recorded as referring to Sir William as 'my mate'. Born in Liverpool, Fred

Gardner first worked for a wheelwright in Stafford. His father was a seaman; his mother and several other relations were a music-hall team—probably a reason for his extensive *repertoire* of chorus songs and dirty jokes. He was the last chairman of Sydenham Palace music hall in Cox Street, Coventry. He was much influenced by the church, and was a sidesman at Holy Trinity. A strong disciplinarian, he was fair, too. In Coventry as in Blackpool, trade was seasonal; like his colleagues he was always reluctant to tell people to go away for the quiet season and glad when he could re-employ them several months later. The notice on his door read; 'Work like Helen B. Merry'. For years he was an 'institution' of the company.

It is worth quoting Harry Teather again on this question of unemployment: 'In response to an advertisement of a vacancy for one storekeeper, a huge crowd of applicants had assembled at the Time Office for interview. I was extremely busy that particular morning and as it would have been physically impossible to interview everyone, I decided that the first man I came to who had the necessary experience, was married and preferably wearing a discharged-service badge, would be selected. I came across my man in the first fifteen; he possessed all my requirements plus three children. When I announced that the position was filled, I was nearly mobbed because several of the men present were fathers of five or more children; indignation was rife that I had not taken account of this factor. I was in my early twenties at the time, but I have never forgotten this little episode.'

Some employees, like the Marsh brothers, commuted daily from the Black Country quite happily—glad to be working so much nearer home than before. Swallow had the ability to recruit labour from firms who made bodies for the bigger motor companies that had fallen on hard times. One example was Hollick and Pratt, who specialised in Morris bodies. Another was Holbrook Bodies, run by Captain Stonehouse with financial help from W.A. Oubridge of the nearby British Piston Ring Company. This coachbuilding firm made Weymann-style bodies for Hillman in the two lower shell-filling factory blocks at Whitmore Park, and were therefore next-door neighbours. When they went 'broke', later, Swallow took over their premises.

The Blackpool-ites did not bring their families south straight away. From the Queens Hotel near Broadgate (Coventry's acknowledged 'centre' then, as now) Lyons and Walmsley moved to lodgings in St Pauls Road, Foleshill, much nearer to the 'new' works. Alice Fenton shared rooms in Holmsdale Road with Connie Dickson who had moved home to Fleetwood but had been working there for only a fortnight when her good friend Alice Fenton persuaded her to come and join her in Coventry. So one Sunday, she had reported to the bungalow in Bispham Road, Blackpool, where Greta Lyons and baby Pat were still living, and William Lyons had whisked her off to be re-united with Alice. St Pauls Road and Holmsdale Road were near one another, on the other side of the Foleshill Road and, after Alice and Connie had been pushed into the gutter by some loafers as they passed the Holbrook Lane fish-and-chip shop one night, Lyons and Walmsley usually chaperoned them to the end of their road after the long day's work. It was not long before the partners found themselves homes in residential Earlsdon, south of the city centre, and the girls moved the other way, to Holbrooks, which provided a less-traumatic walk to and from the factory. They were very independent, however, taking life as it came. From digs in St Luke's Road they moved to a house which they rented in Rotherham Road. Alice was earning more so she bought the downstairs furniture; Connie saw to the upstairs. Alice's younger sister Nancy joined them and, later, when Alice's parents came to Coventry, they all lived in Lythalls Lane.

A group of unmarried male Blackpool 'immigrants' shared 45, Rotherham Road immediately after the girls moved out. They were Harry Gill, Chandos Leigh, Lyndon Smith, and Harry Teather. Gill and Smith had become particular 'buddies', and this was fine while each had a motorcycle of his own. When they decided to buy and share a second-hand Austin Seven the trouble began—not because it had a Gordon England body, but because each felt the other was getting the best use out of it. Both men were to leave the company before it became 'Jaguar Cars Ltd', and they made their fortunes elsewhere. No love was lost between them, yet they had their similarities. Neither was prepared to dedicate himself blindly to the company for what seemed relatively little reward. That each was to be so successful financially may well have been a result of experiencing Swallow's struggle to win—plus (in Smith's case especially) a good share of luck.

Sharing was a way of life at Swallow. Not until the British Leyland days was the company to become really impersonal. Nevertheless, after Swallow moved to Coventry, and the workforce expanded through three-figure to four-figure proportions, the organisation was soon large enough for significant people possibly to be missed from this narrative. It is to my regret that this must happen more and more as the story unfolds. One man who should not be left out, however, is Jack Atkins.

No one could have lived nearer to the Whitmore Park shell-filling factory than the Atkins family, for their house in Holbrook Lane was situated directly opposite the industrial estate road . . . 'Swallow Road'. As a schoolboy, Jack became familiar with the activities of the companies on the site—on the left were Dunlop and Motor Panels. On the right was the famous White and Poppe engine factory, and further up the slope on the same side was Holbrook Bodies. Jack Atkins was looking for a job just as Swallow moved in, and soon he was picking his way up the rutted track to apply for work. In the spring of 1929 he became a wing-fitter's mate. The significance here is not only that this retired trim-shop foreman lives in that same house today, but that Jack Atkins is the only man to have served Jaguar for over 50 years *in Coventry*. (Indeed Sir William Lyons and Harry Teather were the only other people to complete 50 years with the firm, although George Lee did come very close, too, when he retired in 1976; likewise Jack Randle, Radford works director, still with the company in 1985.)

As already indicated, the sudden growth in Austin Seven Swallow production capacity from 12 to 50 and more units a week was of no particular interest to Sir Herbert Austin, and one of the first actions William Lyons took in Coventry was to pursue the possibilities of obtaining other makes of chassis upon which to build Swallow coachwork. He and Walmsley had looked at several makes of chassis while still in the north, as we have seen. The first of the larger Swallow saloon bodies to be catalogued was based upon the obsolescent and therefore readily-available FIAT 509A chassis which, as Michael Sedgwick points out in his authoritative book on the great Italian *marque*, was assembled for a brief period in Vickers' ordnance works in Crayford, Kent. This was done under the auspices of FIAT's British importer D'Arcy Baker, whose 1929 catalogue included the 'Swallow' version at £260, with wire wheels £5 extra, whereas Swallow's own leaflet priced it at £255 below a picture of a car fitted with wire wheels.

The FIAT-Swallow followed the Austin-Swallow and Alvis-Swallow style of two-door saloon coachwork, but was less quaint and more elegant in eschewing 'pen-nib' colour schemes; two-tone colours were there aplenty, with nine combinations from the now-traditional Cream with Crimson to Light Mole Brown with Deep Suede Brown, but the waistline colour-division extended horizontally along the body and bonnet sides and gave the car, with its impressive radiator, a most sporting appearance. However, its 'low' gearing and small engine did not provide it with a sporting performance.

The FIAT-Swallow had been the product of discussions between William Lyons and James Ritchie, who ran the main Scottish FIAT distributorship from his former South Western Bodyworks—where imposing coachwork was once made for Daimler and other chassis—in Renfrew Street, Glasgow; later, Ritchie was to hold SS and Jaguar franchises.

Above left *One of Swallow's earliest recruits, Harry Gill, seen on his Scott Squirrel on 'The Dumps' under which ammunition had once been stored, when the factory had been used for war work* (H. Gill). **Above right** *The big adventure! Alice Fenton (left) and Connie Dickson were still teenagers when they were photographed at Swallow Road soon after moving south. They were, respectively, secretaries to William Lyons and Arthur Whittaker. Already, however, Alice was the boss's 'right hand' on sales matters* (Mrs H. Teather).

Having presumably seen the Alvis as well as the Austin, Frank Hough of Henlys asked Lyons for a similar saloon body on the Swift Ten—one of many makes for which Henlys held a London agency.

As suggested in the last chapter, the Henly organisation was the biggest single external influence in the initial development of the Swallow Coachbuilding Company (as the business became known when sidecars began to become the 'poor relation'). Herbert Gerald Henly, the son of an agent for continental cutlery, began his career articled to an estate agent in Highbury, London, just before the first World War. As duty came before physical fitness, Henly was able to volunteer as an Army Service Corps transport driver, despite having a malformed foot. He was finally 'discovered' in Mesapotamia in 1917 and invalided-out. Back home he decided to make for the heartland of London's motor trade, and it was not long before he was able to rent premises at 91, Great Portland Street, not far from Warren Street (nor from the likes of Jack Barclay either).

By the time of the 1921 London motor show 'Henly & Co' had already obtained agencies for Albert, Austin, Citroën, Humber, Overland, Ruston Hornsby, Salmson and Standard cars. That autumn, Henly representatives were on duty not only on the Albert stand at Olympia but also showing-off the brand new French Salmson *marque* displayed in the 'overflow' section, up the road at White City. An 'invitation' advertisement advised readers of *The Motor* that 'our deferred payment system is at your disposal. 4 per cent extra and no vexatious inquiries'.

Very early in its history Henlys became a partnership between the dapper, gentlemanly 'Bertie' Henly and Frank Hough, the rough, tough former motorcycle trader from Walsall. It might have seemed as though their personalities would clash, but they appear to have worked well together with Hough as chairman (terrorising the salesmen, by all accounts) and Henly (the more gentlemanly) as Deputy Chairman. The name 'Hough', they agreed, sounded 'hard' and would complicate the title of the company which would be 'floated' as Henlys (1928) Ltd with a share capital of £300,000 on November 7 1928. Henly and Hough were joint Managing Directors, with two other board members— Henry Lees Buckley of Splintex Safety Glass Ltd and the Rt Hon Charles Albert McCurdy, PC, KC. (Specific concessions were then listed for Alvis, Clyno, Invicta, Swift, Talbot and Swallow.)

Many famous car sellers have worked for Henlys over the years, not least among them being J.A. Joyce who, like Hough, had met Henly in the Middle East during the war and soon afterwards covered 100 miles in an hour with an AC at Brooklands. (Jack Joyce would sometimes act as Alice Fenton's escort at motor industry functions.) Most important, historically, was the occasion when Reginald Chandler of Hitchin—on the 'bread-line' after working his passage home from an abortive attempt at selling trucks for General Motors in Toronto—breezed jauntily into 91, Great Portland Street when he knew Henly and Hough were away on business, and told a rather surprised Charlie Hayes that Bertie Henly had advised him to report for duty as a car salesman. Business was bad in that year of the General Strike (1926) and the company was, like most, often hard pressed to pay its staff. Chandler worked like a demon, virtually chasing people from Great Portland Street into the showroom—hardly dignified; but then Chandler was broke and hungry. 'Who's that?', Henly asked Hayes curtly when he returned. 'Your new man Chandler', said Hayes. 'Never heard of him', hissed Henly, 'get rid of him'. 'I don't think we should do that, Guv'nor', replied Hayes, 'It's thanks to him we can pay the wages this week!' So Chandler stayed.

It was soon after this episode that Hayes, as mentioned earlier, introduced Lyons to Henly and Hough. Meanwhile, Chandler was making lightning progress through the firm which was growing quickly, too, with additional premises at 155 to 157, Great Portland Street, and Devonshire House in Piccadilly acquired by the time their first Austin Seven Swallow two-seater was delivered on January 21 1928 at an invoice price of £151 8s 9d.

Henlys' official territory covered the whole of England south of a line drawn from the Bristol Channel to the Wash, with the exception of Kent where Martin Walter and Company held sway—although they had to accept 'subservience' to Henlys later, in the context of Swallow at least. When Henlys began advertising 'The Swallow Has Arrived!' early in 1928, they listed not only their London showroom addresses and the service workshop in Hawley Crescent, Camden Town, but gave prominence to their new premises in Manchester. (These were run by George White, son of a successful silk merchant in the

Still no machine shop; but there was a lot a trained whitesmith like Jack Beardsley (centre of picture, in dungarees) could do to help Swallow change from just body-making to full-scale car manufacture. Mean-time, in 1930, the main work was bracketry. Far left, having taken over Beardsley's forge, is blacksmith Bill Stevens.

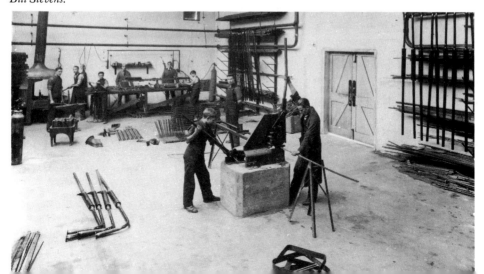

city.) This presented diplomatic problems for Lyons in his relationships with Frank Hough and Stanley Parker, his original agent, but for a while Henlys reverted to London addresses and telephone numbers in their advertising and major territorial claims beyond the agreed line were avoided. As time went on, however, Hough's demanding style gave Henlys the reputation of rough-shod riders.

The FIAT and Swift Swallows were joined at the 1929 Olympia Show by a third and much more important new model—more important because of the effect of the linking of words: Standard-Swallow. There had been no question of achieving full participation at Olympia in 1928, and that year's motor show had co-incided with Swallow's arrival in Coventry anyway. On the other hand, 1929 marked the first Swallow *car* stand ever seen at a motor show. A huge wooden head-board proclaimed 'Swallow Coachwork' in flowing script, with 'Swallow Coachbuilding Co, Coventry' etched clearly below. Beside each car was an oval board on a tripod, naming the car by make and hyphenating this with the word 'Swallow', followed by the rather vague phrase: 'Carriage & Chassis Work, Made in England'. If an Austin-Swallow *was* on show, its presence is not confirmed by the only available picture of the stand in which the relative problems of giving popular cars the

A stand at Olympia: Swallow's first appearance at a car show, in October 1929—the month Wall Street crashed, and yet the month in which Swallow showed its intention to make the grade in the world of the motor car. Left to right: Swift '10', FIAT '9', and Standard '9', all with Swallow coachwork. The last is very much a pre-production model, featuring a bonnet-line that was simply too high for the body. A new radiator cowl was created by Swallow before regular deliveries began, and it formed the basis for the style-setting SS that came later (G. Lee).

1930 Standard-Swallow 9 hp saloon, showing redesigned cowl. The bowler-hatted customer, emphasising the lowness of the roof-line, is The Autocar *technical artist, Max Millar. His car was finished in two shades of blue* (The Autocar).

'low look' are to be seen very clearly. Best looking of the trio was the FIAT-Swallow with its waist-moulding remaining three inches or so below windows and bonnet-top. The Swift-Swallow had a higher bonnet, emphasised by this low waistline; but it was the Standard-Swallow that looked oddest of all—for the 'Big Nine' had a tall and distinctive yet distinctly old-fashioned radiator which made for a ridiculously-high bonnet and negligible windscreen depth.

Looking at the photograph now, it is easy to see why William Lyons was incensed by the strange appearance of his first Standard-Swallow, which almost-certainly remained a prototype. Early in 1930 the car was 're-launched' with a new grille design which was to be developed into the first 'SS' radiator style. In the meantime, Captain Black of the Standard Company took a good look at Lyons' design and soon Standard's own 'peaked' radiator disappeared, to be replaced by one not at all dissimilar to that of the Standard-Swallow!

The only people to make a virtue of the old-style radiator were the Jensens, whose 1929 two-seater on Standard's Big Nine chassis was very dashing-looking, and became the prototype Avon Special. The New Avon Body Company of Warwick was to introduce several more Jensen-designed Standards over the next few years, and the apparent 'parallel' between Avon and Swallow was very marked, for a short period. Allan and Richard Jensen were soon to create their own motor company, however, and despite the styling consultancy work of C.F. Beauvais, Avon faded away as a coachbuilder; strange, then that the Avon name should be revived in the late 1970s—to be associated with, of all things, the Jaguar marque. After a year of turmoil as they settled in at Whitmore Park, Swallow employees felt quite proud to be given the opportunity of going to London to see their handiwork displayed.

Pat Lyons (right) poses with her cousin Barbara, in front of the father's Vauxhall, with its fabric-covered roof and trunk, at Woodside, the Lyons' house in Gibbet Hill Road, Coventry, circa 1931. This car undoubtedly provided several ideas for the first SS.

Among those who went to Olympia in 1929 were Alice Fenton and Connie Dickson. Happy to be together again, the two girls loved the atmosphere of Olympia and their involvement with it. When Bertie Henly and Frank Hough took them for tea in the big restaurant and gave them each a box of chocolates afterwards, the girls were over the moon. The long hours in the dingy Midland shell-filling factory were well worth such brief glimpses of London life in 1929.

The acquisiton of a new company secretary was an important Swallow event. Former Singer accounts man Edward Huckvale was selected from a number of applicants—and the partners being in accord for once! ('He doesn't seem to have big ideas', observed Lyons as they were pondering. 'No, and he's the only one not carrying a rolled umbrella, either', Walmsley snorted.) Huckvale was to stay for the rest of his career, and become a director.

As the new decade began, Swallow Coachbuilding rose rapidly from 'amateur' to 'professional' status. The sidecar business flourished, too, making maximum use of 'off-cuts' that might have been scrapped, but for the presence of the smaller product. Improvisation and self-sufficiency were the order of the day, and Cyril Holland—once again the linchpin of Swallow body manufacture—was busier than ever, creating the adaptions for the characteristic Swallow saloon shape for Austin, Standard, and Swift as those chassis were updated; and for the Morris Minor, although this model was never catalogued. It was, however, displayed by Henlys.

Despite their general impression of frugality, there is no doubt that Swallow paid well with piecework incentives, and employees who 'got their week in' could find *and* afford some free time at weekends. Football fans like Wilf Chamberlain and George Kellie would work through a Friday night if it meant there would be an opportunity to watch Coventry City—then in the third division—play next day. Unattached Blackpool men such as Donald Brown and Chandos Leigh, raced one another up to Lancashire at the end of a Friday shift on their motorcycles. Non-motorists returning north could get lifts—perhaps from Lyons or Walmsley in one of the 'official' Alvises; or from Arthur Whittaker who would charge them ten shillings a trip in the curly-haired chain-smoker's Bullnose Morris—until he married in Blackpool in 1930 and brought his bride, Mary, to Coventry.

The partners' Alvises were replaced in 1930 by a pair of substantial Vauxhall 20/60 'Kingston' coupés. Walmsley chose his, and Lyons followed suit reluctantly. They cost nearly £600 each but were impressive in a modern 'American' way—and, after all, Swallow's own products were still on the small side for regular company director's transport. These early GM-influenced Vauxhalls did have a style that related to the partners' shared tastes. Walmsley's was finished in his favourite colour scheme of brown and beige. Lyons' car was painted ivory, with black fabric roof and trunk, and black wings. By 1930, too, the partners had long since left their St Pauls Road accommodation—'Bugsville' as Walmsley had called it—and brought their families south. The Walmsleys lived first in Morningside; later they moved round the corner into Belvedere Road. Both houses were named 'Swallowdene' and situated in residential Earlsdon. The Lyonses lived nearby, in Eastleigh Avenue, initially; then they moved two miles further south, to the mock-Tudor 'Woodside' on Gibbet Hill, off the fine avenue that leads from Coventry to Kenilworth.

Success brought different reactions from the two partners. Walmsley, a craftsman in many ways, enjoyed the design and development of any new feature; but when it came to making and selling more cars, his enthusiasm began to evaporate. Lyons wanted to move ahead quicker than ever, now that he was experiencing the attainment of his early ambitions. Encouraged as usual by Frank Hough, Lyons moved into the open-two seater market in the winter of 1930-1. Apart from the little Austin, it was the company's first open car since the shortlived Morris Cowley-Swallow. With a tail even more sweeping than Jensen's 1929 Avon Special, the new Wolseley Hornet-Swallow was also Lyons' first six-cylinder product. It was to be supplemented from Autumn 1931 by a four-seater version.

It was another six-cylinder engine, however, that would point the Swallow Coachbuilding Company along its next stretch of road. Henlys, were undertaking most of Swallow's publicity by 1931, giving the impression of an exclusive national franchise. Certainly their 'Swallow Exclusive Coachwork' slogans stood out in the motoring press, usually in the form of whole-page advertisements in *The Autocar, The Motor,* and *The Light Car and Cyclecar.* Catch-phrases such as 'Big Car Comfort . . . Swallow Beauty . . . Austin dependability', 'A Swallow looks expensive', 'If you can't buy a Rolls you can buy distinction', and even 'The World's Most Beautiful Coachwork'.

William Westwater Bett, a former Henlys staffman, had started his own advertising agency in the Strand area of London in 1929. Frequent views of that tall column in nearby Trafalgar Square are said to have led to his naming the company 'Nelson Advertising'. It was natural for Bett to have picked up the Henlys business, formerly handled by Dorland Advertising, and it was he who did so much to give Henlys' and later Swallow's own advertising that exotic aura.

The FIAT-Swallow was not listed after 1930; the last Swift-Swallow advertising was in June 1931. At £269, the Swallow-bodied Swift Ten had been the costliest of the range. Simultaneously, however, another version of Swallow's saloon body, more elongated than any previous one, joined the Austin Seven, Standard Nine, and Wolseley Hornet Swallows. 'The ideal car . . . at an ideal price', read The Henlys/Swallow advertising 'copy' for *The Motor* of June 23 1931. 'The new Standard six-cylinder Swallow . . . Nothing so magnificent, so marvellous, or offering such astonishing value for money has ever been placed before the car-buying public. Here is surely a "dream" car—a car with a £1,000 appearance, a performance equalled by no other £16 tax car in the world . . .' and so on. Lyons had placed emphasis on value-for-money from the outset. This advertisement does nevertheless appear to have marked the first use of the idea of a '£1,000' look. The car in question was based on the Standard Ensign Six chassis, and it took over the role of top of the Swallow range. It was priced at £275.

5: The SS comes . . .
maybe a year too soon? (1931 to 1932)

From the Blackpool days, when Iliffe's northern area manager, Raymond Bailey had introduced him to a number of prospective sidecar dealers, William Lyons and the people of the Iliffe Press publishing group were particularly close friends from the chairman, Claude Wallis, down.

Geoffrey Smith Managing Editor of *The Autocar*, seemed to get any 'announcement' story first. This was natural enough, for was not *The Autocar* the oldest and most respected of all the journals that had grown up with the British motor Industry? (Later, Lyons made sure that *The Motor* got its 'fair share' of the coverage!) Each year, as motor show time came around, Montague Tombs (*The Autocar's* technical editor) would sally forth with artist F. Gordon Crosby and make a tour of Olympia commenting light-heartedly upon the trends he discovered.

Lyons, Walmsley and company, whizzing up and down between Coventry and Blackpool, had had little or no time to think about the 1928 motor show, as we have seen. Maybe, in a spare moment, Lyons had been able to settle down to Tombs' discourse in that autumn's motor show edition of *The Autocar*, under the heading 'Keeping up Appearances':

'What *is* a "sportsman" *[wrote Tombs in the second of three special issues]* or a "real sportsman", or a "genuine sportsman", or even—if you come to that—a "close-coupled" sportsman, anyway?

'Why should all the car makers rush round to their coachwork departments and order coupé bodies for a "sportsman"? Hasn't the fellow got enough perquisites already, what with his "plus-four" bags and his "plus-two" cigarettes, and all the paraphernalia of his "sports wear"? "Palm-Beach-suitings"! Does he have a "sportswife" and "sportskids" to go about with him? If so, the members of his entourage who sit in the back seats of his coupé must have got some funny legs. The illustrator began to enjoy himself very much trying to picture the probable effects on future generations of the habit of regular riding in some of the "Sportsman's" coupés in the Show.'

Sure enough, in that 1928 *Autocar* heading picture Crosby, pipe in mouth, and the diminutive Tombs are seen considering an imaginary close-coupled coupé. It is an interesting sketch, if only a cartoon.

Exactly three years later, came the announcement of Swallow's new cars the SS1 and the SS2.

John Black and Spencer Wilks were senior directors of the Hillman company when Rootes took over the Hillman-Humber-Commer Group. Marriage to daughters of

Left *Full page advertisement in colour, from* The Autocar *of July 31 1931, depicts a 9 hp Standard Swallow saloon but whets motorists' appetites with talk of the 'SS'—still two months away!*

Back in October 1928, this 'self-portrait' of Montague Tombs (the smaller one!) and F. Gordon Crosby headed their annual motor show chat-story. They called it 'Keeping Up Appearances' and Tombs made some rather cynical remarks about motoring fashion. The first SS coupé (see page 71) appeared three years later. Artist Crosby became an SS customer himself! (The Autocar).

William Hillman turned out to be no inducement to either to stay in a subservient role. Wilks went to the Rover Company; Black joined Reginald Maudslay's Standard Company, which was on the verge of becoming too old-fashioned to survive. That was in 1929. Black was what Sir William Lyons calls a 'go-getter'—as he himself has often been described. It was Black who would provide a catalyst for the thoughts of Henly, Hough and Lyons; by 1931, they were seeing that Swallow's style would be as shortlived as that of its rivals if a special chassis could not be produced at a reasonable cost, to accommodate the long low look they wanted to sell. The characteristic Swallow saloon look had reached its ultimate expression, having been 'stretched' from Austin Seven out to Standard Sixteen dimensions.

Reginald Chandler, third in command at Henlys, drew Lyons' attention to the L-29 Cord. Other would-be stylists from Henlys and Iliffe responded to Lyons' search for an ideal selling 'line' and it was Donald Reesby who managed to get nearest. Reesby was head artist at an Iliffe-owned design studio in Hertford Street, Coventry, called British Photo-Engraving; he and his team interpreted some of Lyons' sketches in full colour. Lyons was delighted and, back at the works, with the expert hand of Cyril Holland never far away, the shape was brought up to life-size. Unfortunately, with the roof four feet from the ground, the overall length worked out at about 18 feet—more the dimension for a long-wheelbase limousine! There was still time in which to get the proportions right, though.

After one of his many meetings with Lyons, Black sent his formal letter to the Swallow Coachbuilding Company:

'Dear Sirs, *[he wrote]* Following Mr. Lyons' interview with the writer this morning, we are writing to confirm the points discussed, in order that any doubts and misunderstanding may be dismissed from our minds. The arrangement for the 1932 season is as follows:-

'1. We agree to supply you with chassis of current production types, at net prices recently quoted to you.

'2. We agree to supply you with special six cylinder chassis to suit special body requirements.

'3. The chassis referred to under number 2 above, will be reserved exclusively for you.'

Black went on to outline an agreement that freed Lyons from selling to Standard agents if they did not take up the available supply of 'Swallow' models, and some technicalities about scheduling.

'We feel *[he continued]* this arrangement will work very satisfactorily, and we hope that we have cleared up all the points recently discussed. If there is anything more you wish to know, or if there are any points on which you would like our further co-operation, we shall be pleased to do all we can on hearing from you. Yours faithfully, John P. Black, Director and General Manager.' There was, in general, empathy between Black and Lyons.

Not long afterwards, Lyons—usually the healthiest of men—began to experience sufficient pain to cause him to stay at home for several days. Presently he was whisked off to the Coventry and Warwickshire Hospital. After several weeks of fretting, but now minus his appendix, Lyons was back in Holland's shop. He was aghast at what he saw! The roof of the sleek coupé had been raised several inches. 'It's like a conning tower', fumed Lyons as he surveyed the long bonnet with two rather ugly boxes stuck on the back (one for people, and one for luggage). With Henlys now pushing him as much as he did his own employees, Lyons could hardly complain—nor did he do so for long. Walmsley had done what had proved necessary while Lyons was ill and made the cockpit high enough for the occupants to enjoy *some* degree of comfort! The new car *had* to be at Olympia or, it was feared, a year of Swallow progress might be lost. Lyons accepted the situation, as there was really no alternative. Holland recalls having to walk out of the office while the partners had their inevitable altercation. From such experience, Lyons learned to control his temper; then it became easier to win.

The Standard Motor Company possessed a new chief engineer and designer, Edward Grinham, who had been responsible for the Humber Super Snipe but had not liked the 'post-Rootes' company very much. Grinham and his staff co-operated with Swallow Coachbuilding where Harry Gill's few belt-driven drills and Jack Beardsley's coachsmithy were the nearest things to mechanical engineering yet introduced. The major piece of re-design work for Swallow's special Standard Sixteen chassis related to the springs. Grinham's chief draughtsman Ray Turner drew new, long, flat semi-elliptic springs to fit outside the modified frame members.

The element of haste had been given an extra charge by the following news item in *The Autocar* of July 31, 1931:

'The S.S. and the Swallow

Specially Adapted Sports Type Standard.

"S.S." is the symbol adopted for a new car which will be put on the market in due course by the Swallow Coachbuilding Co., though at the moment it is still in the "unrevealed secret" stage. The car is a marvellously low-built two-seater coupé of most modern line. Aft of the long bonnet is a very smart two door body, and at the back of the body is fitted a big luggage box, the lid of which gives access to the luggage space inside the body, as well as inside the box.

The mechanism of the car has been developed from the 1932 type Standard Sixteen chassis along the lines necessary for the special purpose of a sports car. The S.S. frame is downswept in the centre, the engine mounted well back, the springs are rearranged to drop the frame as a whole considerably lower, and the wheelbase is lengthened. A special type of deep-chested radiator will be fitted, and the gear control will consist of a short lever mounted well back and close to the driver's hand. Additionally, it is proposed to make a similar type S.S., based on the new Standard Little Nine chassis.

The present range of smart Swallow saloons will be continued on the Big Nine and the Sixteen 1932 model chassis.'

The interesting thing is that this 'controlled leak' was accompanied by the same photograph of the Swallow-bodied Ensign as had appeared when that car had been announced in the same magazine barely ten weeks earlier. Moreover, the Swallow Coachbuilding Company gave Henlys a mere one-line 'mention' at the foot of their famous four-column advertisement in the self-same magazine, beginning 'WAIT!—The 'S.S.' is coming'. (This advertisement is reproduced in full on page 60.) Once again it was a Standard-Swallow—a 'Big Nine' this time—that was illustrated. Whatever the reason for this 'teaser' advertising, *The Autocar* of July 31 had effectively committed Swallow to producing *something* new and dramatic for Olympia. Maybe that commitment would not have been made if William Lyons' appendicitis had struck a little earlier?

Anyway, the announcement had the effect of galvanising all concerned into more feverish activity than ever. One man who could not achieve the desired effect was trim shop chief, Irishman Ned Carey. A properly-fitting neatly-stretched fabric covering for the coupé top was necessary, and poor Carey simply could not produce a good prototype. Word quickly passed round north-west Coventry, that an expert trimmer was urgently needed 'up the Swallow'. He was found quickly. The cocky little newcomer worked long into the night. Lyons and Walmsley were there, too, sitting on packing cases in a corner. 'If I can't do it, no-one can', Percy Leeson had pronounced confidently, rising to the bait as he looked at the wrinkled fabric laid over the skeleton of wood and bent wire. Twice sacked for fighting, Leeson had nevertheless become an expert trimmer at Midland Bodies. He completed the prototype before the night was through. From that day on until his retirement from Jaguar more than 40 years later Percy Leeson was responsible for all trimming, and Sir William Lyons still remembers his feeling of relief at seeing the first

1930s fun: Harry Applebee (right) with Austin-Swallow and friends exploring mid-Wales. The picture— on the B4518 at Staylittle—was taken by Len Clarkson, owner of the other Swallow (D. Mudge/ L. Clarkson).

fabric-covered roof and boot completed in craftsmanlike fashion at last. As Olympia show-time approached, however, this special 'Sixteen' was by no means complete and the new car was still virtually a mock-up even at the show. On the other hand, Standard's new 'Little Nine' provided an ideal and simple opportunity for Swallow to stay in the small-car business.

The Austin Seven Swallow was entering its fifth year of production, but despite frequent updating was becoming long-in-the-tooth—at least as far as performance was concerned. It certainly did not command a high price on the second-hand market and so (as when it was new) the little Austin Swallow became a good 'buy' for the impecunious enthusiast. Harry Applebee, starting out on a textile industry career, bought his first car, a 1930 Austin-Swallow, for £20 when it was five years old. 'I chose it for its sporting and out-of-the-ordinary appearance', wrote Applebee not long before this book was written. 'It was reliable and economical but, with 11 or 12 bhp at most, its performance was very poor even by 1935 standards.' Applebee's pal, budding motor engineer, Len Clarkson, bought a similar 1929 model soon afterwards. This did not have the front and rear bumpers like Applebee's car, but both had external water temperature gauges. Clarkson's was fitted with several other 'extras' including fog and spot lamps, imitation 'knock-on' hub caps from Halfords, and a miniature Belisha Beacon as a marker-cum-decoration for the nearside front wing. Clarkson's feelings towards his car (which, like Applebee's, had originally been sold though Parkers', the first Swallow car agents) were similar: 'Reliable and enjoyable, but underpowered'.

Despite their heavy bodies with their 'fashion' extras, these two Austins took their owners on some quite arduous journeys from their North Cheshire homes into the Welsh mountains. 'My best-remembered feature of this car *[writes Harry Applebee]* was the braking system which would have delighted a present-day "L" driver having difficulty in starting on a steep hill without rolling backwards. The hand-brake operated the front-wheel brakes, and the brake pedal the rear wheel brakes—quite independently and with no interconnection. When stopping on an incline, one pulled on the handbrake and left it on the ratchet. The "give" and slight flexibility of the front axle attachment to the chassis then allowed the car to roll backwards a little whilst the front axle stayed where it was, drawing the brake cable tight. On re-starting one left the brake on, the car moved forward, the front axle stood still, the brake cable went slack, and the car moved off—after which the brake lever could be fully released!'

It is easy to see why, even in 1931, no easy paths lay ahead for the Swallow Company. With the FIAT and Swift-Swallows gone, and the Austin Seven-Swallow in its final throes, only the Standard and Wolseley factories were to remain regular suppliers—and not for very long, either. Never intended as a high volume product—at least, at Lyons' proposed scale of operation—the Hornet Swallow was to be fairly shortlived anyway. Thus, the relationship with the Standard Motor Company was crucial to Swallow establishing a *marque* of its own. The Standard 'Little Nine', announced in the summer of 1931, needed a relatively small amount of modification to take a scaled-down version of Swallow's new fixed-head coupé, but there was not a mention of this model when the big announcement day arrived.

Lyons was anxious, always, that the company should create a good impression—but not if it was going to be too expensive to do so. Virtually every Swallow-bodied car 'road tested' in the press came from Henlys. At the factory, other priorities meant that public relations, as such, did not yet figure in Swallow's plans. It was the *Daily Express* that provided the first-ever SS story for the general public. Frank Hough had persuaded William Lyons to let Harold Pemberton come to the Swallow Road works. Captain (later Major) Pemberton of the Lancashire Fusiliers had been a junior reporter before

Sportiest of the Swallow-bodied cars in the early 1930s was the Wolseley Hornet-Swallow. The two-seater had a particularly attractive tail, as seen so clearly here. C.F. Harris was tackling Ibberton, final hill of the 1931 MCC Exeter Trial.

fighting in the first World War with such distinction that his Military Cross had been reconsidered and a Distinguished Service Order substituted afterwards. He won the *Croix de Guerre* (with Palm) too, before returning to Fleet Street, first with the *Daily Mail* then the *Daily Express* for whom he was motoring and military correspondent. He was to cover the Abyssinian and Spanish wars before losing his life in a civil air crash in 1937.

On Thursday October 8 1931, however, Pemberton was in Coventry. His story appeared next day, in the centre of page 11, between items as depressing as any to be found today—one was on the desecration of graveyards and the other reported the third day of Al Capone's trial! This though, was the good news of Friday, October 9 1931:

' "Dream" Car Unveiled
Designed by 22 Salesmen.
The £1,000 Look.
By Harold Pemberton,
"Daily Express" Motoring Correspondent.
Coventry, Thursday.

TO-DAY, at Coventry, I have seen a motor-car for 1932 that has virtually been designed by twenty-two salesmen.

It is a remarkable motor-car in many ways, and will provide one of the few remaining surprises left for the Motor Show which opens at Olympia next Thursday.

It represents a motor-car salesman's dream—the type of motor-car he would like to sell. It will be called the "S.S.". The chassis and engine, which is rated at sixteen horse power, have been made by the Standard Motor Company of Coventry, for the Swallow Coachbuilding Company.

Some time ago the leading salesmen of Henly's Ltd., the motor-car distributors, were summoned to a conference. They were asked to state their ideas of the sort of motor-car they could most easily sell if they were given the opportunity. The "S.S.", which I saw unveiled to-day in preparation for its departure to Olympia, is the result.

The salesmen were unanimous on one point: appearance is the best selling point in these days. "Give us a motor-car with a £1,000 look, but which costs £300, and life will be easy!"

The new "S.S." costs £310. Whether it really has a £1,000 look or not, visitors to Olympia will be able to judge. It certainly has an expensive appearance. "What do customers imagine to be a good-looking car?" was the next question asked. The answer was: 'A car that is low in build, looks slim like a young woman, has a long body, and generally looks rakish."

Armchair Seat

The new motor-car is certainly the lowest-built British car I have ever seen. Two short people can shake hands over the top, and there is ample head room within.

It is so low that footboards have been done away with.

With the sliding roof open, a short man can look down on the seats. This result is brought about by having an under-slung chassis and by placing the springs outside the chassis frame.

The driving seat was also the suggestion of a salesman. It is almost an exact copy of the luxurious armchair in the boardroom of Henlys occupied by the chairman, Mr. Frank Hough. "Why not put that armchair into a car?" said a salesman. So there it is.

The driver lounges back in an armchair, the steering wheel is almost in his lap, and the gear lever, by an ingenious extension, is almost where the left hand rests.

The steering wheel comes below the level of the windscreen, so that vision is almost perfect.

Many other salesmen's ideas are incorporated. They voted for a bright colour scheme. The wood panelling interior matches the bodywork. The car I saw was green externally, and the dashboard was of green wood beautifully engrained.

It remains to be seen if the salesmen's dream is the public's dream. The "S.S." will certainly be one of the most novel cars on view at Olympia.'

Pemberton may have got it wrong (about the chassis being 'underslung') but such unsolicited publicity was something new in free testimonial-writing, although at the time William Lyons had 'not known what to make' of Pemberton's visit to Coventry. He had given him a copy of Donald Reesby's three-quarter-front drawing of the new car, however, and it appeared with the story in the *Daily Express*.

The Autocar's three-page description included the same drawing and a fine 'cut-away' by their leading technical artist, Max Millar, whose own car was, incidentally, a 1930 'Big Nine' Standard-Swallow. The heading was : *'The 'SS' Sixteen Coupé'*; but it is worth noting that even in the first series of SS cars several were to be sold with the larger, 20 hp, engine, option of which was mentioned in the first S.S. catalogue in passing. *The Motor* did not announce the car until the following Tuesday (October 13), when there was a two-page feature, with photographs of the mechanical details. There were two exterior pictures. One was a side view, based on another impression of the car as Lyons had hoped it

Low, but still 'overslung' at the rear;—the SS1 as drawn by Max Millar for The Autocar *on announcement day, October 9 1931. The rear seat was virtually unusable, hence the availability from spring 1932 of a more pronounced trunk to contain a dickey seat. (See page 202.)*

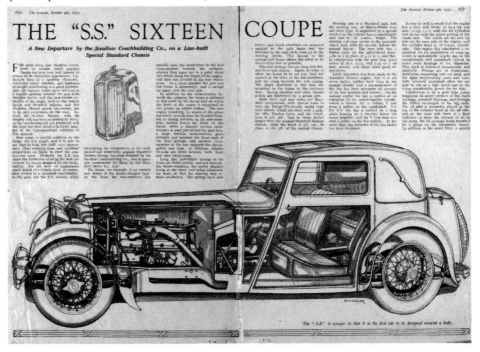

THE "S.S." SIXTEEN COUPE
A New Departure by the Swallow Coachbuilding Co., on a Low-built Special Standard Chassis

might look; this view was definitely copied by Frank Hornby for his 1933 'Modelled Miniatures' which became the first Dinky Toys in 1934—the 'SS1' being Dinky No '22b', price sixpence! ('22a' was similar below the waist and an imaginary two-seater above it. The set of six was completed by a van, a lorry, a tractor, and a tank.) *The Motor*'s second picture was a head-on shot actually based upon a photograph of the real car. These two views, plus the 'Reesby three-quarter', served as catalogue illustrations.

In its issue of October 16, reviewing the coachwork section of the 1931 Olympia show, *The Autocar* described the Swallow Coachbuilding stand (No 72) as follows:

'Naturally the greatest interest on this stand lies in the new S.S. Sixteen coupé, which, with its low build and long sweeping lines, seems the embodiment of speed and efficiency. The body is roomy and comfortable, and the wide doors give easy access. It has a flush-fitting sun-shine roof, a peakless front, and single pane screen, and is finished in black and carnation red.

'The "Little Nine" Standard Swallow coupé has a body on very similar lines and is a most attractive little vehicle, with Dunlop Magna wheels.

'The Hornet Swallow sports two-seater is an extremely popular model and has been considerably improved, the specification now including bumpers, ship's-type ventilators, and two spare wheels, while, of course, the chassis improvements include a four-speed gear box. This car is finished in Nile blue and ivory. The Austin Swallow saloon remains unchanged, as it was considerably improved last year.'

This was the Austin-Swallow's last show appearance, although production would go on until the following summer.

Despite not being in the main hall with the big names, Lyons was delighted and amazed at the favourable public response to his new cars. He knew only too well that the 'Little Nine' Swallow's lines were so much more harmoniously balanced than the 'Sixteen's', and he used real photographs of it for advertising purposes. The terms 'SS1' and 'SS2' for the six-cylinder and four-cylinder models, respectively, *may* have been coined in 1931, but were not yet in regular use.

In another formal letter to William Lyons during that 1931 motor show John Black wrote:

'With reference to recent conversations that have taken place between your Mr. Lyons and our General Manager, we now have pleasure in confirming the arrangements in connection with the 'S/S' models.

'1. We will supply you with the special 16 hp chassis in accordance with the specification and drawings agreed, incorporating the major units of our 16 hp 6-cylinder, and another model incorporating the major units of our "Little Nine".

'2. We will undertake not to supply the special 16 hp chassis to any other firm or person during the present season, terminating on 31st August 1932.

'3. In consideration of the above, you will pay us the sum of £500.0.0 (FIVE HUNDRED POUNDS) towards the cost of dies and tools for the production of the chassis frame.

'4. That you agree to take 500 16 hp chassis between now and August 31st, 1932 and a quantity of "Little Nine" chassis, to be agreed.

'5. The price to be charged for these two chassis types will be—
£130.0.0 (ONE HUNDRED & THIRTY POUNDS) NETT for the 16 hp
£82.0.0 (EIGHTY TWO POUNDS) NETT for the "Little Nine".

'6. You will have complete authority to appoint your own Disributors and Dealers.

'7. If at any time during the present season any new features are incorporated in any of our models or units, which can with advantage, be fitted to either of the above chassis, then you will be advised and asked to co-operate with us.

'8. The above arrangement to apply to the 'S/S' models only and the arrangement to continue definitely for this year, and from then onwards, subject to six months notice in writing on either side.'

Unlike the cars bodied by Avon of Warwick (in which Reginald Maudslay's son John was to have deep involvement later on), the new 'Swallows', as John Black was now acknowledging, were SSs in their own right. What 'SS' actually *meant* was something between Black and Lyons. Now, at last, Lyons was a motor manufacturer with a *marque* of his own!

Henlys' number three man, Reginald Chandler, brought his elder son into the business in 1931, and put him with Joe Argent, the old coachman. Young Gordon Chandler kept the flies out of the chandeliers of Devonshire House, and placed the drip trays neatly under sumps and axles. Years later, as chairman of Henlys Ltd, he recalled with pride the great moment when he and Joe Argent eased the new SS into the showroom for the first time, supervised by their eager eagle-eyed bosses, *and* by William Lyons himself.

At the Scottish show in November, Ritchie's of Glasgow and Rossleigh of Edinburgh showed the SS1 while Scott-Brown & Co of Paisley displayed an SS2 for the first time north of the border. (This firm does not appear to have remained an SS dealer for long, but one

A double-spread in The Motor *of January 26 1932 shows the SS2 as it was, and the SS1 as Lyons hoped it might be!*

Kathleen, Countess of Drogheda, in one of the first SS1s delivered to Henlys early in 1932. It cannot be her own, however, as hers was finished in white with Carnation wings (The Autocar).

is reminded that the great driver of Lister-Jaguars, Archie Scott-Brown, was a son of that Paisley family.) By the end of the year the first production SSs were beginning to be despatched to distributors.

A four-page feature in *The Motor* of January 26 1932 contained photographs of the SS1 taken from hitherto-taboo angles, and the car really did look better in 'real life' than in the artists' impressions—yet there was a double-page advertisement in the same issue with two long, thin ladies looking across the spread to a long thin SS1 (the 'Dinky' profile picture!), one of them declaring 'Irrefutably My Dear . . . The Car of the Year'. That was indeed a special issue of *The Motor*, with road impressions, plus supporting advertising from Rubery Owen (chassis makers), Wilmot Breeden (bumpers), Pytchley (sliding roofs), Protecto (safety glass), Bendix Perrot (brakes) and many other suppliers, and distributors.

Concours d'elegance soon became the happy hunting ground of SS cars as they were already for the Austin, Standard, and Wolseley Swallows of the bright plumage and the pert stance. The SS1 made its *real* competiton début in the 1932 RAC 1,000-mile rally to Torquay. I use the word 'real', since the event *did* involve driving! However, the crucial test, upon which the rally was decided, involved driving as slowly as possible in top gear for 100 yards without actually stopping. Spectators were not awarded prizes for boredom, but cars with the facility of preselection and a 'fluid flywheel' did have an advantage. The SSs did not figure high up in the awards lists, although discrepancies in the various available records do not make it clear exactly who drove what, anyway!—at least as far as Swallow products were concerned. Listed among the finishers was an SS1 entered by Edward Huckvale, the Swallow Coachbuilding Company Secretary. His sons Rex (who also worked for the company) and Denis both think their father is unlikely to have taken part in *any* motoring competition, let alone one of this length. It seems much more probable that the entry was placed by Huckvale on the company's behalf, and that the car was actually driven in the rally by A.G. Douglas Clease. We know *he did* take part, as *The Autocar,* for which he wrote, published a picture of him with the car.

More interesting is that, in the walkover by the 'fluid-flywheel' brigade, one of the best performances was put up by none other than F.R.W. England, the man who, 40 years on,

Wolseley Hornet-Swallow body mounting. Les Iles is nearest camera on the right. Harry Whittit (one of several Whittit brothers) is in the centre. Others are less easily recognised.

would succeed Sir William Lyons as the head of Jaguar Cars Limited! Fresh from his Daimler apprenticeship in London, 'Lofty' England (as he was to become famous) was the runner-up in that first RAC Rally of March 1932. He drove J. Mercer's Windover-bodied Daimler Double-Six in the tests and was eventually beaten only by the RAC timekeeper, Colonel Loughborough, who took part with one of the new 'Daimler' Lanchesters, the 15/18, in which a poppet-valve engine and Daimler's fluid drive were combined.

High performance was to be a thing of the future, and by far the most sporting of all the 'Swallows' in 1932 were the little six-cylinder Wolseley Hornet Specials, which were to be seen doing quite well in all the best trials. Both *The Autocar* and *The Motor* reckoned the SS1 would do 70 mph, although they both made it clear that their first test-runs were in a stiff-engined low-mileage vehicle. They liked the car to look at and to drive but, here and there, possibly, the fainter praise *could* be read as pretty damning. The SS2, although overshadowed by its more powerful partner, seems to have had a more immediate appeal for the testers of *Motor Sport* and *The Light Car and Cyclecar* who were happy with its ability to cruise at 50 mph and reach 60 at a pinch.

Up north, the trade was at war, with Henlys marching inexorably into Stanley Parker's territory. 'Words cannot describe the beauties or the amazing performance', declared Parkers' first SS advertisement in *The Motorist*. George White at Henlys' Manchester branch had got in first, however, with: 'The car of 1933 on sale today. Be years ahead in your buying . . . Buy from Henlys and assure straight dealing'. As Britain's largest motor agents already, Henlys could perhaps afford a somewhat heavy-handed touch at the expense of their rivals. After all, they were still by far the biggest promoters of Swallow and SS anywhere . . . and they needed to be, for the *un*tested aspects of the SS1 in particular soon manifested themselves. In the absence of a proper Swallow service organisation, Harry Gill was sent to London to try and resolve the problems of overheated occupants and uncontrollable carburation—caused through Swallow and the RAG carburettor man (Max Morris) simply not undertaking any kind of cold weather test programme for the new car. Without an engineering department to set standards—although, of course, he had Grinham's co-operation at Canley—William Lyons was having to extract the utmost from his jacks-of-all-trades and Harry Gill was a leader among them. The windscreens leaked and the Pytchley sliding roofs leaked and Frank Hough had good reason to storm round 'like a tiger about the place' (as Harry Gill remembers him).

The troubles that had to be (and therefore *were*) overcome with those first 500 SS1s stood the company in good stead for coping with the life of a car manufacturer in the years that lay ahead. At Swallow Road, the failure of the steam-bending idea for body timber had long been forgotten and the accuracy of the repetitive sawmill work, and of the jigs for frame assembly, made body construction a much more professional job than of old. 'Picked from the best of the world's forests . . . Gliksten's seasoned hardwoods are the finest the world produces.' The Swallow factory itself must have come into this category! When Holbrook Bodies came to the 'end of the road', Gliksten made an offer of £18,000 to the receiver, for the timber in the floors and the structure alone. As suppliers, however, they changed their minds when they realised how badly Swallow needed the two 'Holbrook' blocks for expansion (Lyons finally obtained them for £12,000 early in 1933). Another major modernisation project since the early Swallow days had been the introduction of cellulose in place of the old paint-and varnish early in 1930.

Inadequate rear seating—acceptable (maybe?) in the neat little £210 SS2—was proving an obstacle for Henly salesmen with the SS1 to dispense. Even those first road-test reports of January 1932, while generally maintaining the fulsome praise already lavished upon the SS concept, dismissed the rear seating as being suitable only for small children or luggage; or, as 'Monty' Tombs had written, back in 1928, people 'with some funny legs'! Henlys, finding sales slowing already, took the initiative and by July 1932 were offering ('with the usual enterprise and skill of the SS designers') an SS1 with dickey-seat conversion for £320, only £10 more than the standard model.

By now, William Bett had been joined at Nelson Advertising by his brother Robert, and by a young Londoner, Eric Colbon, who had trained at Arthur Owen's agency. Colbon's words were soon ringing out from the advertisements—'The Swallow Touch That Means So Much' (for the Wolseley Hornet-Swallow), 'The value of its beauty . . . the beauty of its value' (for the SS1) and many more. The 'SS' lettering had been developed into an hexagonal badge by Reesby for advertising (not yet for the car itself) to supplement the existing stylised 'Swallow' symbol.

Although the number of distributors and dealers around Britain was increasing rapidly, Henlys maintained a general stranglehold in the south and even pushed Parker's SS activities into a small territory euphemistically described as 'North Lancashire'. Henlys kept up their promotional work virtually non-stop, and in June 1932 held a grand rally and gymkhana at Heston aerodrome. Owners of Alvis, Rover, SS and 'other makes' found themselves taking part in egg-and-bucket races and *concours d'elegance* at no cost yet with the chance of 'valuable prizes'. Imperial Airways arranged 'around the block' flights, lunches were served, and tea could be taken as the band of the Coldstream Guards struck up. Gordon Chandler remembers how successful the day was, and contemporary reports confirm it. Henlys' 'big sell' was not always the hard one and, in the days before one-make clubs had really 'taken off', this kind of promotion had tremendous appeal.

The Swallow sidecar business, which would go on functioning throughout the 1930s, continued to receive the personal attention of William Lyons. The designs still had his special touch, although there was less chance to be original in this field any more. Some

Above *The Model 4 Swallow was still a popular sidecar in the late 1920s and early 30s. Sidecar department foreman Dick Cronkshaw (wearing cap) works on one, as does Bill Vardy (facing camera, left), also an ex-Blackpoolite.* **Below** *The motorcycle and sidecar were to remain popular throughout the 1930s; starring in this contemporary scene are a 1932-registered 493 cc BSA Sloper and the latest thing in Swallow fashion—the De Luxe Launch (Model 11), complete with rail around the 'deck'* (The Classic Motor Cycle).

Henlys attracted plenty of spectators and competitors to their open days. This one was at Heston in June 1932. The little SS2 appears to be winning the potato-and-bucket race . . . or maybe it is finishing fourth? (The Autocar).

Swallow sidecars even had fluting *à-la-*Vauxhall. A specialist was brought in to market Swallow sidcars. His name was Howard Davies, and his initials—'HRD'—were already famous in the world of motorcycling. Howard Raymond Davies had founded his Wolverhampton company, HRD Motors, in 1924. He had won the Senior TT the following year on one of his new HRD motorcycles. The larger-than-life if not immortal Freddie Dixon rode an HRD to victory on the Isle of Man two years later; but in 1928 Davies sold-up, although his *marque* name continued to be associated with the great machines of Phil Vincent until 1956.

Davies' presence in Coventry in the 1930s helped justify maintaining the Swallow *marque*; and there were still plenty of enthusiasts among its users. An interesting example is Harry Roberts of Walsall, who joined Temple Press as an assistant photographer in 1931, and remembers enjoying his Ariel 500 (ohv conversion) and Swallow combination most of the time although he did experience one accident, when the front sidecar connection came adrift on a left-hand bend. He brought the outfit to a halt on the right-hand verge, but it rolled over slowly. A dislocated wrist did not stop Harry Roberts lifting it clear to free his unhurt but trapped passenger, Ashley Taylor (then assistant editor of *Cycling*). The sidecar—probably a 'Model 7'—was undamaged but its chassis was changed to one of Ariels' own, without a spring wheel which Roberts had come to dislike. Swallow's official sidecar chassis suppliers were Mills-Fulford by now; then, from 1935, the Coventry firm of Grindlays was to provide them. The dropping of the word 'sidecar' from the company title was, however, warning enough that the world of motorcycling was quickly becoming the 'poor relation' at Swallow Road. Mid-1932 would not have been the best time to bother Lyons with sidecars, or any other trivia for that matter. Already another Olympia show was looming large. This year's SS1 simply *had* to be right.

"THE AUTOCAR" SEPTEMBER 30TH 1932

New S.S. Roomy Sports Saloon

Largest Circulation

The *Autocar*

FOUNDED 1895

1933

6: Getting more professional
(1932 to 1935)

'Export business has been amazingly good and before the show closes tomorrow we shall have booked definite orders for 1,000 SS1 cars.' Thus said Frank Hough of Henlys ('frankly amazed at the amount of business') when being interviewed by Tommy Wisdom.

'On a small stand in a corner of the coachwork section [wrote Wisdom in the Daily Herald and the Sporting Life] is one of Olympia's best-looking cars . . . the SS1 . . . Yesterday morning an agent from Holland flew to London to try to arrange a Dutch agency for these cars. He went away disappointed; the agency had already been arranged. "I could have sold 600 of those cars," he said.'

The October 1932 London motor show was a good one. Miles Thomas sales manager of Morris Motors, called it 'the best since the war'. For William Lyons it was a satisfactory conclusion to a year of worry. Virtually everyone agreed that, this time, his big coupé really did look superb. Indeed Harold Pemberton went one better still, in the Daily Express: 'Last year I described the SS1 as the car with the £1,000 look. This year it might be called the car with the £1,500 look. And it costs only £325'. That was the price—complete with Reesby-drawn 'SS' monogram badge—of the 1933-model SS1 2-litre coupé; or £335 if you chose the 2½-litre engine. In retrospect it seems a pity in some ways that the SS marque did not begin here! From now on, even the top typewriters at Swallow Road had a special key that printed the new 'SS' monogram!

What a transformation! With seven extra inches in the wheelbase, the proportions were now beyond reproach—and there was room for four adults sitting comfortably, all under cover! A further re-design of the Standard-based chassis, made exclusively for Swallow by Thompson Pressings, included triangulated cross-bracing in the middle and virtually parallel side-members that passed under the rear axle—real 'underslinging' this time.

A.G. Douglas Clease achieved another major 'scoop' for The Autocar by borrowing a production prototype for a long weekend in the summer of 1932. After waiting around for some last-minute work to be done—like the fitting of new-type door locks and windscreen wipers—the Cleases were able to drive only from Coventry to Birmingham on the Friday evening. During the next four days, however, they covered a good thousand miles and found the new car ran 'as smoothly, quietly, and comfortably as a dream car'. They raced the LMS express train over Shap and Beattock summits ('the speedometer needle swinging steadily up to the 80 mph mark') and reached Tarbet on Loch Lomond on Saturday night. On the Sunday, they crossed Rannoch Moor in pouring rain and found the roof and windscreen leakproof (a pleasant discovery after the shortcomings of the car's

Left *Right second time! The 1933 SS1 was well-proportioned and genuinely attractive, with its longer chassis, underslung at the rear. For the first time, Swallow booked the cover of* The Autocar *(September 30 1932) and took a* Motor *cover soon after.*

predecessor). Against a 'howling gale', however, it proved impossible to enjoy to full advantage the newly-completed high-speed road through Glencoe. Later in the day, they made an anti-clockwise circuit of Loch Ness; work had begun on the new main road, the state of which 'beggars description' (wrote Clease): 'It is a mass of pot-holes, ruts, and boulders, and resembles a cart track . . . Nevertheless the new SS1 averaged 26 m.p.h. over it!' After a night at Fort William the Cleases took the rugged 'Road to the Isles' occupying 2½ hours for the outward trip to Mallaig, during which they were held up by 'two other well-known cars which found 15 mph their reasonable limit', for the loose surface had 'many an outcrop of rock or water-worn gully'. Without impediment, however, the 43 miles back to Fort William were completed in a creditable 1¾ hours. The weather had improved, and the long gradient of Glencoe was achieved at between '60 and 70 m.p.h.'. During the final day's run from Loch Lomond to the Midlands, which was 'uneventful', 46 miles were put into an hour.

In his announcement-day article (*The Autocar*, September 30 1932) Douglas Clease concluded:

'Speed it has in plenty, rapid acceleration, powerful braking, but above all the road-holding which is uncanny in its steadiness when cornering at high speed. This is undoubtedly due to the underslung rigid frame and long flat springs giving a low centre of gravity but, what is important, this steadiness is not gained by any sacrifice of comfort. The steering, too, is light and precise, with sufficient self-centring action. The body is roomy and comfortable and the seating and upholstery are such that no fatigue was felt at any time during or after this quite strenuous 1000 miles test, a fact which vouches for the excellent driving position, easy-working and well placed controls, and good vision.'

The latter was sometimes criticised unjustly, incidentally—often by people suspicious of long bonnets. In fact, it was easier to see the nearside front corner of the SS1 than it was from the driving seats of most of its high-bonneted contemporaries. On another page of that *Autocar* (the cover of which featured the new SS1), a 'cut-away' by Max Millar was supplemented by a drawing of the new armchair-style rear seating which made the new SS1 a real four-seater (within the wheelbase) besides helping disguise the intrusion of the transmission tunnel. A major improvement was that the cooling of engine and passengers were now more effective, thanks to improved radiator and bulkhead designs.

The SS2 was changed only in detail for 1933, apart from acquiring a four-speed gearbox. 'Janet' in *The Standard Car Review* for November 1932 looked at the bonnets and boots of eight different variations on the Standard theme and presented a witty 'character-study' of each (and its driver!):

'Piratical, long, low, and a mite rakish *[she wrote of the SS]*. Ladylike, yes, but by no means demure. Snug and intimate, clothes to match must look pasted on. Lay alongside and exact your toll of envious admiration. *The Driver*—labelled modern and cocktail-drinking by her would-be critics—inspires all modern playwrights. Plucked eyebrows—tinted nails but quite self-possessed and capable for all her aura of femininity.'

Some of the other drivers 'Janet' imagined are just as interesting!—for example 'carefully careless clothes' and 'essentially masculine talk' (Little Twelve Maltby coupé); 'likes the thin edge of things' (Little Twelve Patrick Special Sports); and 'rather blasé' (Little Twelve 'Avon' coupé). At Warwick, the New Avon Body Company were still doing wonders of design in line and colour on *standard* Standard chassis, and irritated William Lyons by their regular *concours d'elegance* successes, quite often at Swallow's expense.

At the 1932 motor show, the range—SS1, SS2, and Wolseley Hornet Swallows—were all displayed together. They were still in the coachwork section, but at least *The Autocar*

The exposed spare wheel of the first 1933-model SS1 coupé is seen in this pre-release photograph, taken on the old 'Road to the Isles' (for The Autocar*) in the summer of 1932 by A.G.D. Clease* (The Autocar).

picked out the SS1 as a *marque* in its own right for the purposes of the special Olympia editions. Not until January did *The Motor* (co-inciding with one of Henly's shows) do full justice to the 1933 SSs. Then, however, it gave them six full pages of editorial coverage, including one devoted to 'Disclosures of an Attempt to Produce the World's Most Beautiful Sports Car'. Written by 'Fingermark', the story suggested that Frank Hough had been 'doodling' in a deserted corner of Henly's Camden Town service depot for several years before William Lyons had taken the resultant ideas to create the first SS1. 'Before the first car was produced Mr. Hough, who is Henly's chief, showed me one of the preliminary drawings', declared 'Fingermark'. (Sir William Lyons recalls the self-restraint he needed when he read this!) 'It quite took my breath away. Here was something quite new in motorcars—something that seemed to suggest motoring in 1950, perhaps. One can only speculate upon what SS stands for *[went on the article]*. It might be for super-sports, or for Swallow sports, which is more likely for the cars have been cradled in the home of the Swallow Coachbuilding Co . . . ' Then, as now, the SS name was being nurtured carefully as a *marque*, although careless writers and advertisers would still call the cars 'Standards' from time to time.

The 1933 SS1 examined by *The Motor* was fitted with an RAG horizontal carburettor, whereas the car Clease drove to Scotland had been fitted with an SU unit. It was the RAG that would be standardised for the remaining pre-Jaguar years, however. 'RAG' had been so named in honour of Max Morris's benefactress, Miss Rose Garstin; and Morris had set up his business in London, where the brothers Norman and Sidney Robbins were, for a time, RAG's testers. Sidney (who is still in charge of the family business, Robbins of Putney, the Bentley specialists) remembers being sent out to Ascot to work on the carburation of F. Gordon Crosby's own SS1; it is also interesting to note that Sidney Robbins had previously worked at Henlys.

First serious overseas competitive event for the SS1 was the 1933 Monte Carlo Rally, in which a single SS1 started from John O' Groats. V.A. Prideaux Budge and his crew got only a little way into France when a parked vehicle materialised on a blind, icy bend, to cause the 20 hp car to skid and crash, bending its front axle as well as the bodywork. The two hours lost while the axle was heated-up and straightened could never be recovered fully, and Budge was classified 58th at the finish. It was a tough and bitterly cold 'Monte' in which starters from sub-arctic Tallinn took the first 14 places. The best British finisher was Lord de Clifford in his Bentley fitted with a Gardner diesel engine; he was placed fifth.

Car for a star: Mr and Mrs George Formby with their two-tone SS1, with prophetic registration letters.

Budge was pleased with the performance of his car, and entered it for the second RAC Rally in March but he did not figure in the results; nor did W.V. Cross (20 hp SS1), A.G. Douglas Clease (16 hp SS1, complete with radio) or Coventry solicitor and SS director-to-be, Noel Gillitt, whose SS2 was not the only rally car needing external assistance to clear the stop and re-start test on one of Hastings's notorious steep hills.

In terms of sales, however, Swallow were beginning 1933 well, and by now—thanks largely to Ben Mason, Standard's own export manager—had nominated several continental agents. The first of these were P. van Wijngaarden for the Netherlands, Georg Hans Koch for Austria, Loppenthin and Feilberg for Denmark, C. Santos (Lisbon) and Wilfred C. Ennor (Oporto) for Portugal, Paul Kutsukian for Belgium, and (*not* via the Standard Co) *the* original European Swallow appointment, Emil Frey for Switzerland. The Copenhagen distribution was soon transferred to Bohnstedt Peterson, however, while Lagerwij's of The Hague replaced van Wijngaarden in a very short time.

There was no export sales department as such. All sales policy was in the hands of William Lyons himself, ably backed by Alice Fenton. Their first nominated distributors beyond Europe were the French Motor Car Company's three main bases in India—Calcutta, Delhi and Lucknow—with John Clarke of Johannesburg opening up South Africa. One of the original SS1s *had* gone to Atkinson's, the Standard distributors for Cape Town, in 1932; but Lyons cannot have been at all pleased with their insistence upon calling the car a Standard despite a favourable newspaper report on the 'sports car that is quite different . . . Cape Town's snappiest car'. Clarke was not a 'Standard man', however, and it is clear that, already, the SS car was not necessarily going to be sold 'on the back' of the *marque* from which it was derived.

At home, there were already over 100 nominated SS agents by the spring of 1933, 18 of them being classified as distributors. Henlys retained their stranglehold on the south, as well as the newer franchise for Manchester. The remaining northern territory was shared between Glovers' of Ripon and Harrogate, Hatfield's of Sheffield, Loxham's of

Preston, Thompson's of Hull, Pointing's (soon replaced by Appleyards) of Leeds, Albert Farnell of Bradford, and the first one of all, Parker's of Bolton. P.J. Evans had been first in the Midlands; now the Birmingham firm was surrounded by Atkey's of Derby, Attwood's of Wolverhampton, Browett's of Leicester, Cobridge of Stoke, Shuker's of Shrewsbury, and Truman's of Nottingham. Ritchie's and Rossleigh covered Scotland, Tom Norton of Cardiff ruled Wales, and Harry Ferguson's brother, Victor, looked after Northern Ireland from his Belfast premises. (His company was called Victor Limited.) Alice Fenton did all the work of establishing agreements and good relations when it came to discussing deliveries.

March 1933 saw another step forward for Swallow, when an attractive open tourer was announced on the SS1 chassis. It was a *full* four-seater, too, in which the rear-seat passengers could settle down well inside the car *and* its wheelbase, in SS 'armchairs', rather than add to the wind-resistance as was more usual. Soon, production of the last Swallow-bodied Hornet Specials meant that the Swallow car range was now 'all-SS'. The co-operation from John Black of Standard was acknowledged in the announcement that he would receive the first of the new tourers. Lyons and Walmsley each had one soon afterwards. Lyons', like Black's and most of the other early tourers, was finished in black—much more distinguished-looking than the bright and sometimes garish colour schemes for which the Swallow concern had acquired a name. Walmsley's new tourer was painted beige. Clease borrowed a black one from the factory, and took it north for the second Scottish Rally, in which he finished eighth overall, the sixth in his class—a good result, in fact the best by an SS to date. In the coachwork competition held afterwards in Glasgow's Kelvingrove Gardens, the SS won its class, ahead of Lieutenant Commander Maltby's special Riley Lynx. Ronald Pelham-Burn's carnation-and-buff SS1 coupé (17th in the large rally class) looked an even better bet for the *concours*, but was beaten by several other closed cars. In the following month, July, Clease did well again—this time in the Motor Cycling Club's three-day Scarborough Trial and Rally, to win *The Northern Echo* trophy.

This particular tourer (KV 5523) was then taken back to the works and prepared for use by the Viennese distributor Georg Hans Koch who had entered it for the Alpine Trial with Lyons' approval. Indeed three other tourers were being prepared, too, for Lyons had decided to permit himself the risk of a team entry in one of Europe's toughest events. The three works cars were painted red (KV 5363 for Humfrey Symons), white (KV 5905 for Charles Needham) and blue (KV 5906 for Margaret Allan), and were driven out to the Merano start in fairly leisurely fashion with Symons acting as unofficial public relations man and photographer. Symons' work appeared regularly in *The Motor* and in the daily press, and his reputation as rally-driver was high; indeed Symons had brought an Essex Terraplane into second place in the Scottish Rally only recently. He was already the holder of a Glacier Cup (the prize for a penalty-free drive in the Alpine Trial), as were Needham and Miss Allan. The four tourers looked splendid, with bumpers removed and a spare wheel in each wing.

Apart from free loan of the cars, the SS team was 'on its own'. From the 1933 model year, all SS1s had alloy cylinder heads—exclusively approved by Standard—and these proved to be the main source of trouble in that year's Alpine Trial which was, for the SSs at least, a tale of warped metal and blown gaskets. On the way to Italy, lack of power proved chronic, and Symons had wired Lyons. Lyons cracked the whip with Morris of RAG and Grinham of Standards. As a result, Norman Robbins was sent out by train, and, after a brush with the customs over the new cylinder heads he had about his person, he replaced the heads (for supposedly-more-effective ones) at Merano before the start—but to little avail.

The effort put in by RAG is worthy of further digression, however. Before taking his own life in 1936 Max Morris had (as Norman Robbins puts it) 'charmed many people to part with their brass'. RAG carburettors were advertised on London buses and also through Morris' connection with Maserati which he had established via Giulio Ramponi (for whom he had worked briefly). Norman Robbins took the brunt of any problems experienced with the SS's carburation. The RAG carburettor was of the plunger type, and some petrol mixtures left gummy deposits; so that sticking throttles were a frequent problem on the road, let alone in crucial tests on such events as the 'Monte' and the RAC Rally, when good throttle response was vital. Robbins or his assistant John Rye maintained constant representation in Coventry, in order to satisfy Grinham and his staff at Standard, and it was they who carried out the carburettor-setting when the bodied SSs were sent to Canley for final tests. This 'presence' was at RAG's expense, so perhaps it was not so surprising that the little firm could not stay in business.

Returning to the 1933 Alpine Trial, however, we find that three of the five SSs did in fact complete the whole event. Koch and co-driver Karl Reitmeyer fought on, to finish an excellent 14th overall. They were also sixth in the Bugatti-infested 2,000-3,000 cc class. Needham and Munro, their problems increased by steering gear that was threatening to seize-up, nevertheless managed to take eighth place in that class with the sole surviving works car. The Austro-Hungarian Graf Orssich, came a creditable 11th in class with his SS1 coupé, one of the first to be sold in Austria by Koch. The other two SS tourers made their way homewards in convoy, but Margaret Allan and her co-driver, Colleen Eaton, had to give up and leave the blue car in France. They shared the final stage of the journey in the crippled car of Humfrey Symons and James Wright. Incidentally, that red machine's only other claim to fame was as the official course car for the 1933 Manx Grand Prix meeting when, it was claimed, P.D. Kissack lapped the famous TT course with it at an average speed of 60 mph 'on several occasions'.

From that autumn the SS1 and SS2 were offered in saloon form, with an extra side window instead of the dummy hood-irons of the fixed-head coupé. Both had the 'leather-grained' stretched fabric roof and trunk material—applied by Percy Leeson and his 'pupils'. The SS2s 'grew-up', gaining big-car looks from a longer chassis; an SS2 open tourer did not appear until the following spring.

SS's aluminium cylinder heads were cast by the Coventry Motor Cylinder Company, and it was in discussion with this firm that William Lyons, obviously disappointed with the by-no-means dishonourable failure of his first Alpine assault, became acquainted with Harry Weslake's ability to transform engines. Soon Weslake was called in and began work on improving SS engine reliabilty and general liveliness. As an independent consultant, Weslake was to be associated with the company for many years.

Despite the adequacy of SS performance, and the nice things people said and wrote about it, the fact remains that—in 1933 and 1934 at least—its lack of vivacity needed the prompt remedial action that the *marque*'s styling had so recently received. 'Adequacy' was not enough for a leader like Lyons! On October 26 1933 he registered a subsidiary company called SS Cars Ltd, with a capital of £10,000 in £1 shares. On the engine question, Henlys came to the rescue, for they now possessed the whole British concession for Studebaker Corporation. A Studebaker Commander was brought to Swallow Road and, for a while, serious consideration was given to the fitting of an American straight-eight in the all-British SS! This project was, however, dropped; as was a McEvoy-Pomeroy Zoller supercharging exercise! Not only did Weslake start work on an overhead valve conversion for the Standard 'six', but Lyons had made up his mind to overcome the lack-lustre technical specifications of his products by forming an engineering department of his own at the earliest opportunity.

As shown already, one 'department' run largely by Frank Hough of Henlys, and to some extent by the less outgoing Lyons, was that of publicity. In 1934, the Swallow/SS organisation was joined by a Londoner, Ernest William Rankin—35 years old, educated at Beverly School and the Barnes & Putney schools of Art, and a first World War Lieutenant of the Middlesex Regiment. (Later he became a Dunkerque veteran, and would serve, like so many others whose careers were interrupted, in Italy and the Western Desert. He was to become a major during the second World War.)

In 1930, Ernest (or 'Bill' as he was usually known) Rankin—with six years' experience advertising General Motors products behind him—had gone in for an open competition to brighten up the image of Watney's, the brewers. Not only had he won it; he had created the 'Red Barrel' that is now one of Britain's most famous trading symbols. Who better, then, to promote the rise of SS Cars Ltd, than Rankin? Very soon, he founded an SS Magazine, mainly for the trade, and acted as 'go-between' for the new SS Car Club in its contact with the factory. As well as his liaison work with the Bett brothers and Eric Colbon at Nelson Advertising, and starting a public relations service for the company, Rankin made sure that SS and its enthusiastic customers would really appreciate one another; like Mercedes-Benz and other great *marques* of the world's motor industries, Lyons' cars were to establish a clientèle among whom repeat orders would account for a large proportion of the manufacturer's business continuity.

Rankin was also present at SS Cars in time to monitor their performance in a second Alpine Trial sortie. This time there *was* a 'man from the factory' to help try and bring success to the young Coventry company—none other than Harry Gill. Harry Teather's recollection of their night out at the Ritz dance hall in Earlsdon, behind the Coventry Technical College, is not shared by Gill. One of the 'Alpine' cars in Gill's care was stolen from outside the hall, and Teather had to drive Gill over to Nuneaton at dead of night in his Bullnose Morris to collect it from the police. Gill kept being stopped all the way back to Coventry for driving a 'stolen' car.

1934 was a better year for SS cars in rallies, although it was in 'comfort' rather than 'performance' competitions that the *marque* tended to shine. Lyons entered another team of three SS1 tourers for the Alpine Trial—but only Douglas Clease's *Autocar* long-term-test-cum-rally car (KV 7570) was factory-owned. Clease used it for the RAC and Scottish rallies, too, but it should be emphasised that anyone acquiring any car on the basis of its placing in a British event would have been very unwise, for there was not yet a UK road event that could be classed as a serious test. By comparison, even to finish an 'Alpine' was at least an indication of a car's and its drivers' competence, and this kind of prestige was something SS needed.

The second and third official 1934 Alpine SS team entries came from Sydney Light and Charles Needham. Light was a well-known motorist and yachtsman, and the first customer for a 1934-model SS1 tourer, with which he had promptly won his class in the Monte Carlo Rally comfort competition. Such competitions were not considered interesting by the 'Alpine' organisers, however, and their event was a 'no-nonsense' one. Light's car had a puncture and went off the road on the fourth day, but the marking system was such that the team was still placed third in its category.

Like the Cleases, Needham could not quite maintain his set average towards the end, but the SSs did not overheat so badly this time, and his run was much less agonising than the year before. Although the car was his own, Needham did, of course, have factory support in the form of Harry Gill as co-driver. Back at the works, it was a little quieter than usual on the SS assembly lines without that gruff Yorkshireman to chivvy things along. Gill did not find his Alpine experience particularly memorable; but then co-existence between *any* Lancastrian and *any* Yorkshireman is supposed to be well-nigh impossible, so perhaps the crew of Gill and Needham did well to last-out the five days of the trial?

The racing driver Norman Black gave the SS2 tourer an ignominious début when he and Reuben Harveyson ran out of time without turning a wheel on the fifth day. It was said that neither had woken up in time! It was left to a private entrant, F.W. Morgan, to make the best individual SS performance. He drove very well indeed, and brought home a prize for finishing fourth-equal in the 2,000-3,000 cc class, his 20 hp SS tourer being beaten only by two Hotchkisses and a Panhard. Although not a sports car of the ultra-specialised type—such as, say, the Frazer Nash—Coventry's SS was beginning to gain respect in the motoring world. Every SS was road-tested, each road-test including a mechanical check at the Standard works, Canley, where Sid Lawrence was one of the most useful of contacts. For example, it was Lawrence who persuaded SS that a bigger water pump impeller should be brought in to aid cooling.

In the winter of 1933-4, Lyons let it be known that he was looking for a service manager, and former Blackpool men Harry Teather and Lyndon Smith were among the keen applicants; but neither got the job. It went to a Standard man, Digby Paul, who was provided with premises consisting of a space between existing 'shell-filling' factory buildings, suitably roofed-over! Among the first to join him in the new SS service depart-ment were foreman George Dewbury, Freddie Ford, Charles James and Len Wells from Standard, who were to stay with SS and Jaguar for many years, as would Bill Hucker on the stores side. Soon afterwards, Fred Perry—one of the expert body-makers who had moved from the Midlands up to Blackpool to build Austin Seven Swallows in 1927—became the service department's ace coachwork repair man by virtue of his ex-perience in the production body shop.

An SS man with two jobs at this time was Clifford Dawtrey who not only took respon-sibility for inspection but prepared the first SS handbooks as well. In his spare time he en-joyed camping with his family, and built himself a caravan. Then he made another; and when he began making this into a third occupation, and Lyons sacked him, he went into caravan-building full-time! Ex-Blackpool men George Kellie, Lyndon Smith, and painter Harold Marsh and several other Swallow men—including Wilf Chamberlain—would assist Dawtrey in the evenings and at weekends. One of the helpers was David Blain, usually known as 'Doug' or 'Jock'. (He and Lyndon Smith later went into partnership with Dawtrey; Marsh left SS for a time, too, to run the painting side.) Blain had done a full apprenticeship and worked for Horace Barnes (soon to join SS, too) at White & Poppe's factory by the entrance to Swallow Road. Their engine designs and machining techniques were admired throughout the industry, and when they were taken over by Dennis Brothers of Guildford and closed down, Blain was one of several talented White & Poppe men soon to make their mark with Swallow; in fact he played football for the Swallow team, managed by sawmill king Fred Gardner, through whom he got the job.

All metal-working in the mid-1930s was still being done in one of two out-houses on the sloping grassy area between the shell-filling works and Swallow Road, and it is interesting to note that all these old buildings are still much the same today externally. (Dunlop use most of the old main factory as office accommodation nowadays.) Jack Beardsley was in charge, of course, Bill Stevens having taken over the actual forge shortly after Swallow's arrival in Coventry.

A tool-maker by trade, David Blain—together with Bill Carefoot—was the first professional machinist to join the company. He operated its first machine—a small centre-lathe which, like all the early tools, had been acquired second or third hand from one or other of the less resilient of Coventry's many motor car or motorcycle factories as they sold-up. From making bracketry for bodies, chain links for production lines, and many more jobs that any other firm might have 'bought out', Jack Beardsley's coachsmithy had rapidly graduated into a tool room which could also produce small body components such as headlamps mounts, windscreen-securing nuts and the like, as well as small pressings.

William Walmsley was never short of ideas, and in 1934 had two very attractive two-seaters built, powered by the 20 hp engine. These special SS1s were not prototypes of anything in particular, but may well have inspired the SS90 just the same. Walmsley was as frivolous as ever, though, and even fitted one car with a firebell—shades of the days 15 years before, in Stockport, when his revving-up awoke the neighbours. Increasingly, he was now a model railway addict and many was the Swallow craftsman who visited his home to make or fit a part, or—in the case of Harold Marsh—paint the scenery.

The Walmsleys' teenage son, Bobby, now went to Bloxham School in Oxfordshire. Lyndon Smith would sometimes borrow one of Walmsley's SS1s for weekends, in return for acting as Bobby's chauffeur to and from the school. The friendship between Walmsley and the Smith family continued even after Lyndon Smith, still in his early 20s left SS cars in high dudgeon following his aforementioned failure to land the job of service manager.

The model railway was becoming a passion with Walmsley, and Blain's centre-lathe was 'working overtime', turning bits and pieces for it—'foreigners', they would have been called had Bill Walmsley not had a stake in the business. 'You're not asking me to pay for this lot *twice*, are you?' he would say, when Lyons tackled him about it. It even reached the stage of Walmsley failing to obtain material from the stores without a requisition, and not unnaturally this led to further animosity.

At the 1934 motor show, SS Cars at last had its own stand in the main hall, thanks largely to the intervention of Peter Henry, Armstrong-Siddeley's sales manager, on William Lyons' behalf at a council meeting of the Society of Motor Manufacturers and Traders. Lyons had wanted a manufacturer's stand for the previous three years and believed that his strained relationship with Sir Herbert Austin, the SMMT President, may have contributed to the delay in getting one.

The SS range was really blossoming now, with four engine sizes and two chassis, each with the choice of coupé, saloon or tourer coachwork—plus a brand new 'fast-back' saloon. Available for the SS1 chassis only, it was called the Airline and, with Rankin on hand to boost the publicity, it brought SS more show headlines than ever before. 'One of the most practical expositions of streamlining yet applied to the modern car', wrote 'Tim' Thomas in *The Motor Trader*. 'Dignity is attained by sheer simplicity of line . . . a sense of "airiness" is gained by the use of very long windows' reported *The Birmingham Post*. 'A perfect example of non-freakish streamlining', volunteered *Time and Tide*; yet William Lyons disliked and dislikes this car more than any of his other creations, and probably knew already that it would be obsolescent within a year. Never again was there to be a 'fast-back' SS or Jaguar saloon body from Coventry; Lyons felt he had allowed himself to be swayed by fashion in the 'year of the streamline'. The SS Airline was, however, the best looking of a bunch that included Chrysler's 'Airflow', Singer's 'Airstream', and Triumph's 'Flow-Free'.

William Lyons had accepted presidency of the SS Car Club and his wife presented the prizes at Bournemouth, the base for its first major weekend rally in November 1934. Among the prize winners were the SS1s of Leslie Hatfield (the distributor for Sheffield) and Tom Crumbie of Adams Brothers and Shardlow, the Leicester printers who did so much of the early SS and Jaguar catalogue work. Bertie Henly put in an appearance at the rally headquarters—the Burlington Hotel, Boscombe—during the weekend.

In that month, too, Lyons prepared a purchase option agreement and on the 20th, Huckvale wrote formally to Walmsley advising him of SS Cars' first annual general meeting, to take place at the works eight days later. At the meeting Walmsley gave notice of his resignation; the partnership was over. Each of the 10,000 £1 shares of Swallow's

Towards the end of 1934, Coventry MP Captain W.F. Strickland bids 'good-bye' to Richard G. Taylor with his first consignment of SSs for North America. Advertising manager Ernest Rankin (left) and the rest of the SS management very soon wished they had said good-bye to Mr Taylor somewhat earlier. The photograph was taken in Swallow Road, beside the main office block.

nominal 'subsidiary', SS Cars Ltd, was divided into four five-shilling ordinary shares; the capital was increased to £30,000 by creating 80,000 new ordinary five-shilling shares. Lloyds Bank had already been acting as agents for Williams Deacon's Bank, and the Swallow/SS account had been transferred; now Lloyds were appointed official nominees. (Lyons had, however, retained the Blackpool firm O. & W.B. Haworth, and their Alan Mather still audited the acounts).

Before any official announcements were made, there came the news that one Richard G. Taylor had been appointed sole Transatlantic concessionaire for SS. Taylor achieved this by the simple expedient of registering the name 'SS' in North America, so that no one else—not even Lyons—could use it there. He was photographed with a Coventry MP, Captain Strickland, and Ernest Rankin with a fleet of SS cars lined-up behind them in Swallow Road. One of these cars, an Airline, was to be displayed at the forthcoming New York show—a dealer's rather than a manufacturers' show—and Taylor was the only foreign car promoter to book space until, at the last minute, other exhibitors staked claims to show the 'PA' MG Midget and a Type 57 Bugatti with coachwork by Gurney Nutting 'who does trick things with Bentleys', said the *New Yorker* adding: 'I imagine the SS, which is also British, will capture the fancy of sports-car owners'.

New York's Mayor La Guardia opened the show in Grand Central Palace on January 5 1935. After it was over, *Time* magazine reported thus:

'Since English Rolls-Royce Ltd. became so vexed last year with the Rolls-Royal Company of America that the latter is now Springfield Manufacturing Company, another pioneer opportunity is obvious. But are U.S. citizens ready to pay some 18,000 dollars today for a brand new English Rolls?

'Figuring that they are not, pioneer Richard Taylor, famed English racing driver [sic], has made eight flying trips to the U.S. in the past two years selling the S.S. with phenomenal success in California and Florida. As every swank Briton knows, there are few cars on His Majesty's roads swanker than an S.S. Last week pioneer Taylor chalked up an amazing record at the close of Manhattan's Motor Show.

'From an obscure stand on the top floor among the accessories he had sold five S.S. cars per day retail for some 2,400 dollars each, plus several times that number wholesale to eager new U.S. dealers.

'Explanation of this pioneering boomlet: Every S.S. is guaranteed to do between 85 and

90 m.p.h., between 20 and 25 miles per gallon, comes equipped with extremely low-slung English four-seater body having slide-open "sunshine roofs," cocktail trays opening behind the front seat and other Mayfair niceties.

'Finally an S.S. has won the premier award at every *Concours d'Elegance Automobile* held for the past four years in Cannes, Deauville and Biarritz.

' "I'm a weak man", says pioneer Taylor, "I was so shot to pieces during the war that I have really no strength at all. Would you believe that I was able to drive an S.S. from here to Palm Beach in one full day—1,200 miles? That gives you some idea." '

Clearly the journey had affected his capacity for terminological exactitude. Although several sales *were* made, more than ten years would pass before Lyons began offering left-hand steering; and when the big export drive started it would not be Mr Taylor doing the selling.

While Mayor La Guardia was touring the Grand Central Palace of New York, Britons at home on January 5 were opening their papers to another story. The *News Chronicle* told it simply: 'Negotiations are nearing completion for the flotation of S.S. Cars, Limited which is to be converted into a public company, with a capital of £250,000.'

Here is how *The Financial News* of London elaborated upon the situation, on January 10 1935, under the heading:

' 'S.S. Cars' Dual Offer

Lists open to-morrow for an offer for sale of 100,000 6½ per cent. Cumulative Preference shares of £1 each at 21s 6d per share and 140,000 5s Ordinary Shares at 10s 6d per share in S.S. Cars, Ltd.

This company, which was incorporated in October, 1933, has acquired the successful business hitherto carried on by the Swallow Coachbuilding Co. Ltd. Its activities are mainly concentrated on the production of the S.S. car which has achieved outstanding success in this country, on the Continent and overseas.

100 p.c. Increase in Sales

This success is reflected in the increasing sales over the last three years. The period from July 31 last to date, in comparison with the corresponding period last year, is stated to show an increase in sales of over 100 per cent., and the number of orders in hand is also stated to be substantially greater.

The combined profits of the businesses for the past three years to July 31, 1934, were £12,447, £22,349 and £37,645 respectively. Net assets, exclusive of goodwill, and including the additional working capital now being provided, less preliminary expenses, are shown as £179,857.

Cover for Preference Dividend

According to the figures set out above it will be seen that the profits for the year ended July 31 last cover the Preference dividend over 5½ times, leaving a sum equal to 28 per cent. on the issued Ordinary shares.

The Preference appear an attractive high-yielding investment of their class while the Ordinary shares have possibilities.'

William Lyons was now in sole charge, the Chairman and Managing Director of SS Cars Ltd. Arthur Whittaker, who had progressed quietly from his faltering sidecar-selling days in Blackpool to become a highly efficient general manager, joined him on the board. Noel Gillitt, the solicitor, remained a director of the re-formed company—joined by Thomas Wells Daffern, already an active director of the Coventry Permanent Building Society.

7: The year of the Jaguar (1935)

William Walmsley took his money and left. His interest in cars and sidecars was still there, but to him 'going public' held no attraction. Each of the partners had probably realised inwardly for a long time that their ways would part. When it did happen, it was a 'clean' enough break. There had never been any apparent desire by Walmsley to obtain personal publicity, and Lyons found no reason to offer it.

Before telling the 1935 story, it is only right to turn attention to William Walmsley as he was leaving the company finally, in January 1935, nearly 15 years after making his first sidecar. By this time, or very soon afterwards, Blain, Kellie, Marsh, and Smith were working full-time at Clifford Dawtrey's Airlite Trailer Company, making cheap canvas-over-ash-frame caravans in Clay Lane. Walmsley had taken a financial interest already; now he saw Dawtrey's business as a new outlet for his design ideas. One of the most interesting was a caravan with a roof that could be raised by placing screw-jacks under the front.

Walmsley bought himself a Bentley and used it for towing, although advised not to by

Mr and Mrs Clifford Dawtry (left) and Mr and Mrs Lyndon Smith (right) pose for a 1936 Airlite publicity shot at Maxstoke Castle, a favourite spot with motor industry photographers. As well as Dawtrey and Smith, 'Jock' Blain and William Walmsley were listed as directors of the Airlite Trailer Co (L. Smith).

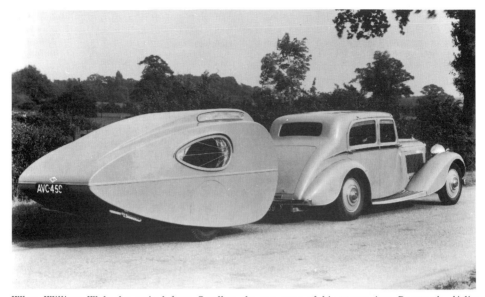

When William Walmsley retired from Swallow, he put some of his money into Dawtrey's Airlite company—and some of his design ideas, too. This streamlined caravan 'split' in the middle to give it extra height when parked, with soft weatherproof material filling the resultant 'gap'. Walmsley later wrote-off his beautiful Bentley (L. Smith).

Derby. It is thought that he was not towing with it when he wrote it off in a monumental accident all on his own. 'Just Dad's luck', said Bobby when he heard afterwards that father had stepped out of the remains with only a sore thumb. Walmsley went out and bought a Studebaker after that—probably Bertie Henly's salesmanship again!

After Airlite Trailers had been wound up—never having really got 'off the ground' properly, Jock Blain and Harold Marsh returned to 'the old firm'. Lyndon Smith moved out to a plot of land immediately opposite the site of an old staging inn, 'The Blue Boar', near Dunchurch on the main London road out of Coventry, selling a few caravans and living in one himself. When the adjacent filling station came up for sale, Smith was able to buy it thanks to a £1,500 loan from Walmsley. Lyndon Smith sold the petrol and his wife Dorothy ran the site café, helped by his parents who had moved down from Blackpool. They made ends meet, keeping things ticking over while he worked as a fitter for Armstrong Whitworth during the war. After the war he returned to Dunchurch and was able to build up the business. Then came his second big break; a site development plan he was considering in 1955 coincided with publication of the M1 route. Four years later he snared the contract to build at Watford Gap—the first motorway service area. Today the 'Blue Boar' group he started has moved into the multi-million pound bracket!

Thanks also to Walmsley, Dawtrey had got going again in 1938 with a new company, Coventry Steel Caravans, still at Clay Lane—apparently utilising extra space recently vacated when Cross & Ellis had given up car body-making and stuck to the retail trade. Dawtrey's new 'Phantom Knight' was a very heavy caravan, constructed of steel over ash. Then during the war, the company did light engineering work in the old Quinton Barrack at Parkside until Dawtrey and his small team were bombed-out.

The Walmsleys' biggest personal war-time tragedy was the death of their son Bobby, who was pilot of a Typhoon that crashed into the cliffs near Dieppe. He was still in his early 20s.

Left *When Airlite was wound-up, Dawtrey started up again—this time calling the business Coventry Steel Caravans. After the war, premises were eventually found in the Corn Exchange in Market Place, Warwick. The main hall itself is supposed to have inspired Dawtrey in the design of his mobile homes and banks which, in 1948, were Britain's costliest standard caravans. (Coventry Steel Caravans).* **Right** *William Walmsley in his later caravan-promoting days* (Mrs Winnifred Walmsley).

William Walmsley did take some further interest in the Dawtrey saga for a while. From the rubble, Coventry Steel Caravans re-emerged in 1943 at Leek Wootton (near Kenilworth—the present site of Broad Lane Caravans.) There, in a field, an office was erected and used for two years. Without going into detail it is worth recording that the caravan, for which that office was actually the prototype, became one of the most ingenious (though expensive) vehicles of its type on the market. The 'Coventry Knight'—which replaced the 'Phantom'—was made not in the field but three miles away in Warwick's old Corn Exchange; the architecture of this strange 'factory' is said to have inspired Dawtrey when he was designing his unusual mobile homes (often used as banks for open-air events, too), which were made largely of prefabricated alloy extrusions and perspex.

Ronald Lown, head of Coventry Steel Caravans (later part of Caravans International, at Newport Pagnell) was working at Warwick with Dawtrey in the late 1940s; he had joined him from Daimler via Rover. Lown remembers Walmsley coming to the Corn Exchange Works in Warwick with a number of ideas—some of which were adopted. It seemed to Lown as if it was really a hobby. Clifford Dawtrey left and tried starting yet another caravan business, Silver Knight Trailers in Leamington; it went wrong. He died by his own hand.

Walmsley drove Jaguar cars himself in the 1950s, and Sir William Lyons remembers meeting him and having a chat outside the service department at Browns Lane once. As an apprentice, I remember seeing a Mark Eight and matching caravan (in Walmsley's favourite caramel) parked outside a house in Holyhead Road, Coventry, which I was told belonged to Sir William's former partner. Walmsley's first wife, Emily Letitia, had divorced him and both had re-married—she to Norman Robbins. (When RAG had come to an end Robbins had joined Robin Jackson at Brooklands; later he had moved on to Lagonda.)

Walmsley had always suffered from pernicious anaemia; in later life his health was failing generally. The making of intricate components and mechanisms for his model railway continued to occupy and fascinate him. In 1960, he moved back from Coventry to the Blackpool area once again in the hope that he would get better; but he got worse, and died at Poulton-le-Fylde on June 4 1961, leaving a widow, Winnifred. He had been approaching his 69th birthday. Arthur Whittaker and Edward Huckvale attended the funeral on behalf of Jaguar Cars Ltd.

Having explained briefly William Walmsley's involvement in getting the Swallow, Coventry Steel Caravans and Blue Boar companies started, it is now time to return to the narrative for 1935.

*   *   *

There was much to occupy everyone at SS cars in that year. Several of the earliest distributor appointments had not worked out well and a new man was taken on at the new year. At Brown and Mallalieu's in Blackpool, back in his early days, Lyons remembered one of the more senior salesmen telling him he would 'never make it' when he left to join Walmsley. Lyons had told him; 'you wait; when the company gets big enough I'll send for you'. Now it was happening and Eric Warren was appointed SS's northern area trade sales representative. (It had been thanks to Warren that Whittaker, the Metropole Garage apprentice, had got his Swallow job in 1923.) In the south, of course, Henlys still saw to most trade matters. However, a bitter blow was struck when, suddenly, in January 1935, Henlys chairman and joint managing director, Frank Hough died at the age of only 46. He had decided to go into hospital for a simple hernia operation, but an air embolism got into his blood stream and that was that. Bertie Henly took charge at headquarters, and Reginald Chandler—whose sons Gordon and Douglas were both working for the organisation by now—became second in command.

In Coventry, the SS sales organisation was building up slowly. Alec Blythe, a former Triumph man who had gained much of his early experience working in East Africa and South America, and joined Swallow in 1932, was now assisting Alice Fenton in her dual role of secretary *and* sales assistant to William Lyons. She had been helped for some time, too, by her younger sister, Nancy. The new service manager, Digby Paul, needed a secretary, however, and Nancy Fenton got the job. Further attempts were made to get the North American market organised, for the line-shooting Richard Taylor had soon disappeared from his Waldorf Astoria address. In Europe, SS began to appear at motor shows, too, starting with Brussels and Amsterdam early in the season.

Sydney Light bought a shiny black SS1 Airline in time for the 1935 Monte Carlo Rally, but it was beaten in its *concours* class by the *Grand Prix d'Honneur* winner Pascoe's attractive Talbot. The Honourable Brian Lewis, more racer than rallyist, set off last from John O'Groats but reached Aberdeen first, in a new works SS1 tourer with Reuben Harveyson. They won the unlimited *concours* class for open cars as Light had done the year before. In all, four SSs completed the road section, but none was well placed, Lewis being best at 55th. The second major SS Car Club rally was run in February gales. Arthur Whittaker joined in for once, and he took a second-class award despite losing time on narrow roads near the finish at Buxton.

March saw the announcement of two new 'mid-season' SS1s—the attractive drophead coupé and the short-wheelbase '90'. The latter was a two-seater, and the Honourable Brian Lewis took one of them on the RAC Rally that month; the car ran out of time, after stopping with failed clutch-withdrawal mechanism. Later Lewis did a spectacular but unofficial run in the eliminating tests. Eight SS drivers, including Douglas Clease with the new drophead coupé, won first class awards. Major Sir Alfred Hickman's badge-

bedecked Airline could gain only a second-class award, despite his warthog-tusk mascot. Harry Gill and Ernest Rankin took an SS1 saloon and gained a third-class award; they did win their concours class, though. Gill says that this and the 1934 'Alpine' were the only two rallies in which he ever competed, other than club events. Rankin, on the other hand was to take part in several more events on SS's behalf. There was no Alpine Trial in 1935, and it is doubtful if the company would have participated anyway, for there were so many projects related to the company's future that needed to be given priority.

The first priority was to create an engineering department. Harry Gill and Cyril Holland were never short of stylish coachwork exercises, but there were only the aging SS chassis to fit them on to; and Harry Weslake was well advanced with engine development. (Later, Lyons was to bring in driver-engineer Dick Oats as consultant, too.) Not only was there an urgent need for a new chassis, but, more important, a first-class engineer who could co-ordinate and bring a complete motor car all the way from design to production line. Through Edward Grinham of Standard, and his deputy—Lewis (brother of Clifford) Dawtrey—William Lyons met, interviewed, deliberated and finally chose William Munger Heynes, who had been doing Grinham's stress-engineering job at Humber.

Much of Heynes' success, and his knack of bringing out the best in his staff later on, came from the understanding of humanity that had followed a strict, strictly-organised, yet happy childhood as one of six highly-individual brothers. (One of the other Heynes boys was to work for the New Avon Body Company of Warwick, which at one stage looked like becoming a rival to Swallow in the low-priced-luxury-and-style stakes). Bill Heynes was born on the last day of 1903. His real ambition was to be a surgeon, but such a large family could not afford the long period of study. His grandfather was a farmer, but Heynes' idea of becoming a vet came to nought, too. Vets had a bit of a reputation for booziness in those days, and his parents did not approve. Heynes did take some of the examinations though. His first job was in his father's cabinet-making business in Leamington Spa, but he did not enjoy the work at all. Then one of his many aunts—this one was treasurer of the Leamington Croquet Club—put him in touch with the motor industry for the first time, and discussions led to Heynes beginning his apprenticeship at Humber in 1923. One of his first discoveries was the willingness of car-making people at all levels to share their engineering experience and wisdom. It was Lewis Dawtrey who got Heynes his first job after he had served his time, when the works manager, Oliver, had not been able to offer him anything. Unlike his equally-inventive brother, Lewis Dawtrey did not make a habit of taking chances, and Heynes (who became Dawtrey's assistant in

due course) learned from him that common sense and slide-rule should always be used together. Another man who encouraged Heynes was 'Jock' Wishart, Humber's engineering chief-to-be. From him he acquired a taste for design, and Heynes remembers in particular the Wishart theory that 'if it looks wrong, it cannot be right'. Says Bill Heynes: 'It wasn't infallible; but I've found it remarkably consistent!'

Heynes' first-ever design exercise (for an Institute of Automobile Engineers paper) was a four-cylinder motorcycle engine featuring twin overhead camshafts and hemispherical combustion chambers. Among his other designs was a four-speed synchromesh gearbox for the Hillman Minx, one of the popular cars of the then-new Rootes empire. He was also involved in several experimental independent front suspension layouts for the Hillman. In 1932 he married Evelyn ('Dutch') Blunt, Grinham's secretary; and in April 1935 he arrived at Swallow Road to begin his career as Chief Engineer of SS Cars Ltd. With one draughtsman, Percy Smith, to help him, Heynes had no time to lose, for two complete cars were required for the Olympia Show, barely six months away. Soon he would form a small team, led by former Hotchkiss engine man, Laurie Hathaway—whom he had known at Humber. Hathaway would be his right-hand man on the mechanical side. Bill Thornton, who had been Triumph's body designer, came to SS as the body-engineering link between Bill Heynes and Harry Gill.

One of the first things Heynes learned, on arrival, was the failure of the pretty little curving-tailed SS90 prototype (ARW 395) in the RAC Rally. In his *News Chronicle* 'road-test' the Honourable Brian Lewis avoided mentioning the clutch trouble, confining his criticism to the suspension and steering. 'Ideal for competition work', he observed, 'but I had other ideas about it at three o'clock in the morning on top of the Grampian Hills! I am assured by the manufacturers that the production cars will have slightly shorter rear springs and the steering will be made more direct. This should improve the character of the car enormously, as one felt that for a car capable of about 90 mph these two points required consideration.' Lewis entered the same car for the Shelsley Walsh May meeting, but it took well over 50 seconds to get up the hill, although it came third in its class. Heynes drove a supercharged SS1 tourer to the same meeting (see picture opposite). It seized-up on the way home.

The SS90 would hardly get beyond the prototype stage as it happened, but more than 20 slab-tanked 'production' versions did find their way into the public's hands. Jack Beardsley remembers 'cutting and shutting' the chassis to create the SS90, all of which had the same sequences of chassis and engine numbering as the SS1; the '90' had its own

Above *In Blackpool for the big SS Car Club rally of 1935, (left to right): Mrs Whittaker; Edward Huckvale, Mrs Huckvale (with young Tony Whittaker), Mr and Mrs Cyril Holland, (?), Mr and Mrs William Heynes, Arthur Whittaker, and two friends* (C. Holland). **Below right** *Cyril Holland winning the SS2 class in the timed test at Blackpool in 1935. He took part in the SS Car Club event at Scarborough a year later and was again successful* (C. Holland).

production body-number sequence, however, and this was to be carried on by its successor, the '100'. These cars were 'SS1' in width and 'SS2' in wheelbase.

A.G. Douglas Clease had *his* first go in a '90' on the Scottish Rally in June. He was second in his class in the *concours*; but although his works car (AVC 477) did well in some of the tests it was not placed in the rally 'proper'. Eric Boyd took delivery of *his* SS90 just in time to compete, and was fourth equal in the acceleration and braking test at Pitlochry; but he retired with clutch withdrawal symptoms. So it took Matthew Wilson and his SS1 tourer to provide any kind of showing in the Scottish Rally results—third in the unlimited open-car section behind a Ford V8 and a Railton. Just behind *him*, in a 3-litre Talbot, came Gunnar Poppe of the famous old Coventry engine-making family. A week later, the SS90 scored its only 'win' ever—though an unofficial one—driven by none other than William Lyons himself! Here is how it came about.

There was already a tradition of Swallow employees being taken to Blackpool for their annual day out at the company's expense; Lyons and Whittaker had only recently accompanied some 300 people—about half their workforce—on the fourth such outing. Now, for the second time in a month, Lyons was heading north for Blackpool. On this occassion it was for the SS Car Club's first national rally, organised by the founding secretary, G. Moxon Cook of Croydon with, no doubt, some encouragement from Ernest Rankin who managed to ensure wide press-coverage. It was to be the biggest SS club event yet, with over one hundred entries from all over Britain and even one from Sweden. This was just the opportunity to show the SS90 to enthusiasts, so Lyons grabbed AVC 477 as it arrived back from Scotland and headed north at high speed early on June 22, a glorious Saturday morning. The competitors were making a long weekend of it, spending two nights in the Imperial Hotel, and the special tests had already begun when he reached Clifton Drive—a fine new concreted promenade on Blackpool's South Shore.

The main test was really a 'sprint with obstacles', over half a mile in length, and W.G. Vaughan (SS1 tourer—70.8 seconds) was quickest. Sammy Newsome, the Coventry distributor, came second (SS1 Airline—72.4 seconds); the small-car category was won by Lyons' original body draughtsman-cum-craftsman Cyril Holland in (according to *The Light Car*) a 'well-handled' SS2, taking 85.6 seconds. Much interest was naturally shown in the new SS90, and Lyons agreed to do two unofficial 'exhibition' runs at the end of the morning. He drove fairly carefully on his first run, but at the second attempt really showed-off the car's comparative agility—not to say his own driving skill—by completing the course in 64.0 seconds!

Most people then made their way across town to Stanley Park where, did they but know it, Alice Fenton (though not a driver then) had sat at the wheel of an Austin Seven-Swallow and a Morris Cowley-Swallow for the company's first official publicity pictures only eight years earlier! On this occasion the spectacle was to be an air show organised by Lieutenant Owen Cathcart-Jones, RN, who (with Kenneth Waller) had broken the record from England to Australia and back a few months earlier, flying a Comet. Now his flying team (which Rankin had fixed up with six SSs for the summer, including an Airline model for Jones himself) was performing one of its series of Jubilee Air displays, to tie-in with the SS Car Club Rally. It is interesting to note that the equally-famous aviator, Jim Mollison, had bought one of the original SS1s in 1932, but had been photographed not long afterwards with his wife, Amy Johnson, for a Delage advertisement looking for all the world like Bonnie and Clyde!

Some lucky SS club members enjoyed a free flight around the tower before hurrying back to the 'Imperial' for the mayor's tea-dance. As Honorary President of the club, William Lyons was host to Kaye Don and other guests of honour for dinner that evening. There was brilliant sunshine once again on the Sunday, when the somewhat bloated party emerged on the Middle Walk for the *concours*, won by John Eaves (SS1 tourer). It had been the SS Car Club's biggest and best event, and a happy weekend for Lyons—happy in the knowledge that the receiver for the Sunbeam car and commercial businesses had accepted an offer from the machine tool company, Alfred Herbert Ltd. Herberts had told Lyons that they would dispose of the car assets to him! Indeed it had been widely reported that 'SS Cars Ltd. will take over the name, goodwill, and patents of the Sunbeam Motor Company Ltd., and will produce a range of Sunbeam cars at their modern factory in Coventry'.

Lyons and former Sunbeam racing-driver Kaye Don must surely have chatted about the exciting prospect during the weekend? A few days after Lyons' return to Coventry, on Monday July 2 1935, the *Birmingham Post*'s story read:

'Enquiries at Coventry yesterday failed to clarify the position regarding the reported sale of the assets of the Sunbeam Motor Car Company, Ltd., of Wolverhampton, to Motor Industries Ltd.

'A "Birmingham Post" reporter was informed by an official of Alfred Herbert Ltd.,

Left *SS cars final line, 1935, with an Airline on the left and a tourer in the foreground.*

Right *William Heynes at Swallow Road, 1936, with his first engine test bed.*

which was originally reported as having purchased the assets of the Sunbeam Company, that his firm was not willing to make a statement regarding the matter as the position was uncertain at present.

'SS Cars Ltd., of Coventry who, prior to Saturday's surprise development, had been announced as having purchased from Alfred Herbert Ltd., the name, goodwill and patents of the Sunbeam Company, was yesterday in conference with its legal advisers. Later, Mr. W. Lyons said: "Beyond the fact that this latest development is most surprising, we are unable to say anything at the moment, as the matter is under legal consideration." '

The Rootes moguls had moved in, and were about to add the Sunbeam name to *their* empire. The name of 'Sunbeam' was not to elude William Lyons for, in 1961 via Guy Motors of Wolverhampton, the former Sunbeam commercial vehicle business was to become part of his Jaguar group!

A more direct hit on Lyons' pocket was made by the secretary of the SS Car Club who had absconded with the funds at Blackpool; so Lyons paid the big hotel account. 'Either we have no owners' club, or you run it', Rankin was told by Lyons, not in the best of moods. Rankin ran it from then on . . . .

SS cars were now being used and eulogised by a wide cross-section of the population. There were the 'colourful' show-offs, like Leonard Plugge, who combined his honeymoon (to Honolulu in 1935) with a drive in his SS1 across North America to promote his inter-national Broadcasting Company. He claimed he had once owned the world's first radio-equipped car. It is difficult to resist quoting the whimsical *Memphis Press Scimitar* repor-ter who had the job of meeting the Englishman and his 'low slung' car:

'Capt. Plugge arose somewhat "early" this morning to accompany a Press-Scimitar reporter from Hotel Peabody, where he and his wife spent last night, to a near-by garage. It was, to be exact, 11.30 when he met the reporter in the Peabody lobby.

' "I never meet people before about 12 or 12.30", Capt. Plugge said in his clipped British accent, "but I overlooked the fact that I had come into another time belt. So", he laughed, "I am able to see you an hour earlier."

'Capt. Plugge takes great pride in his car, which he has named the "Aether VI". It is an English-made Swallow, powered by a Standard engine. At the garage, he climbed beneath the wheel and showed the reporter the myriad gadgets which make it one of the most completely equipped automobiles in the world.

'All fittings, including steering wheel, gear shift, hand brake lever and instrument board are in ivory with chromium trim. Upholstery is in green leather.

' "Yes", Captain Plugge said, "I am proud to say the Aether VI is beautiful. She must be—she has taken ten international prizes in 'affaires of elegance'—beauty contests. Eight of the ten were first prizes".'

Then there were the 'showbiz' customers, like 'The Two Leslies'—Leslie Sarony and Leslie Holmes of variety and radio—with their pair of Airlines, Jimmy Nervo (of Nervo and Knox), and the 'ukelele man' himself. It was the familiar high-pitched voice, calling her name through the window, that alerted Alice Fenton to the arrival of fellow-Lancastrian George Formby to chat to her while his SS1 was being attended to, in the Swallow Road service workshops. There were sportsmen such as R.E.S. Wyatt, the England and Warwickshire cricket captain, and Bill Pacey whose racing Bentley was developed and prepared by Walter Hassan at Brooklands.

By 1935, even some of the great recordmen—Sir Malcolm Campbell, John Cobb, and George Eyston among them—were prepared to endorse the SS as a worthy *marque*. The police too, were beginning to take to the SS. First recorded 'handing-over' was an SS2 tourer by Norman Redfern of Parkers (who still held sway in Bolton) to Inspector Morris; not long after, E. Nugent Christie, chief constable of Bedford acquired an SS1, too. The press were still paying tribute to the SS1 and SS2 ranges. Use of the Weslake-modified cylinder head and twin RAG carburettors for 1935 and 1936 made sure that their performance—if not consistently responsive, as some rallyists found—could justify the superlatives that tended to be lavished upon them.

The Motor bought a 20 hp SS1 tourer (AYY 940) from Henlys in 1935 and covered 10,000 miles in the first four months, after which it was reported: 'A broken fan belt on one occasion has been the sum total of departures from reliability and one of the strongest impressions remains the effortless performance and comfort which have made really long journeys untiring and rapid.'

The car was run-in very carefully and, on decarbonisation, the engine showed 'no traces of wear' and was 'extremely sweet and smooth running', much of the smoothness being attributed to the stiff seven-bearing crankshaft. Ride and handling were praised although 'personal preference inclines us to keep the Andre shock absorbers very tight on the front and very nearly as tight on the back'; and the low build of the car did not stop it from crossing the Wrynose and Hard Knott passes without grounding. The car would cruise at 70 mph 'indefinitely' and a maximum speed of 84.5 mph was recorded with the screen flat. Comfort and detailed finish were appreciated.

If the SS1 had not been a good or genuinely enjoyable car four years earlier, it was now—and everyone marvelled more and more at its excellent value. Most expensive of the range were the 20 hp drophead coupé at £385 and the SS90 at £395. Cheapest of the SS1s, the 16 hp open tourer, was still only £335. There was less choice for the SS2 owner, who was offered only the saloon, tourer and coupé styles—and the latter type was not listed at all for 1935 and 1936, although the occasional fixed-head coupé *was* still being made during those two final SS seasons.

Henlys still did most of the SS press loan work. One of the last SS2 impressions was gained from a run to Donington and back by *The Light Car* who, when collecting the car, noted how deeply affected Bertie Henly had been by the loss of his friend Frank Hough. It was found to be 'a car with real symmetry of outline coupled with practical features which are attractive and useful', these including space for four people and their luggage, and such points as a get-at-able tool kit in the boot lid and triple-hinge doors. 'The performance of the car is good. It will cruise very happily in the fifties, has a smooth clutch and a very snappy gearbox, and holds the road well'. For 'good', I would read 'adequate' performance, especially in view of the remarks of *The Light Car*'s editor, Eric Findon, on another occasion when he said that the Triumph and the Hillman Aero-Minx could 'run rings round' the SS2.

The over-weight, underpowered lower end of the SS range filled a niche of the smart-car market—but not a high-performance niche. No SS2 or subsequent '1½' ever won a worthwhile competitive event, and fortunately not many were made to try. In view of the product's low price, Rankin had published an article in the *SS Magazine* (Vol I, No 2) for distributors and dealers under the heading: 'There is no mystery about SS quality'. This is how it began:

'Not infrequently the examination of an SS by a prospective purchaser ends with the question, "How do they do it for the money?" . . . a question prompted by surprise that special coachwork of such obviously high quality can be offered at so moderate a price.

'In the absence of any explanation, many have felt that there is "a catch in it somewhere", a simulation of quality no more than skin deep. Yet there is no mystery about it. If all the materials are examined, both seen and unseen, it will be found that they are of the finest quality. All upholstery is of real soft tanned leather; carpeting is of the deepest pile; solid castings are used to the total exclusion of cheap metal pressings for even the smallest of details, whilst the cellulose finish is of a standard unequalled even by cars in the four-figure class.' It went on to point out that only prime ash was used for the frame and finest cemented alder for the plywood, that body manufacture was in 'the best traditions of bespoke coachbuilding practice, by means of a highly organised jig system', and the inspection system was 'highly organised and rigidly enforced'. Accompanying the story was an invitation to dealers, to bring their customers to inspect the works. There was now a proper office block, with an 'SS' motif over the doors. Like the inside of an SS car door, these doors featured a 'sun-ray' pattern. The surface of Swallow Road itself was much improved, and no longer so discouraging for visitors. Although old, the wooden-floored factory buildings were quite well-lit and, now that all four blocks were being used, there was some justification for offering visitors 'every facility for observing the modern methods of production and assembly'. On another page dealers were exhorted to follow-up the SS Cars share offer (which had received the equivalent of 20 columns of editorial coverage in 51 newspapers and periodicals) with local advertising.

The sidecar shop continued to be busy, too, although Lyons was keeping a dubious eye on that market. He had, however, registered a new private company called the Swallow Coachbuilding Co (1935) Ltd to deal separately with that side, with £10,000 capital. The *marque* 'SS' now dominated 'Swallow' officially—not *vice-versa*; but a new name was about to overshadow them both.

Now that SS Cars was moving forward at such a pace, there was a growing feeling that the next new product should have a name of its own. The word 'Standard' kept cropping-up—with *and* without the 'Swallow' bit. If 'SS' did not stand for anything in particular, the public were not getting much chance to believe it. William Lyons could not spare any length of time to concentrate on such matters, and it was left to the Nelson advertising agency—the Bett brothers and Eric Colbon—to work on a list of names and present them to him. They were delighted at the opportunity of giving the new car a new image for, despite some bright covers on *The Autocar* and *The Motor* (and such catch-lines as 'Speed . . . Grace . . . Silence' and 'Speed . . . Silence . . . Luxury') they had not yet managed to persuade the public or even themselves that the SS1 was *quite* the ultimate in motor cars. They could see the utter determination with which Lyons was attacking the world of motoring, and it was their job to support him with a strong name to back up the attack. Many of the animal names they selected were either too wishy-washy or had already been put to us by other companies. The name that kept coming to the top of the list was 'Jaguar'—and it was that name which caught Lyons' imagination. It reminded him of his old school and motor club chum Arnold Breakell who had been older than Billy Lyons and joined the Royal Flying Corps. Afterwards he had regaled Lyons with his stories of working as a mechanic upon aero-engines. There had, of course, been a 'Jaguar' aero-engine, but it was now obsolete. Permission was therefore sought from Armstrong-Siddeley to use the name, and that was granted willingly.

In his first few months with SS, Bill Heynes found his former chiefs Ted Grinham and Lewis Dawtrey particularly helpful despite the preoccupation of their new 'Flying Standards'. With their assistance plus the co-operation of suppliers' engineers, and the advice and encouragement of William Lyons, Arthur Whittaker and all his other new colleagues, Heynes got down to the task of meeting his engineering deadline. With the body jigs already well advanced, the new cars were clearly going to be 'coach-built', in much the same manner as the existing models. Major panels were to be bought-out, as for the SS1 and 2, largely from the Motor Panels factory—handily situated on the Whitmore Park estate, too, but nearer to Burnaby Road. Motor Panels' chief executive, Albert

The first SS Jaguar saloon, in 'mock-up' form. The spare wheel finished-up on the other side . . . or perhaps two had been considered, like the SS1 Airline?

Smith, and his bicycle had been beating a path between factories for several years already, 'The Swallow' having brought him good business.

Jack Beardsley, Harry Gill, and all the other departmental chiefs did the usual act of 'in-house' preparation—building their own moving tracks for the first time. Incidentally the 'railway lines', visible in some interior photographs of the factory, were relics of the 'munitions' days of the first World War and never used by the later tenants. John Black, now having virtually taken over from Maudslay at the Standard Company, agreed to manufacture the over-head valve 'Weslake' version of the 2.7-litre engine exclusively for SS, while continuing with side valves (and an abortive V8) for the 'Flying Standards'. His company would also go on supplying side-valve engines for a final season of SS1s and SS2s, the latter's 1.6-litre '12' being carried over to a small version of the new four-door 'Jaguar' saloon. The '90' two-seater and SS1 four-seater tourer bodies provided ready-made open coach-work for the new *marque*. They were called the 'SS Jaguar 100' and the 'SS Jaguar open tourer', and would be made in small numbers only. The latter looked vir-tually identical to the SS1 tourer, in which 'disguise' the new ohv engine was tested most before announcement.

It was the beautifully-proportioned and styled ohv SS Jaguar saloon upon which, for some time at least, the company's future would depend. The recent arrival of Triumph assembly in the former White & Poppe plant at the end of the drive, and that of Bill Thornton at SS, have led to who-came-first arguments in the past; but it was the new 'Jaguar shape' that appeared before and far outlived Triumph's Dolomite saloon. The new SS also had an imposing 'Jaguar' radiator grille, which suddenly made a Coventry car look as though it *might* have started life in Derby. MG were up to the same game with their two-litre SA saloon—unfamiliar territory for Abingdon.

Amid the feverish activity of the pre-Olympia count-down, SS advertising began to hint at a sensation to come. As usual the press helped in this build-up of interest. Humfrey Symons, who had driven for SS in the 1933 Alpine Trial, hinted at the various motor show 'surprises' in his syndicated newspaper column on September 18 1935, under the heading: '"Hush Hush" Plans of the Car Magnates—Mystery Models Promised for Olympia'. (He went on to refer to an 'entirely new SS which bristles with interesting mechanical features and has striking coachwork'.) Three days later, Rankin arranged Lyons' famous trade luncheon at London's Mayfair Hotel, where guests were invited to guess the price of the new SS Jaguar saloon. Even taking into account the obvious reason for being asked, they came up with an average answer that was still about £250 too high!—the new car would cost £385, Lyons told them. If William Lyons had not already become a legend even within motor trade and industry circles, he did so that day.

Show advertising centred around the bigger saloon, which was sometimes incorrectly illustrated with 'streamlined' proprietary sidelamps, as fitted to the SS1 Airline. 'The High Performance Car for the Connoisseur' read one of the somewhat disappointing slogans. The *editorial* promise was more forthright. 'A credit to the British automobile industry' declared *The Autocar*, beaten for once by their rivals at Rosebery Avenue: 'With a distinguished appearance, outstanding performance, and attractive price as the main characteristics, the new SS Jaguar range represents an achievement of which Mr. Lyons and his technical staff may well feel proud.' Thus *The Motor* did its bit to launch the very first 'Jaguar' motor car on September 24 1935.

8: Birth-pangs of the new breed
(1935 to 1939)

Could William Lyons himself have envisaged, in 1935, that fame and fortune were only just around the corner? Perhaps so, but it was going to take a little longer than he would wish, because of two factors of which he was already aware. One was the likelihood of another war, still a little remote; the other was the immediate problem of modernising the means of body-making—the very business at which he had made his name. Within a fortnight of the announcement of the new Jaguars, Cecil Kimber introduced his MG SA saloon and it *might* have been a direct competitor had it not become the subject of several modifications intended to make it compete even more. Its production was delayed and, as Jaguars began to appear on the roads, the MG men (who had previously looked at SS with what Wilson McComb calls 'justifiable contempt') now began to appreciate and probably envy the adventurous Coventry firm which had no Nuffield Group to push *it* around.

First deliveries of the 2.7-litre SS Jaguar saloon were made well before the turn of the year, and the Honourable Brian Lewis was able to give the model its competition *début* in January 1936, taking second place in class in the Monte Carlo Rally coachwork competition. As the SS Jaguar was already known to be a fine performer with a chassis to match, it did not seem to matter so much that it was a long way down the leader-board in the general classification. The SS Jaguar saloons were already shedding some of the flamboyance of their predecessors . . . or was it something to do with the clientèle? SS1s and SS2s *were* made in 1936, but not very many. The SS Jaguar 100, although the most exotic car of the range, was announced quietly. Maybe enthusiasts would think it identical to the

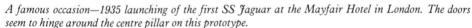

A famous occasion—1935 launching of the first SS Jaguar at the Mayfair Hotel in London. The doors seem to hinge around the centre pillar on this prototype.

Casimiro de Oliveira takes the SS Jaguar to its first outright race win abroad, at Vila Real, Portugal, in 1937.

SS90 which had had such a poor start to life? Nevertheless the '100' was described from the outset as being 'primarily intended for competition work' and 'sufficiently tractable for use as a fast tourer without modification'.

T.H. (Tommy) Wisdom of the *Daily Herald* and *Sporting Life*, a successful race and rally driver already, got together with Coventry theatre proprietor and SS distributor S.H: (Sam) Newsome to persuade his friend William Lyons to let him run in the Alpine Trial, which was back on the international motoring calendar once again for 1936—taking place mainly in politically-stable Switzerland. Wisdom and his wife Elsie ('Bill') took the 2.7-litre SS Jaguar 100 through the event penalty-free—a marked contrast to previous SS performances! In the special tests he was beaten only by Descollas in a 3.3-litre Bugatti, who lost road marks anyway. So, if there had been a general classification, Wisdom would have been placed first.

Motoring enthusiasts around Europe quickly turned and gave a more respectful glance in the direction of the small Coventry firm whose products had been so outpaced in Europe's toughest road competition twice before. Now here *was* a new force to be reckoned with! This particular car (BWK 77) was to have further success not only in rallies and hill-climbs but, briefly, in racing, too. When the 3.5-litre engine was being developed, a high-compression version was fitted to this car and, in stripped form, this '100' lapped Brooklands at over 118 mph—much quicker than any other pre-war Jaguar ever went.

Unmodified, the SS Jaguar 100 could *rally* against all-comers, including the BMW 328, with a good chance of success; however, Lyons' appreciation of the bad as well as the good publicity to be had from competition work was so sharpened by experience that on at least one occasion he was able to persuade private entrants to withdraw from a *race* they could not hope to win. There were exceptions, of course—like F.J. McEvoy's class win in the 1936 Marne Grand Prix at Reims and de Oliveira's 1937 victory at Vila Real. The latter was a very close-run thing. Casimiro de Oliveira was already one of Portugal's top drivers, but the opposition for his 2.7-litre SS Jaguar 100 was quite strong, including a BMW, an Aston Martin, and two Adlers—Trumpf models of the type which had done so well in Alpine Trials.

De Oliveira was dicing for the lead on the twisty street circuit when a stone flew up and broke his goggles. He made a quick pit-stop, re-joining the race behind Max zu Schaumburg Lippe's German-prepared, lightened Adler, Alfredo Rego's BMW, and Mario

Teixeira's Aston Martin; he caught up again, however, and the crowd were delighted when the Portuguese-driven SS won, holding off the Adler and the BMW by less than one second after 90 miles of hard racing. De Oliveira would become better known as a Ferrari driver later in his career, winning the 1951 Portuguese Grand Prix at Oporto and finishing second in 1952 and 1953. Back in 1937, however, he gave Jaguar what was almost certainly the Coventry *marque*'s first continental outright race victory.

As mentioned earlier, Lyons always believed in 'testimonial' publicity, and soon after the birth of the 'Jaguar' name he got Ernest Rankin to compile a booklet containing press road-test reports and owners' letters. One of the letters was from Paul Marx of Buxton who wrote about his car: 'Having written so many impatient and hasty letters while waiting for my Jaguar "100", I somehow feel urged to write to you, on completion of 9,000 miles, a slight appreciation of the car. The performance rose far above my expectations and fully justified my confidence in giving the order at the last show without having a trial run. The "pick-up" is quite astonishing, but what impresses me most is the way the engine keeps its tune. Beyond a slight adjustment of the tappets, I have not had to put a spanner to the engine . . . By taking out owners of sports cars in the £700 region, I had already broken several hearts on telling them the price.' (At £395 the '100' was the costliest car in the first Jaguar range.)

What Paul Marx did not tell the company was that he would take his car to North America—and race it. What little is known of Marx's programme provides a fascinating glimpse of the transatlantic club scene of the 1930s. Marx found himself among true enthusiasts when he met the Collier brothers and the rest of the ARCA gang, *and* even finished seventh overall in their 1938 'championship'.

The wealthy Colliers—Barron Junior, Samuel and Miles—always had a taste for road-racing and, with a few friends, had created the Overlook Automobile Racing Club some years earlier. This strictly amateur organisation had begun with the holding of impromptu races through the Collier family's country estate (called 'Overlook') which sprawled across several New York hillsides. In 1933 it had become the Automobile Racing Club of America, a grand title for an association that promoted 'European-style' road-racing for amateurs. By the time Marx arrived on the scene, membership of the ARCA had risen to well over 100. The Colliers had cornered the market in MG-selling whereas SS and Jaguar were to remain relatively rare in America until their (late) introduction of left-hand-drive in the 1940s, because of the Richard Taylor monopoly.

The ARCA gave their events authentic-sounding names, and Marx may well have been amused when he found that the 'New London TT' was, literally, a weekend 'tour and trial'—a long, rainy road-run plus driving tests! Finishers reached the Hotel Mohican at New London, Connecticut, in the early hours of a Sunday morning, soaked to the skin and about as testy as the inhabitants they had woken-up *en route*. The winner was OARC founder-member Tom Dewart's MG from the Cord of George Weaver—famous, later, as a racing driver and for his creation of (and entanglement with) the circuit near his home at Thompson, Connecticut. Marx's SS Jaguar came third, in full road-trim complete with small over-riders on the front bumper which was itself a non-standard item. These three competitors were the only ones to make a good job of the road-section and every other car, including the MGs of Miles and Sam Collier, incurred high penalties.

The ARCA's 'prestige event' of the year was its speed hill-climb to the top of Mount Washington, New Hampshire's highest summit at nearly 6,300 feet above sea-level. From the west, hardy spectators could approach via the rack railway; the road wound its way up from an elevation of about 1,700 feet at Pinkham Notch on the east side. It had been used for motor competitions on and off from 1899, but it did not become a regular event until the ARCA gained use of it once a year. Here was real road-racing for the amateur!—and much safer than the typical ARCA competitions held on small, rough, country or street circuits within arm's length of unprotected spectators, for there was only one car on the start-line at a time! Known as the 'Climb to the Clouds', Mount Washington's private eight-mile toll road passed through thick woodland; eventually, however, the driver 'broke cover' and found himself on rough, rocky moorland with very airy views—either that, or wrapped in low cloud. A spectacular venue, Mount Washington was (apart from Pike's Peak) North America's greatest hill-climb course.

For 1938, the clouds *were* low and drizzle had saturated the woodland road, but the rain had stopped when the competitors arrived at 5.30 one Sunday morning. These amateurs *did* take their motoring seriously! Marx took the Jaguar up in 13 minutes 22.6 seconds, comparing well with (exactly) 13 minutes for the Ford-Amilcar special of ARCA President, George Rand. In a class of his own, however, was Lemuel Ladd in the V8-powered 'Old Grey Mare' which skittered over the loose shingle to record an almost unbelievable 12 minutes 17.6 seconds—a hill-record which was to stand until well into the post-war era, when the Jaguar name would fare even better. Meanwhile Marx's fourth place overall—behind the Ford Specials of Ladd, Rand, and McMillen, and ahead of the Colliers' and other MGs—was a performance that backed-up the evidence from Wisdom's Alpine Trial success: that the SS Jaguar 100 was fast, reasonably controllable on loose surfaces, and could take quick altitude changes in its stride.

Quite what went wrong a fortnight later in the ARCA's third annual 'Round the Houses' race at Alexandria Bay (near the Thousand Islands of the St Lawrence) is not clear, but there was apparently very little car *or* driver reliability to be seen! It is not known why Marx failed to finish, but the Jaguar—stripped of its wings and windscreens—made a fine sight dashing along the main street of the small New York state town, its driver bare-armed and bare-headed. The rules were few, and there were several crashes. No one was hurt, although an occupied wheelchair was narrowly missed by a detached Chrysler wheel. Even the winner, Miles Collier (supercharged MG), had had to disengage himself from a pile-up *en route* to victory.

The Automobile Racing Club of America's last event was to be the amazing World's Fair Grand Prix of 1940 at Flushing Meadows, part of New York city itself. As usual, pure luck prevented anyone from being killed; the winner was Frank Griswold (Alfa Romeo). When America joined the war in 1941, George Rand wrote a 'winding-up' letter to all members, and the ARCA was disbanded. Others may well have raced SSs or Jaguars in America during the 1930s, but the racing must have been even more informal than that of the ARCA! Paul Marx's visit to America in 1938 *does* seem unique. He certainly appears to have been the only man to use an SS Jaguar in those ARCA meetings. Since those days, Jaguar has become one of Britain's biggest dollar earners, and won many American races too.

It would be impossible, though enjoyable, to follow up all the letters that appeared in the SS 'testimonial' booklet. One man wrote that 'despite strenuous thrashing in trials and on the track, the car is still running perfectly. I have owned a good many fast cars but I can honestly say that none of them has given me as much pleasure as my 100'. His name was E.H. Jacob, and his successes included an outright victory in the Welsh Rally of 1937. He was a member of the winning team then, as he was in the RAC Rally which was beginning to include some competitive tests to make it more than a boring drive followed by a grand polish! Ernest Rankin was a member of these teams, and in fact organised them on behalf of the company and the club. As he was now acting as secretary to the SS Car Club, he could 'wear two hats' when it came to entering teams for rallies.

Rankin arranged at least two sprint meetings at the works ('The Coventry Speed Trials'), enlisting the aid of Fred Gardner as chief marshal, John Witherall as a starter and

Paul Marx (SS Jaguar '100', No 18003) looks as unprotected as the spectators at Alexandria Bay, New York, in 1938 (A.S. Barnes).

others from the works besides keen SS owners like Tom Crumbie who was responsible for printing Rankin's poshest catalogues. It was Rankin, too, who organised rallies to Scarborough and elsewhere, *and* several race meetings at Donington between 1936 and 1939, press-ganging more from the trade and the works to help. At Scarborough, the best SS2 performance was, as at Blackpool, achieved by the original 'wood-butcher' (as he was called), Cyril Holland. Lyons was, of course, the SS Car Club President; Vice-Presidents were Bertie Henly, the Honourable Brian Lewis, Professor A.M. Low, and Sir William Sleigh, one or more of whom usually appeared as stewards. Company secretary Ted Huckvale and his elder son Rex would be joined by auditor George Pye (who had come to SS from Haworth's of Blackpool) on the general marshalling roster; Freddie Ford of the service department was in charge of pit and paddock marshalling while his boss, Digby Paul, did the scrutineering with A.G. Douglas Clease of *The Autocar*. Clease was also on the organising committee with former racing driver, Jack Joyce, of Henlys, Leslie Hatfield and several more including, of course, the hard-pressed Rankin.

Among the other notable 'regulars' when the SS Car Club went to Donington was Charlie Lodge from the sales department. He was the timekeeper, and he assisted Laurie Hathaway with the handicapping, too. The SS Car Club was certainly a leader among active one-make clubs of the 1930s, and there is no doubt that it fostered good relations between company and client. The Blackpool incident of 1935 had put Lyons on his guard, though. More than ten post-war years would pass before Sir William sanctioned an RAC-affiliated club bearing the name 'Jaguar'.

1936 and 1937 were great years of consolidation for the Jaguar *marque*, consistent production being helped by the dropping of the SS1 and SS2 during 1936 and by making few changes to the Jaguars. From £24,209 and £27,367 in the two previous years, SS's net profit for the year ending July 31 1937 went up again to £34,292 and a best-ever dividend of 12½ per cent was paid. Almost coinciding with that happy knowledge came the last of the basic stages in the 'professionalisation' of the company. It was a lesson learned in the hardest possible way—through major losses in production.

Among the newcomers to the SS management at this time was W.C.E. ('Ted') Orr who came from the Standard Motor Company as works manager. It was usually known within SS Cars what people's jobs were, and official titles were generally avoided. In some cases relationships were indeterminate and therefore somewhat abrasive—a case in point being

Harry Gill and Ted Orr, each of whom could be pretty abrasive without help from the other!

While the coachbuilt saloons were being made, MG had developed their 'big' saloons, and were advertising them 'For Space . . . For Grace . . . For Pace' by 1937. 'That's a good line', thought Eric Colbon at Nelson Advertising, and filed the idea away in his mind—at least he must have done, probably unconsciously. In Coventry, the disaster began as the new all-steel 'trial' body was cut up into separate components, which were to be contracted-out to several different body-pressing specialists. With the old system of coachbuilding, it was fairly easy to 'adjust', and get a good, even fit around (say) the doors. Now, when it came to assembly the new bodies would not fit together.

The 1937 show, where the all-steel car was announced, was another success story. The tourer was dropped from the range, which now consisted of saloon and drophead coupé models with 3.5, 2.7, and 1.8-litre engines, all with overhead valves. The bodywork was broader but visually similar except that the spare wheel had been moved from the wing to the bootlid—first with a 'sunken' cover, then (for the show) totally hidden. Because of the weight of the lid, the wheel was quickly moved again to a compartment beneath the floor, which needed the rear bumper hinging down for access. The bumper was secured with wing-nuts! The SS Jaguar 100 was still listed, with a choice between the two bigger power units. The 3½-litre '100' was, in fact, the company's first genuine '100 mph' car.

That winter saw the SS works in turmoil, because of all the new bodywork problems, and was virtually at a standstill until well into the spring of 1938. With the planned increase in output—and the need for a wider-than-ever variety of skills—up went the labour force to well-nigh 1,500; but it could not be utilised to the full for many months. Rubery Owen made the doors and the roof; Sankey of Wellington the quarter-panels. Pressed Steel and other firms were involved, too. After much argument, and eventually even some compensation, the maze of production lines that had grown up at Swallow Road ground into action on a near-continuous basis. There were metal-workers now, many of them induced northwards from the American-owned Briggs concern at Dagenham. Spot-welding and tricky bends were smoothed with pounds (if necessary) of lead; as demand for the coachbuilder's art became less, so the need for skilled lead-loading increased. The other 'life-savers' of the new system were the dingers who, with uncanny ease, could smooth and stretch pressings that did not match. The new craftsmanship was on its way, and it was not long before coachbuilders in Britain, Switzerland, Belgium, and elsewhere were beginning to try building special coachwork on SS Jaguars. Mechanical unity of the SS

Left *1937 pressed steel prototype, showing spare wheel position. Although it lost its external mouldings, the bootlid still carried the spare for that year's show. Back in Coventry, though, there was some frantic pre-production redesign work! . . . and the wheel went under the floor.*

Right *William and Greta Lyons with their two elder children, Patricia and John, at Wappenbury Hall, their home since 1937— roughly when this picture was taken.*

Jaguar was complete; the SS chassis was now as choice a one as any for a coachbuilding house to select when planning a new exotic or luxurious body style. Over the years, many individuals would try and improve upon the body designs of William Lyons and the Jaguar team. There were some glorious failures, but few that could be compared with a 'Coventry Original'.

For a while, it had looked as though SS Cars Ltd might actually make a loss, but the summer recovery averted that. When the financial year (ending July 31 1938) showed a drop in net profits by more than £12,000, this is how Lyons reported to his shareholders:

'The past year has been a very anxious one for your directors, owing to the failure of certain material suppliers to deliver by the dates stipulated in their contracts, and subsequently to maintain satisfactory supplies, in consequence of which, until the last three months of the year only a very limited production was obtained.

'As late as April it appeared that the year's trading must inevitably show a substantial loss, but after that date we were able to overcome the major part of our difficulties, and have since arranged an amicable settlement with the suppliers concerned.'

The dividend was down to five per cent and the net profit to £22,218. (Henlys, who would have expected about half the total SS business for the year, dropped from £56,700 to about £38,000 net profit.)

Lyons ended his 1938 speech with typical confidence, and spoke of a successful start to the new season. He mentioned competition success, emphasising that these were achieved by private owners, picking out the 3½-litre SS Jaguar saloon of J.O.H. Willing as 'most outstanding'. Although it had finished only 42nd 'on the road' it achieved the top position—*Grand Prix d'Honneur*—in the 'comfort' competition at Monte Carlo. This must have been especially satisfying, for it automatically reflected great credit upon the quality of the new all-steel body, once it had reached the 'finished' state.

The summer of 1938 saw William Lyons relax sufficiently to go to the South of France for a holiday, and to take part in the SS Car Club's Donington meeting consisting of a series of short handicap races. He made several false starts in his enthusiasm to get away, but the results spoke for themselves; his 3½-litre '100' made the quickest lap of the day at an average speed of 68.81 mph, and the best race average at 67.37 mph. This was a 'trade' race, in which 'Sammy' Newsome (65.93 mph) was second and Bill Heynes (63.07 mph) third, in similar cars. It is significant that several of the drivers present raced their cars at Brooklands, Crystal Palace, or Donington quite regularly, yet could not match Lyons' speed that day (although they were not competing against him in the same event); H.E.

Ormrod's SS90 is sent on its way in the SS Car Club 'trade' race at Donington in 1938, soon to be over-whelmed by the flying SS100s of Lyons (DHP 734, No 31), Newsome (DDU 822, No 30), and Heynes (DHP 736, No 32) in that order.

Bradley averaged 66.84 mph in his race and other 3½-litre '100' race speeds included K.W. Raspin (66.25 mph), G.E. Matthews (65.45 mph), and G.A. Burgess (64.52 mph). Best 2½-litre '100' race speed was that of A. Goldman who won the final handicap race at 61.95 mph, with C.E. Truett's car next quickest at 61.79 mph; Michael Head, who was to become famous as a driver of post-war Jaguars, could not do better than 55.10 mph. Incidentally, the inner circuit of just under two miles per lap was used; although the average speeds were given to two places of decimals, timing was in whole seconds! It seems likely that, had he decided to take up *the sport* as a hobby, Lyons would have been among the very best of club racing drivers; as it was, his determination on his rare track appearances matched that of his approach to matters of business.

Storm clouds may have been hovering over all Europe, but for SS Cars Ltd the financial year that began on the first of August 1938 was to be Lyons' sunniest by far. For the first time, output for the 12-month period would exceed 5,000 cars and Bill Heynes urgently needed another senior engineer. From the moment Wisdom intercepted him in the pad-dock during the September 1938 race meeting at Brooklands, it did not take Wally Hassan much time to make up his mind. Wally was born in 1905—one of six children. (Another coincidence they discovered soon after he met Bill Heynes was that his grandfather, like Heynes' father, had been a cabinetmaker.) His father was manager of the Upper Holloway branch of a large gents' outfitting chain, and knew Sunbeam's London service chief. In 1920, he took Wally out to Hendon to see him in the hope of finding the lad a job. They had been out of luck with a railway training, and had already looked without success at AEC in Southall, and at Daimler's London depot. On their way home from Sun-beam . . . yet another wasted journey . . . they noticed a factory being built nearby. The factory was for a new *marque* called after its creator; presently 15-year-old Wally Hassan became the 14th 'clocker-in' at Bentley Motors.

Hassan's next 18 years were filled with practical experience. When Bentley Motors gave up racing (shortly before failing and being bought by Rolls-Royce) he spent six more years—mostly at Brooklands—working on and building Bentley specials for Woolf Barnato and Bill Pacey. After a brief spell with ERA at Bourne in 1936-7, Hassan was invited back to Brooklands by Thomson & Taylor to work on John Cobb's Railton-designed land speed record car—which he did; he also made a 4.9-litre Bugatti-powered racing car for Dick Wilkins.

Hassan had already received the benefit of Jaguar experience, when Heynes had provided him with information on the 'works' SS Jaguar 100 (BWK 77) for a similar car he was preparing at Brooklands. He moved to Coventry late in 1938 and, as SS's chief experimental engineer, was given the job of developing an independent front suspension system. He was not totally divorced from competition, however, and was soon extracting even more performance from the works car (in which he had already seen Wisdom lap Brooklands so quickly), and in its 'open-wheeled' form—looking not unlike Sir Malcolm Campbell's Sunbeam 'Tiger', only smaller—the SS Jaguar was propelled by Sam Newsome up Shelsley Walsh hill in 1939 in 42.95 seconds. (This very respectable time was to be beaten when, in 1973, its restorer David Barber managed 41.67 seconds—but that was done with modern tyres fighting a more modern surface.)

A particularly effective job was done by Wally Hassan for the 1939 Monte Carlo Rally. Jack Harrop of Manchester, whose driving of SS cars had impressed Lyons greatly, was provided with a Hassan-prepared 3½-litre saloon (DKV 101) for the winter classic. Five other Jaguars were entered but Harrop's was the only competitive entry. Even so, Harrop was prompted to write to Rankin beforehand: 'I am astounded at the marvellous appearance of the car, but I am doubtful whether you really appreciate the extreme conditions in which this car has to travel'. He added a reminder to Heynes that two Rollo tow ropes were needed, with five-ton breaking strain, and stressed 'the absolute necessity of raising the existing chassis crossmember that carries the spare wheel to enable the car to be trayed from the gearbox right to the tail'. That Harrop meant business was brought home forcibly when he told Rankin that the Gourock Rope Work Co of Liverpool was making some rope-ladders for him.

Harrop's co-drivers were the well-known Cheshire engineer, George Mangoletsi, and William Currie, a Manchester cotton merchant. Mangoletsi was detailed to report back to the works from Athens, Harrop's chosen starting point; 'Everybody raves about the appearance of the SS but they say it is impossible for it to get through the Balkans, and the official odds are, I believe, 100:1 that we don't get as far as Belgrade—well we will see. Personally I do think it is a little low. The roads even round Athens which they call good are the very devil. However, Jack is very optimistic and we certainly have the weather with us, . . . The favourite for the Rally is Gordini with an 1100 c.c. Fiat . . . the BMW came through from Germany on the rally course . . . very battered indeed, one especially having gone down a ravine. Everything is quite O.K. . . . but the engine doesn't seem

The 1938 Earls Court surprise: a one-off SS Jaguar 100 fixed-head coupé. It is seen here with its subsequent owner, Gordon March, at the wheel.

Greta Lyons and 'Bill' Wisdom did the 1939 RAC Rally together with this 3½-litre SS Jaguar saloon. They are seen here afterwards at Brighton.

quite as healthy as it might be . . . sorry that the snaps we took at Dover were no good, but the weather was terrible . . . In spite of all the alleged difficulties we will do our best to "bring back the Cup".' An official and cryptic pre-rally bulletin backed-up the warnings: 'With the present weather conditions all over the continent it is not expected to be a joy ride but a gruesome struggle against the elements in which pronostics(!) as to best and easiest route are buried under ice snow and mud to say nothing of the cold'.

Somehow 'third man' William Currie kept a diary, and noted the initial trouble with heat caused by the undershield covering the exhaust system and the almost continuous bumping on 'large rocks . . . it was quite impossible to avoid'. They thought they were out of the rally when, at Sofia, they heard that the route to the Dragoman Pass was blocked by a landslide; guided by flares held by Bulgarian soldiers, they were able to detour via what Currie described as a river bed. Later Currie slid the car into a ditch, but they were still up to time at Belgrade. Despite buckling a wing in Austria (Currie again), they managed to reach Grenoble for the start of the first eliminating test without penalty. This 355 kilometre test was divided into five sections. The third section was effectively a special stage, being only 12 kilometres in length. 'Harrop took off his coat and jacket and worked at the wheel like a demon as he took the hairpins in beautifully controlled slides, rushing the car through in excellent fashion. We later found out that we had made the second fastest time of the whole rally.'

The pressure continued and while Currie slept, Harrop and Mangoletsi rushed into Monaco with about two minutes to spare after seven stops to pour water over steaming brake drums. Without time for clocks or adjustments came the acceleration and braking test on the Quai Albert Premier, and Harrop's run was done carefully to avoid penalty if the brakes should misbehave. They did not; but who can say they would not have done if used harder? Nevertheless, the Jaguar was still tenth equal in the rally, and the Barclays Bank Silver Cup (for best performance by a British car) was won—the first-ever important competition award for an SS touring model.

In reply to Lyons' wired greetings, Harrop wrote: . . . sorry we were not able to sweep the board . . . wish you could have been here to see the sad looks of the Humber chaps. They had set out to win the Barclay Cup and were really sure of it after the second test and told everyone so . . . Congratulations on building a really tough car and thanks for giving me the chance to prove it.' Having made his contribution to Jaguar history, Jack Harrop was to die at war . . . the war that was to change the face of Britain, its industry, and its people.

9: Sidecars, Stirlings and survival
(1939 to 1945)

Even before the war, with output approaching a weekly target of 200 cars, more construction had been in hand at Swallow Road. A major acquisition by SS Cars Ltd, was Motor
Panels (Coventry) Ltd, whose factory was also on the Whitmore Park estate. The new
subsidiary's board consisted of Albert Smith and the SS directors. A Scot named Tommy
Dean from Briggs Bodies was general manager, and Harry Gill was moved over from the
SS factory to work under him. Gill took offence at what he regarded as a snub, especially
in view of the recent arrival of Ted Orr from Standard. He began looking elsewhere and,
early in the war, he left, joined de Havillands and worked at Hatfield on the
Mosquito—where Grinham and Turner of Standard also turned-up for a while. Gill later
returned to the Midlands and became his own master. This big, tough Yorkshireman
(who may have rubbed a lot of people up the wrong way but who had turned so many im-
possible-looking jobs into practical propositions when, as he put it, 'we were all amateurs')
remained very active, making a great success of his business life in engineering and
building. He continued to admire Sir William Lyons and (one suspects) *vice-versa*. He did
tell me that he would not have been as well-off financially if he had stayed at SS. Perhaps
he would have preferred to be his own boss from the start—who knows?

At the time, Lyons had quite enough 'on his plate'; the body crisis and the purchase of
Motor Panels had left him in a very tricky position when war came, and his 'new'
bankers, Lloyds, put him in the position of having to guarantee the SS account personally
for some time. Another man might not have had the strength of character to carry on but,
from the time it was realised that contracts were there to be obtained, the war was simply
another challenge to Lyons to maintain the business he had set up.

Originally it was thought that the Manchester bomber would become a production
reality, and that SS would get a large slice of the manufacturing contract. When that
project was dropped, SS Cars became official repairers of Whitley bombers, as well as
manufacturers and fabricators of parts for the Stirling, the Mosquito, the Spitfire, and the
Lancaster. Aided by the war ministry, a new factory was built, up Swallow Road, and
some machining work was done there; for all their creative work, Jack Beardsley and
Wally Hassan had had only a handful of ancient machine tools before the war; now
ministry contracts began bringing in more up-to-date equipment. This factory was used
mainly for work on large aircraft. Armstrong-Siddeley—to whom SS had become sub-
contractors on the 'Cheetah' radial aero-engine—had commandeered a boot and shoe factory called Black's at South Wigston, near Leicester. It was re-floored to take machine
tools, and Jack Beardsley was put in charge of it, on behalf of SS Cars. Bert Langley was
the chief tool-designer, and Bert Maling his draughtsman. It was Beardsley's own
capacity to take great strides forward as an engineer and as a manager during the
'Wigston' period that fitted him ideally for the even bigger responsibilities he was to take
on after the war, and for 20-odd years beyond.

Coventry city centre after the blitz. Although barely three miles away, the SS factory was badly damaged only once.

Also in the SS team was Jack Randle. In 1935 he had joined the company aged 15, working for Harry Teather in the stores (*and* he was tea-boy for William Lyons!). After a brief spell with Armstrong-Siddeley he returned to SS Cars in 1940, and moved with two or three hundred others to South Wigston in 1941 after the new Swallow Road factory building had lost much of its roof in the *blitz*. After Randle had spent a period as machinist (and, briefly, shop steward), Beardsley promoted him—and it is interesting to note that each was to become responsible for the company's Radford works much later in his career, Randle retiring as plant director in the summer of 1985.

In Wally Hassan's little experimental department there was, of course, no car development and, apart from some machine-tool conversions to electic operation from the old overhead belt-drive system, his skills were not being put to best use in Coventry. Hassan moved to Bristol as a carburettor development engineer for a short time, and among the people who helped him were Charles Newcombe (to find a house) and Philip Weaver (to learn the intricacies of Claudel-Hobson aeroplane carburettors), both of whom were to become associated with Jaguar themselves. Hassan and Weaver were unhurt in the daylight raid that killed sports-car maker Adrian Squire, also doing war-work at Bristol. In Coventry there was much sadness too, as the bombs kept on coming; not least for Bill and 'Dutch' Heynes who lost their first son, Simon, when their house in Beechwood Avenue was destroyed. 'Dutch', already peppered with shattered glass, had to wait for many agonising minutes while the makeshift ambulance was *strafed* on the way to hospital.

After one of the worst raids William Lyons arrived in Swallow Road, having driven around the city via Browns Lane, dreading what he might find. It was the morning after an incendiary bomb had wrecked part of the roof of the newly-constructed factory building, and there was rubble everywhere. What he remembers better than anything, though, is the remark of one man who nodded a friendly greeting as Lyons got out of his car: 'Sharp again this morning', he said. In fact, the Swallow Road plant was not nearly as badly damaged as those—like, say Daimler's main Radford works—nearer the city centre. There, of course, people were losing their homes in a trice. It was not like Dresden in

Germany; but Coventry really did suffer. By the time billeting was being organised officially, Greta Lyons had housed more than 20 homeless Coventry people in the estate around Wappenbury Hall, their country house seven miles out of the city, to which they had moved from Gibbet Hill a couple of years before the war. When the authorities came, she had to tell them there was no room for more evacuees. One lot of 'nomads' had been picked up by the Lyonses in the Eagle Street area, having obviously lost their home. A greengrocers was still open there; the words chalked on a blackboard propped against the remains of the building caught Greta Lyons' eye: 'Here we stay because we must, and here we'll stay until we're bust.' This was, of course, typical of stories told by everyone who had to cope with living in and around war-time Coventry.

Alice Fenton now shared a house on the Tamworth Road with her ill and elderly parents and her sister, Nancy, who, as the service department was virtually disbanded, worked for Claudel-Hobson who occupied the former White & Poppe and Triumph Gloria works at the north end of Swallow Road. (Later she moved with that company to Wolverhampton before going to Morris Engines in Coventry.) In April 1941, Alice wrote to her great friend Connie, with whom she had shared home for seven exciting years after they had come to Coventry as teenagers. Since 1936 Connie had been married to storekeeper Harry Teather, and lived in the Cheylesmore district of Coventry. In 1941, however, Connie was back home in Fleetwood for the birth of the second of three sons. Work was not offering any excitement, Alice Fenton confided, and most of her acquaintances seemed to have 'hibernated' or gone 'as dead as ditchwater'. However, she was going steady and 'having a marvellous time. We have been to every dance hall in the Midlands, and have defied black-out, bombs and everything else to keep alive'. By keeping alive, she meant 'living life to the full'—not just 'existing'.

One department at Swallow Road, Foleshill, that was able to continue more-or-less its normal activity in war-time was the sidecar shop, with Howard Davies still selling hard. Elsewhere in this book will be found a comprehensive record of SS's war-time production, which included nearly 10,000 sidecars for several different war department uses. The success of these contracts was due to the efforts of Davies; Lyons and Davies were to disagree over the matter of commission. Davies left, and towards the end of 1944 William Lyons and Eric Sanders (managing Director of the Helliwell Group) negotiated the sale of the Swallow Coachbuilding Co (1935) Ltd. Helliwells used the Swallow name not only for sidecars but also for an advanced scooter which *The Motor Cycle* described as being 'of pleasing appearance, yet readily accessible for maintenance, easy to manoeuvre, simple to drive, comfortable, practically skid-proof, and economical'. Despite this unsolicited praise, the 125 cc Villiers powered Swallow 'Gadabout' was to last only a few years, from 1946. Tube Investments Ltd, became owners of the Swallow name and continued sidecar production; briefly in 1954-5 they would enter the car market with the TR2-powered Swallow 'Doretti—a pleasant-looking 100 mph sports-tourer.

In 1956, still called by its old title and still making a few sidecars, Swallow Coachbuilding would be absorbed into the shrinking world of British motorcycling via Watsonian—the famous Birmingham company which made complete sidecars and (according to Wilfred Webb, when I met him in Stockport) supplied William Walmsley with his first chassis back in 1920. To conclude this digression, it should be added that long-serving Watsonian director C.G. Bennett thinks the nice idea of this 'Swallow connection' is quite likely to be correct; but Watsonian do not have the records to prove it. Watsonian still make a few sidecars, but have not put the 'Swallow' name to them for many years. At the time of writing Watsonian's biggest single contract is for Land-Rover body panels. C.G. Bennett has told me that the Swallow Coachbuilding Co (1935) Ltd, is still registered by Watsonian, ready for use if a suitable product comes along . . ..

Meanwhile, back at the war, in Coventry, SS Cars had gained one of its top directors of the future. John Silver had done most of his production engineer's training with the W. & T. Avery Company at Smethwick. In the 1930s he had worked at General Motors accessory factories in Birmingham and Dunstable, Lucas of Birmingham, and BSA at Small Heath, so when he joined SS Cars in 1942 he already had a fine reputation. In the years to follow, Silver was to enhance that reputation even more. He was the company's first *real* production engineer and one of his early jobs was to get the manufacture of the main sections of Meteor III jet aircraft fuselages under way. (SS Cars took this contract from under Standard's nose. Captain, soon to be Sir John, Black—who was not only still boss at Canley, but also chairman of the 'shadow' factories scheme—was not amused.) Later, Gloster test pilot Eric Greenwood was to fly a Meteor low over Swallow Road to give SS people their first experience of jet propulsion. As the production record shows, amphibious trailers accounted for the greatest quantity of any single war-time SS product.

Another brilliant man to join SS cars as war began was engine designer Claude Baily, formerly of the Anzani and Morris factories; he was to become Bill Heynes' chief designer. The Hassan family had hardly settled into their house near Bristol when news of an exciting new War Department project brought Wally Hassan back, hot-foot, to Coventry in 1943. Baily and Hassan got down to their work with zest. What was needed was a parachutable self-propelled vehicle. That meant light weight. The first prototype had a 10.9 hp V-twin JAP engine mounted behind the driver and a distinctive nose like a Volkswagen's. It was called the 'VA'. A second prototype, the VB had a Ford 'Prefect' engine in the front. Both featured independent suspension all-round, and the latter might have been approved by the Wheeled Vehicles Experimental Establishment who bought it, after tests in Long Valley and other well known military training areas in the Aldershot area. Before either SS cross-country car had been tested in a parachute drop, the exercise was abandoned when parachute development itself took a step forward, making the 'real' Jeep safely droppable . . . but only after Hassan had watched several break their backs upon impact.

One of the problems of war was the setting of standards. The people of SS Cars were well versed in the art of creating something out of very little, and William Lyons himself went on record later as being quite frustrated by the formalities of munition work. Repair time which he felt should take (say) a month, could be extended indefinitely and sometimes it was a whole year before a particular Whitley bomber was on its way by trailer to Tachbrook aerodrome near Leamington Spa for flight testing. Many an enthusiast, seeking factory assistance with a rebuild, is perplexed by the discovery that the only real help is likely to come from the vehicle itself—or from another of the same type. The fact that nearly everything was jigged and not set-out on paper means that accurate drawings have existed only from war-time onward.

One of the first assignments for Tom Jones when he arrived at SS in 1940 was to measure up the various small parts of a sidecar body—and *then* make a technical drawing! He drew the fold-up military sidecar which SS Cars had been commissioned to build as an experiment, but which, like the VA and VB cars, was never put into production. For a while he was 'seconded' by Claude Baily to body-men Bill Thornton and Bill Robinson, to draw the structure of a future saloon that was to be the Mark Five. When Jones returned to the chassis drawing office, the body draughtsman who took over was Cyril Crouch. Today, Crouch and Jones are, respectively, Jaguar's chief body and chassis engineers. Continuity is the essence of the engineering department, and it should be added at this point that another draughtsman to join SS cars in war-time (the son of Newsome's Corporation Street garage manager) was a quiet man, who had already worked briefly at Standard, named R.J. Knight. Bob Knight was to be in charge of Jaguar

Arthur Whittaker (left) and Edward Huckvale meet one of the Whitley 'ferry' pilots at Tachbrook aerodrome, Leamington.

engineering from 1972 to 1980. Back in the 1940s, he was soon beginning to carve his special niche as one of Britain's best motor-vehicle engineers.

When the new post of company accountant was created, the irrepressible and non-conformist Fred Gardner was very suspicious. Like all good accountants Arthur Thurstans, who left Lockheed in 1943 to join SS Cars, was soon introducing organised systems into each department. He found co-operation virtually everywhere except in the sawmill, Fred Gardner's factory within the factory. Thurstans had to advise Lyons, who rang Gardner in his presence; it took Lyons several minutes of persuasion as well as an 'ear-bending' from Fred (he was one person Lyons addressed by his first name) before Gardner agreed to toe the line.

The purchase of Motor Panels Ltd, had not been a success for the company, and Lyons sold it to Rubery Owen Ltd. Autonomy on the body-making front was not to be. On the other hand, war had helped build-up the machine shop facilities and then, as peace appeared over the horizon, so did an opportunity of the type William Lyons always seemed so quick to recognise and act upon. Sir John Black told Lyons that the Standard Company would be pursuing a one-model policy—the Vanguard—after the war and he would no longer be able to supply him with power units on an exclusive basis. Lyons immediately offered to buy the machine tools for the 2.7- and 3.5-litre ohv engines. Hardly had Black time to say 'yes' when Lyons' cheque was there on his desk and the equipment on its way from Canley to Foleshill. When Black wanted to change his mind a little later, of course, Lyons was not interested. A suggestion that SS and Standard should join forces was met with a similar rebuff. If Black believed that nearly 15 years of co-operation between the two companies would soften William Lyons, he had another think coming!

Having failed to obtain a major SS shareholding in the 1930s, Black was madder now than ever, and told Lyons that Standard would be buying the car business of Triumph. Lyons had been offered it in 1939 but, unimpressed by the facilities and figures, had veered off that acquisition. Having warned Lyons he would put SS out of business, Black made his announcement that 'we are free to produce Triumph cars of character, and distinction'. On November 15 1944 *The Motor Trader* gave the following background information:

'In September 1939, Triumph was acquired from the receiver by Thos. W. Ward, the Sheffield iron and steel engineering concern with quite a few interests in the motor trade; no financial details of the acquisition were published.

'The Triumph Co. had a capital of £300,000, and the receiver appointed by the bank, had been in possession for about three months. During the war the company has been making aero engines and aircraft components.

'Gossip had it that Thos. W. Ward intended to go into the motor industry in a big way, and proximity of the SS Factory to Triumph may have had something to do with merger rumours which have turned out to be untrue.

'Before the war Triumph Dolomite range of models scored many successes in competitions, and in the "specialist" market the Dolomite had possibilities as a strong competitor of SS, Riley and M.G. The first named has always been associated to a greater or less degree with Standard, and the other two are, of course, in the Nuffield Group.

'Judging from the announcement he made about the purchase of Triumph, Sir John Black's intention is to go after this specialist market.

'I understand that there is no truth in the story that SS will enter the mass production market. The company will continue to build the same type of cars as in pre-war days.'

That last comment was one of many similar ones to be seen in the press. Some elaborated, like *The Motor World* (November 17 1944) under the heading 'No Mass Produced SS Cars':

'Rumours that SS Cars Ltd will enter the mass production market after the war are officially denied. Mr. W. Lyons, managing director of the SS company, informs us that it is true post-war plans provide for considerable expansion of their pre-war activities, but manufacture will be concentrated upon cars of even higher quality than in the past. It is also intended to take full advantage of the export markets established with considerable success before the war.

'Naturally SS Cars Ltd are anxious that the goodwill of SS owners should not be prejudiced by unfounded rumours.'

Rumours, all rumours!—but no-one suggested where they might have begun.

In February 1945, SS Cars Ltd announced that it would take the *marque* name it had been using for nearly ten years, and in March 'Jaguar Cars Ltd' was approved.

*   *   *

Over the next year, and more, Britain's businesses concentrated on salvaging what they still possessed, what they had acquired, and returning to as normal peacetime trading conditions as the many restrictions allowed. Noel Gillitt had gone to Kenya and stayed there. Alan Newsome had been his assistant from 1936. A motoring enthusiast himself, Newsome has happy memories of fast drives to the coast in one of the two special Avon drophead coupé-bodied SS Jaguar 100s commissioned in 1939 by his brother 'Sammy', the Coventry distributor. Returning from the war to his own business, Alan Newsome became Jaguar's solicitor, and eventually a board director.

A regrettable departure as war ended was that of Cyril Holland, the original Swallow 'draughtsman', and master jig and body maker. He had been invaluable on Whitley work, although frustrated by the government aircraft inspection department's plodding working pace. He had also done some mock-up car-bodies from Lyons' sketches as he had done so many times over the two previous decades; but he was a coachmaker, first and foremost, and it was his opinion that he would not be offered a senior position in peacetime, as more modern body-making techniques became necessary for Jaguar. Moreover, unlike most of his colleagues, he had first-hand experience of war; now the sight of shot-up

The 'new' factory, with the old one beyond. Swallow Road is on the right. The nearest two (of the four) blocks of the old shell-filling factory were Swallow's first Coventry foothold.

Whitley cockpits sickened him—and he was angered by the way he felt Howard Davies had been let down. He moved to the Bournemouth district, and spent a few years experimenting with new methods of soil-less fruit growing. After that he went into partnership with Arthur Whittaker of Jaguar, in a small engineering business; later still he ran his own small works. Holland's role as 'interpreter' of William Lyons' ideas was inherited in part by Fred Gardner's sawmill. The official body development shop, working closely with the Pressed Steel Company after the war, was managed by Bill Robinson. He was assisted by Harry Rogers who would look after the experimental body shop at Browns Lane later on.

Jack Beardsley and his men completed their Wigston contract work and came back to Foleshill. Some ministry equipment was adaptable, some was not. Much of his time was spent rushing round Britain's machine tool sales, sometimes with tool designer Joe Corcoran but often on his own. Lyons left Beardsley with decisions-to-purchase that involved large sums and high risk. Having made up his mind on certain courses of action, often after much deliberation, Lyons did show the ability to delegate as Jaguar grew. When it came to the biggest decisions, such as acquiring Daimler and Guy later on, or merging with the British Motor Corporation, his fellow directors were not consulted. As the majority shareholder, such decisions were his alone. One of the more unusual purchases was a pair of Pratt and Whitney borers, which Beardsley had to inspect far underground near Calne in Wiltshire, where they had been used in the manufacture of rifles. (He identified them as being just the thing to bore the holes through the twin camshafts of Jaguar's own new engine.)

In the summer of 1945, Arthur Whittaker—as director and general manager—issued the story of the company's war-time activities, and in the same week it was announced that Major E.W. Rankin, RAOC, had resumed his role as Jaguar's advertising and public relations manager. Within days, he had begun re-establishing publicity and press contact and, on September 21 1945, the first pure-Jaguar motor cars were announced. The most significant difference from their predecessors was the fact that the 'SS' hexagon had disappeared. New 'J' and 'Jaguar' symbols signified total realisation of William Lyons' dream—to become a complete and completely independent manufacturer of British luxury cars. The Jaguar successes that were still to come are now legendary.

10: Jaguar Cars Limited . . . very limited! (1945 to 1948)

Every department of the factory had been disrupted to some degree by the war. One section that had virtually disappeared was the service department. In the 1930s, Digby Paul—the ex-Standard man who came to SS to be service manager, thus relieving Arthur Whittaker of one of his many direct responsibilities—acquired an assistant. His name was D.H. ('Dan') Warren. After the war, Digby Paul became a manufacturer's agent in the field of industrial diamonds. He lived in Kenilworth and, as a Jaguar owner, returned to the works service department from time to time as a customer. Late in 1945, Colonel Warren was demobilised from Chilwell and returned to Jaguar as service manager. He was awarded the OBE in the 1946 New Year's Honours List, for technical services to the RAOC. With a year, however, he left the company once again—'with regret'—having received an invitation from the Control Commission to become assistant transport controller in Germany.

As a result of a sequence of events set in motion by his old racing chum Wally Hassan, the exceptionally tall, 35-year-old 'Lofty' England was appointed Jaguar Service Manager by William Lyons in September 1946. From 1927 to 1932, Frank Raymond Wilton England served an apprenticeship with the Daimler Company at its London depot. Then began whirlwind years, spent mostly as a racing mechanic—first with the Birkin and Couper company. 'Couper' was Mike Couper, a great competition driver, mainly with Talbots, who would become a Jaguar dealer one day. 'Birkin' was, of course, Sir Henry Birkin, the racing driver. Dorothy Paget, who had already sponsored part of Birkin's career, now owned the small company which, while England worked there, was preparing cars for racing—Bentleys, MGs, and Lord Howe's Alfa Romeo, for example. The Bentley connection meant that England used to go to Brooklands, and it was during this period that 'Lofty' and Walter Hassan first met. At Birkin and Couper's, England helped build a prototype tractor, and designed an electrically-operated motor-racing game for fairground use. The former was before its time; the latter put the company in financial trouble. When it finally 'folded', England took a job at the old Hooper works in Jubilee Place, Chelsea, where Alvis had their London service department.

While working at Birkin and Couper's, England got to know Charles Newcombe as a friend, and as 'about the best welder/fitter/machinist I've ever known . . . Charlie was a real perfectionist'. In 1934, England and Newcombe joined Whitney Straight Ltd—as did ex-Birkin men 'Jock' Finlayson and Bill Rockall—and spent the season in Italy together, preparing Maseratis with Straight's chief mechanic, Giulio Ramponi. Straight, a wealthy American Europhile, raced successfully and organised his team as a business; later he became an air transport tycoon.

England acknowledges that he learned a lot from Newcombe (who would leave Bristol and became Jaguar's chief inspector after the war). When Straight gave up racing at the end of the year, England and Newcombe joined ERA. Then, late in the summer of 1935,

New name! Jaguar employees swarm down Swallow Road and out into Holbrook Lane. Note the bricked-up doorways on either side, a relic of when no one would share the resurfacing cost with Lyons.

England returned to London and the Alvis service department, which was in the Great West Road by then. It was an even shorter stay this time. 'Lofty' England told me the story: 'At the end of the year there was the Alvis London Service Dinner, held at Hammersmith. Charles Follett, who for some years had been the London distributor, made the speech for The Guests. To our surprise it wasn't very complimentary to Alvis. (At that time we didn't know he had fallen-out with Alvis management and was either about to lose or give up the distribution of Alvis cars.) When I was walking through the car-park with my chums Harry Dashwood and Fred Scarborough—we were in "digs" together in Chelsea—we saw Follett's car and thought that, as he hadn't been nice about Alvis, he might have some trouble starting it. So one of us disconnected the ignition switch rod— the snap-on ball-joint type that was standard on cars with no ignition key. Next day I rang in from an outside job to find that much drama had ensued; so I decided it was best to get another job quickly. I rang Charlie Newcombe and arranged to go back to E.R.A.—then took full responsibility for the dastardly deed'.

In 1936, England worked for Richard Seaman. When Seaman joined the Mercedes-Benz works Grand Prix team, England took the role of mechanic in charge of three ERAs, an ex-Straight Maserati, a Delage, and a Delahaye for the Chula-'Bira' White Mouse Stable. The first sign of any settling-down occurred in 1938 when he went to Alvis again, but this time in Coventry! He began as service engineer and was soon made superintendent of the works service department. He volunteered for the RAF in 1941 and, after completing his flight training in the USA, was seconded to the USAAF as an instructor. Returning to Britain in 1943, he flew Lancaster bombers regularly on daylight bombing raids.

'Lofty' England's father—a director of a Unilever subsidiary—had encouraged his son in his enthusiasm for motoring, and while still at school in Finchley Lofty was running a 1921 Douglas motorcycle, bought for £10. As mentioned in an earlier chapter, England drove a customer's Daimler Double-Six to second place in the 1932 RAC Rally. He made time to go motorcycle racing, too, mainly at Brooklands and on the

A real machine shop of its own!—and Jaguar can make its own engines. One of the original Swallow machine men, Ted Gough (right), supervises the setting-up of three Shardlow vertical crankshaft lathes.

Isle of Man. He rode a Cotton in the 1935 Lightweight Manx Grand Prix, retiring early with a carburation failure, but when he returned in 1936 things were different—it was his best race ever! From sixth place after one lap, England and his 249 Rudge Python-engined Cotton moved up through the field to take second place just before the finish. He did his lap-scoring by keeping six pieces of chewing gum held under a rubber band, one to be eaten at the start of each lap. He was beaten only by Denis Parkinson (248 Excelsior), who was to go in for commentating later on. Another feature of that meeting was the in-spired performance of Austin Munks who—following a shooting accident—rode his 350 Velocette one-eyed. Munks, who became a Jaguar dealer in Lincolnshire, won the Junior Grand Prix by seven seconds after more than three hours of flat-out riding. In his final event on the island, the 1937 Lightweight Tourist Trophy, England was given a 'works' ride on a 248 Cotton-JAP, but could not match his own previous lap times, and retired at Crosby on Lap Five with a broken valve collar. Omobono Tenni (Guzzi) won this race from 'Ginger' Wood (Excelsior)—later a familiar figure at Jaguar as SU Carburettors' technical man.

Back at Alvis as assistant service manager, Lofty England tried car racing too, and was quickest away from the start-line in one of the first post-war races—the 1946 Brussels Grand Prix for two-litre Sports-cars. Driving Gerry Dunham's special 12/70 Alvis, which could lap Brooklands at over 110 mph in 'the old days', he settled down in third place behind St John Horsfall (Aston Martin) and Leslie Johnson (BMW). Then, towards the end of the race, a float chamber came adrift and three more BMWs relegated the old Alvis to sixth at flag-fall. It was soon after this small addition to his already vast wealth of com-petition experience and practical engineering knowledge that Lofty England came to Swallow Road to take charge of the servicing of Jaguar motor cars.

The board of Jaguar Cars Ltd now consisted of William Lyons, T. Wells Daffern, Ar-thur Whittaker and William Heynes. Heynes was appointed in May 1946. The addition of Heynes to the directorate reflected his great achievement in building up an engineering team and a high reputation for the Jaguar *marque*. It was also an indication that, soon, there would be a series of great new motor cars and power units. What the public did not know was the use to which Lyons, Heynes, Baily, and Hassan had put their weekly anti-incendiary-bomb duty 'look-out' sessions. Hassan recalls that, towards the end of the war, they would sign-on at six o'clock on a Sunday evening and spend their duty hours discussing the Jaguar cars of the future together. From William Heynes' published engineering papers, and many subsequent writings on the subject, the story of the first 'all-Jaguar' engine's birth and early life is well-known. It is worth stressing, once again, that Lyons did not want *just* high performance; as with the car itself the engine must *look* powerful too. In the end, he ignored recommendations to retain simple push-rod operation for the valves; Jaguar engines *would* have two overhead camshafts each.

With so many more employees now in so many trades, especially since the inclusion of so much sheet metalwork, trade unionism had, of course, become an integral part of the Jaguar scene. In Autumn 1946, a year after the resumption of car manufacture, a mass meeting for all employees was held in the main assembly shop, to clear the air of some discord that had resulted in differences of opinion and stoppages of work, and at the same time put across a plan to deal with all problems by constitutional procedure. The shop stewards' committee chairman Charles Gallagher, the convenor P. Bentley, and 25 shop stewards were joined by William Lyons and works manager Ted Orr. Gallagher set the meeting into lively action, and Lyons responded quickly. 'If we do not work hard now', he warned 'I feel that times are going to be very difficult'. The meeting had started at 4.30 pm, but even after the longish speeches, members of the audience (estimated to be 1,400 strong—virtually the whole workforce) were ready for a question and answer session. 'What about the forty-hour week?' shouted someone. Lyons was on his feet in a trice. 'It's something we would all like; I would like it . . . but . . . if we are to hold our own against the competition which is on the way we must get things done, and get them done *now* while the sun is shining for us . . . I am not condemning the forty-hour week, but it is no use living in a fool's paradise'.

The meeting was long, and ended on an optimistic note. The very few who had missed it could read the full report which took up five full pages of the first edition of a new magazine, *Jaguar Journal*, edited by Rankin on behalf of Lyons who had introduced it 'as a link between management and employees', as he said in the foreword. There were two more pages stressing how vital it was to produce more cars, and the other half (there were 16 pages in all) was taken up with social news—including 'This month's personality'. Appropriately Harry Teather was the subject and it was noted that, as chief storekeeper, the second-longest serving employee now had a staff of more than 50 under him. On the back page Ernest Rankin, as chairman of the formation committee, called for a meeting to elect a Jaguar Sports and Social Club general council. It was not long before Jaguar Cars had its own clubroom and a full-time social club secretary. The *Jaguar Journal* was the company's first magazine since 1935, and Rankin kept it going fairly regularly for nearly five years. As regards labour relations, that open meeting had marked the public declaration of Lyons' acceptance of the unions' role, but he never wavered from a policy of total refusal to negotiate during unconstitutional strikes. The policy worked well, except on rare occasions.

With steel and other essentials so restricted, it was very much a seller's market in the late 1940s, although Lyons regularly warned his workforce that the situation could not prevail for long. It was certainly no time for the firm to be spending money on motoring competitions, however, and in any case the sport would take some time to re-establish itself after a six-year absence—with compensation only in the wide selection of hastily-built airfield runways and perimeter tracks now gathering weeds all over Britain. Indeed the war changed the face of motor racing, not only because of the sudden transfer from German to Italian Grand Prix car dominance, but also as a result of the budding drivers whose careers might have blossomed. Surely the greatest driver never to realise his full potential because of the lack of worthwhile events in his day, was Jean-Pierre Wimille?

Unlike many of the other great names, he never had any connection of any kind with Jaguar. Later, the first three 'official' world champions—Giuseppe Farina, Juan Manuel Fangio, and Alberto Ascari—would all become Jaguar owners, although they never raced them personally. Meantime however, several well-known drivers acquired the old SS Jaguar 100 model.

In North America 'Johnny' Von Neumann bought a 3½-litre car that had found its way to Canada, and he told *Road and Track* that it had been fitted with a Winfield cam and high-compression head which improved the already brilliant performance of the '100', producing 109 mph and 0 to 50 mph within seven seconds. He was pleased with a standing-start quarter-mile time of 17 seconds and with the car's reliability. When John Cobb was at Bonneville salt flats in 1947 (to become the world's first 400 mph land-traveller) Von Neumann drove from Los Angeles to Salt Lake City to see the action; then he returned to take part in the Palos Verdes road trials and won, without re-tuning the car. 'In the suspension', he said 'the makers were able to combine a racing car's stability with a reasonable degree of softness. It rode and handled as a 100 mph car should.' That might have seemed somewhat fulsome praise in the ordinary way, but Von Neumann was a fine driver in his own right and among the cars he was to handle soon afterwards was the modified Porsche of Max Hoffman who considered him worth flying from California to New York to race it.

In Australia, Keith Thallon of Brisbane recorded a 17.3-second 'standing quarter' in 1948 with his '100'. He was also reported as achieving 'the second highest speed recorded by a motorist in Queensland' (according to the *Brisbane Telegraph*) when he covered a 'flying' quarter-mile at 103.45 mph on 'a special course' with the car in standard trim, complete with guards and lamps, but with windscreen and hood down. Earlier in the year Thallon's '100' and Walter Mathison's smaller-engined model had performed well in Queensland's Strathpine airstrip races. Thallon had also broken the sports car record for the Queensland hill-climb course. The SS Jaguar 100 was still competitive!

Among Britain's best known post-war exponents of the '100' were Tom Cole, 'Curly' Dryden, Les Leston, and 'Spike' Rhiando, all of whom became better-known as racing-drivers in other types of car. Cole sprinted and raced his '100' to such good effect that Lofty England lent him a works 3½-litre engine; like Marx before him, Cole took his car

Far left *Economy drive: Bill Rankin shows off the post-war Jaguar catalogue—the same information but one-tenth as much paper.*

Left *Lofty England, newly-appointed as service manager* (Ron Easton, The Autocar).

Right *Now a Jaguar director, Bill Heynes, with his chief designer, Claude Baily* (Ron Easton, The Autocar).

to America where he spent a large proportion of his time. Dryden was a ex-RAF man who kept a pub; as with Rhiando, he was a ground-floor member of the 500 cc racing movement. 'Spike' (real name Alvin) Rhiando was a Canadian who spent a lot of time in Britain, and actually won the first big 500 cc race at Silverstone in 1948—after Stirling Moss had trouble, it should be added. Rhiando *may* have raced his '100' on the public road only! Towards the end of the war he won an unofficial sprint. His opponent was a friend riding a Triumph Tiger 100 motorcycle on a dual carriageway near Ipswich. One reason for Rhiando's easy 'victory' on that occasion was the fact that his car—which he had bought 'blind' when away from England in 1942—happened to be the ex-Truett machine. In a letter to *The Autocar* he referred to the special crankshaft, connecting rods, and pistons, Scintilla magneto, 'bronzed' head, and large-bore SU carburettors and asked for readers' opinions as to its chances in post-war racing. These modifications had been done at the works, and this car was probably the fastest 2½-litre SS Jaguar 100 of all. 'I could do a lot to the frame, weight-cutting', suggested Rhiando—already the owner/racer of several midget speedway cars and motorcycles, besides having an SS1, an SS2 and an SS Jaguar saloon—and, judging by the many chassis drillings visible under the car's well-restored body today, Rhiando followed-up the idea!

Les Leston used his '100' in sprints and trials, and afterwards had it fitted with a frantic all-enveloping aluminium body with curved perspex from a light aeroplane around the cockpit. Almost as strange was Paul Pycroft's conversion of another '100', winner of the first-ever car race at Goodwood. Although an SS Jaguar 100 had been 'placed' in the very first post-war speed event—a sprint up the drive of Naish House near Bristol in 1945— it was not until the following year that the *marque* was to enjoy its first straight victory of the 1940s when Scotsman Noel Bean made best time of the day up the interesting half-mile hill-climb at Bo'ness near Linlithgow—a location now part-buried under a housing estate. Today, an authentic '100' is a car to be treasured, yet coachbuilders in several countries—notably Belgium, Czechoslovakia, and Switzerland—gave the model their own strange and exotic interpretations of what the sports-car of the future would look like.

With the government's steel allocation dependent solely upon export performance, Lyons put all his energy into overseas markets, and among the first to show were the Low Countries. Five ambassadors to Belgium ordered 3½-litre Jaguar saloons in the spring of

1946 and soon afterwards three Jaguars won their respective classes in the *concours d'elegance* organised by the city of Brussels in conjunction with the Belgian RAC. One of those winners was a young woman of imposing countenance and unavoidable presence; her name was Joska Bourgeois, and she was the new importer of Jaguars. Soon her excellent sales rate took a blow, however, when her government slapped a top limit on the value of imported cars. Joska Bougeois and William Lyons responded by arranging with Van den Plas—coachbuilders who tried-out one or two of their own designs on Jaguar chassis, but were no longer connected with the London Vanden Plas company—to assemble Jaguars in Brussels. Ted Orr sent Bernard Hartshorn and a team of about a dozen men from the works to Belgium and early in 1948 Lyons himself inspected, tested, and approved the first 'foreign' Jaguar. The restriction was lifted within two years, and only for a brief period—at Mechelen, under British Leyland rule in the 1970s—would Jaguars ever again be assembled in Belgium. In between, they would be assembled in other countries including New Zealand, Mexico, Ireland, and (on the biggest scale of all) South Africa.

In Switzerland Emil Frey and Marcel Fleury continued to service the German and French speaking areas respectively. Other European distributors to continue 'where they had left off' when the war ended were Georg Hans Koch—whose wife would continue to run Jaguar's Austrian business after his death—J.W. Lagerwij of The Hague (whose business was assisted by arranging local Pennock coachwork to be fitted to Delahaye chassis), and Charles Delecroix for Paris. Among the newcomers to the Jaguar selling fold was Erik Sommer; his son, Ole, took over the Jaguar business for Denmark after Erik had been killed during some cross-country truck trials in Germany. The Sommers built several cars bearing their own name, the first being fitted with a two-cylinder Jowett engine. This highly-organised firm is now the biggest Volvo agency in Denmark, and one of many respected businesses lost to Jaguar after the formation of national sales companies by British Leyland; yet Ole Sommer remains an avid enthusiast with a fine personal collection of historic Jaguars. As an engineering consultant, he even designed an aerodrome crash-tender for high-speed cross-country use—powered by the V12 Jaguar engine! German and Italian representation for Jaguar did not settle down so quickly, although eventually the right kind of specialists were selected.

During the very hard winter, early in 1947, 8,000 square feet of the 'new' factory were destroyed by fire, but interruption to the export drive was minimal. At the same time, the first regular exports of Jaguars to the USA were beginning. Pre-war, exports had been few; in the company's youth there had been no provision for left-hand steering, required in most countries, the production would not have met demand. Now conditions for making one's name overseas were ideal, and William Lyons—fighting successfully to win the best possible steel allocation—took the advice of Bertie Henly. Upon his return from South Bend, Indiana, where he had been to see his Studebaker colleagues, Henly told Lyons about an emigrant Austrian opportunist, Max Hoffman, who was already opening up the Volkswagen market in America and had good premises on Manhattan's Park Avenue. Lyons decided to let Hoffman handle Jaguar's business. A chance meeting with a Californian visitor to Britain, who had diverted to the Jaguar works while on a tour to Warwick Castle, was to lead to a second major appointment.

Another big market to open up rapidly, thanks to a change of importer, was Australia. Jack Bryson had a fairly small agency for Morgans and motorcycles when he cabled Jaguar offering to take 2,000 cars in the first year; he was given the franchise, and from then on it was often Jaguar's inability to supply that kept him from achieving his target sales. Bryson built up his business in Melbourne and Sydney, while three other distributors were appointed—Anderson's in Brisbane, Brooking's in Perth, and Dominion Motors in Adelaide.

People did things with cars in the 1940s they would not dream of doing now. First Les Leston (seen in the Harrow Car Club Moss Trophy Trial) put cycle-type wings on his SS Jaguar 100; then he decided to give the car a completely new streamlined body! (The Motor and Thoroughbred & Classic Cars respectively).

Around the world the names 'Jaguar' and 'MG' were becoming associated more and more with British export enterprise. At about this time Percy Shortley, who had come to Swallow in the early 1930s to assist Ted Huckvale, was sent with his costs specialist John Witherall to meet W.O. Bentley and Alan Good at Lagonda's works. They had a nice lunch, and Witherall certainly felt he was in exalted company; but the news they brought back decided Lyons not to buy Lagonda, leaving that to David Brown and Aston Martin.

At home business *was* developing, however, although there were still precious few cars for the hungry public. The importance of a personal service for customers was recognised as an essential asset. Pre-war, Henly's premises at Hawley Crescent in Camden Town had been recognised as the SS service centre for London. In 1947, at Wally Hassan's recommendation, Lofty England appointed Philip Weaver as London service representative. Weaver had stayed on at Bristol when Hassan moved back to Coventry in

Left and right *The hunting of the Snark? No matter what hideousness has been seen* en route, *few Jaguars ever reached the production stage without being totally satisfying to the eye. These two beasts were early efforts in the immediate post-war search for a big Jaguar saloon shape.*

Below right *Lucien Bianchi's father-in-law, Jacques Herzet, had this done to his SS Jaguar 100 post-war.*

1943. After a short period of 'familiarisation' at Swallow Road, Phil Weaver went to London, and he and his family lived in a caravan beside Henly's garage near Heathrow. Jaguar's London service headquarters from then on were at another Henly location, in nearby Brentford. Weaver was based there for several years, looking after Jaguar customers—among them Les Leston, who took his SS Jaguar 100 there regularly before he had it re-bodied. Another competition model which Weaver came to know well was BWK 77, the works '100' run by Newsome and Wisdom. One of its last 'official' appearances was at Bouley Bay in 1947, where Elsie (better known as 'Bill') Wisdom won the ladies prize. Harry Hawkins of the experimental department took the car to Jersey for her from Baginton (Coventry) airport in Universal Flying Services 'Aerovan'. Soon afterwards this car, the fastest of all pre-war Jaguars, was sold to George Matthews who had been rallying and racing SSs quite successfully since 1936. As a weekend hobby Phil Weaver maintained the car for Matthews and attended sprint and race meetings with it. In the 1970s BWK 77 was restored in its 'open-wheeled' state, complete with high-compression engine, and has proved itself capable of dealing with ERAs—reliability permitting.

As well as serving home market customers, Phil Weaver went to Europe from time to time to develop the facilities. Sometimes he was accompanied by the factory spares manager, Arthur Hignett. The service department was expanding and Lofty England badly needed the right man to look after the workshop. When England had first been with Alvis, the chargehand for whom he had worked on the engine section in their London workshop was Bill Norbury; Norbury had served that company in Coventry and London for many years when, in 1947, the Jaguar post became available. Reticent at first, Norbury was soon persuaded not to let anyone else beat him to it! England's faith in the new man was fully justified. As superintendent and later manager of Jaguar's service repair shops, Bill Norbury was to spend more than 25 years with the company, always winning respect for his handling of one of the trickier Jaguar 'front-line' jobs. 'After Bill arrived', said England recently, 'Jaguar service never looked back'. Norbury was respected in the workshop, too. 'The reconditioning shop took a long time to do a set of thick-wall bearings, and even then the oil-pressure was never much good. One day I got Bill to scrape a set of 1937 "2½" bearings; he did the job in his usual quiet way, and very quickly produced oil pressure never seen before'. Those are the words of Lofty England.

Since the earliest home distributor appointments, several changes had taken place. One

of the most significant, back in 1935, had been when John Ernest Appleyard took on the SS agency for Leeds. His two sons were great sportsmen. The elder, Geoffrey, was killed in the war. When 'number two son', Ian, left the forces, he decided to take up motor-rallying. After an impressive drive in the 1947 Alpine Trial—in which he would have finished much better than eighth (third in class) if he had not run out of tyres and, on one occasion, road!—Ian Appleyard managed to replace his '100' (EXT 207) with another car of the same type from the Jaguar works. One car had been stored in the large stables at Wappenbury Hall near Princethorpe—the Lyons family home—throughout the war. Now it was prepared and sold to Appleyard, who took the Jaguar *marque* name to the forefront of international rallying by winning the 1948 Alpine Trial and coming second in the following year's Dutch Tulip Rally. (This famous car, LNW 100, has since been burned-out and restored; it is now owned by Henlys.) That Tulip Rally performance marked the end of the 100's competitive life. At first it had been considered sporting in looks only. Now it had beaten BMWs and Allards often enough to prove itself a genuine, worthy sports car—especially with an expert at the helm.

Towards the end of 1947, recovery from the war was sufficient for Jaguar to re-introduce

the two-door drophead coupé on the six cylinder chassis. Every corner of the experimental and development shops was devoted to exciting new projects, and by 1948 the most important ones were nearing fulfilment. London's first motor-show for ten years was to be held in the autumn, and Lyons had promised the government and himself that Jaguar would do great things for Britain as the country began to rise above the austerity that had been forced upon it for so long.

In February 1948, Lyons got Rankin to tick-off the press for suggesting that Jaguar had been 'earmarked for extinction and would not be allocated steel'. In March, the revived 'export' drophead coupé made its début alongside the Jaguar saloons at the Geneva show. Emil Frey had already anticipated the demand for cabriolets in Switzerland—as he had done in the 1930s—and commissioned two local coachbuilders to make them. These were built on 3½-litre chassis, by Ramseyer of Worblaufen (near Bern) and by Reinboldt and Christé of Basle, and duly appeared at Geneva, too.

The same month saw William Lyons stepping briskly up the gangway of the Queen Elizabeth at the start of a five-week tour to set up his North American sales and service network. For the time being, he left the Eastern United States to Max Hoffman, but he made several appointments in the west. There were S.H. Lynch in Dallas, James Baird in Seattle, and no fewer than three distributors in California. Foreign Motors of Santa Barbara, International Motors of Los Angeles, and the well-known Norwegian, Kjell Qvale of Burlinghame. Not yet listed but soon to rule Jaguar's western activities was Charles H. Hornburg Junior, the friend of the Earl of Warwick who had shown an interest in selling motor cars when Lyons had met him in England. The Jaguar chief recognised Hornburg's flair for selling—as he had Bertie Henly's 20 years before—and, on the basis of that assessment alone, Lyons came to an agreement with the enterprising man who would soon have his own showroom on Sunset Boulevard. During that visit Lyons and Hornburg held a reception and display of Jaguars in Hollywood, and Clarke Gable booked the first order—for a new drophead coupé—on the opening day. Lyons enjoyed visiting the studio where Gable was working, but 'the tea was terrible'.

When the first editions of John Bond's new *Road and Track* magazine heralded the new era of sports cars in America soon afterwards, Louis van Dyke of International Motors was in there quickly with the first of a series of whole back-cover advertisements for Healey, Jaguar, and MG cars. Lyons' expedition included a tour of Chrysler and Studebaker factories and a trip to Canada where he found taxation causing imported car prices to be one third up on the USA. There was much still to be done to establish as big a market as Lyons was banking-on in North America, and he was not happy with Hoffman's ill-concealed attempt to obtain a monopoly. For the moment, however, Lyons was able to take a little relaxation on board the *Queen Mary* before getting into the real stride of being a captain of industry. A Vice-Presidency of the Society of Motor Manufacturers and Traders awaited his arrival back in Britain—and so did the launching of the two new cars that would take Jaguar to the top of Britain's export league!

11: Export or else! (1948 to 1950)

Anyone lurking in the vicinity of the experimental department at the back of the old Swallow Road works in 1948—or even earlier—could have seen the evidence of much trial and error in the body-styling line, but little to suggest that Jaguar was about to introduce some of the most beautiful cars the world had ever seen. He or she might also have heard some interesting new engine noises emanating from the engine test-beds!

The Jaguar twin overhead camshaft XK engine story forms a large proportion of the *whole* Jaguar success story. It may not seem a particularly modern design now—even with its electronic fuel injection, or when installed in military vehicles of today, and it was certainly never revolutionary—but, had it not been for this combined Baily-Hassan-Heynes-Oats-Weslake effort, the Jaguar motor car would have been too tame an animal to win the races and rallies, the sales and prestige, on a world scale. So, despite all that has been written before, no Jaguar history can ever be complete without paying the highest possible tribute to the men who created the Jaguar XK engine.

The public first heard of it in September 1948, when a two-litre four-cylinder version pushed Lieutenant Colonel 'Goldie' Gardner's steamlined special along the *autoroute* at Jabbeke, near Ghent in Belgium, at over 176 mph. For Jaguar this exercise was overseen

A really smooth prototype, getting very near to the ultimate 'XK' shape.

Phew! Wally Hassan mops his brow during preparations to the twin-cam four-cylinder Jaguar engine, fitted to the Gardner special to take records on the Belgian motorway at nearly 180 mph in 1948 (The Motor).

by Wally Hassan, and the engine was a race-tuned unit developing 146 bhp at 6,000 rpm—with a safe maximum of 6,500 rpm. This was a clear indication that development at Jaguar was well ahead of production—so far ahead that many four-cylinder engine sets were manufactured before the decision was taken not to produce it commercially. An interesting note in Bill Heynes' famous Institution of Mechanical Engineers paper, *The Jaguar Engine*, says (of an engine described as the 'XK Four-cylinder'): 'This has been slightly re-designed in its latest form but, at the present, full details cannot be given as the engine has not yet been released to the market'. That was in 1953 so, even five years on, the idea was still alive! Heynes also refers, even then, to V8, V12, and other engine configurations that had been mulled-over in the old Foleshill firewatchers' 'think tank', when BMW practice had been one of the big influences.

It was *not* the new engine in *any* of its guises that was the subject of Jaguar's new-model announcement of October 1 1948. The car of *that* day was designated the 'Mark Five'—I am aware of no *good* reason why—and an attractive, well-made interim model it was too, concentrating upon all the best features of the existing models. Its main improvements were mechanical; the new chassis was more rigid than any previous Foleshill product, and featured a full hydraulic braking system and independent front suspension for the first time. Bill Heynes had been a Citroën disciple ever since the *Traction* had appeared—well ahead of its time—shortly before he joined the company. Soon afterwards he had designed a short-wishbone torsion bar front suspension which Hassan made and fitted to a 3½-litre saloon. This car was destroyed in the blitz by a direct hit; post-war photographs showing its registration number (DKV 120) depict another car.

The Mark Five Jaguar was in many ways a great car, but its successor was well on the way to production even when the Mark Five was announced. Hardly a competition car, the Mark Five nevertheless performed with distinction in the Monte Carlo Rally several times, Cecil Vard of Ireland proving the greatest master of its safe but slightly unusual handling on more than one occasion. The Mark Five came as a saloon or drophead coupé in 2.7 and 3.5-litre forms. There was no 1.8-litre model, although it might have been considered had Sir John Black not needed to keep the tooling on Standard territory, to provide a power unit for his new Triumph roadster and razor-edged 'Renown' saloon.

The last batch of small '1½-litre' Jaguar saloons was made in 1949 and went to members of the company. Perhaps someone suggested that future Jaguars would be too exotic for 'executive' use? When supply of that engine ended, so did the last business link between Black and Lyons. In 1953 Sir John Black had a rather bad motor accident (as passenger in one of the new 'rival' Doretti cars) *and* took a bad decision—to fire his boardroom colleague and technical chief, Ted Grinham, for no apparent reason. Black was still convalescing when, in January, 1954, the Standard-Triumph board visited him and 'asked' him to resign as chairman and managing director following 'consultation' with his doctor. His former personal assistant, 37-year-old Alick Dick—they had first met through Dick's uncle, who was married to another Hillman sister—became managing director in his place. It was a sad but, perhaps, inevitable day for the man who had contributed so much to the forming of Jaguar, and wanted so much to have a part of it. Sir William Lyons has paid tribute to Black's 'energy and success' on more than one occasion.

*   *   *

As the 1948 Earls Court motor show approached, Ernest Rankin was busier than ever. He had organised the Mark Five's trade introduction with a big convention at the works on September 30 that showed all the ingenuity of a man brought up on Swallow company practice. William Pethers and his Hippodrome Orchestra (by courtesy of Sammy Newsome, who doubled as Coventry's impresario!) had played *Lovely to Look At* from a disguised social club boxing ring as the curtains had parted to reveal the new cars. What the guests did not see was the spares department timber that would be made into crates and packing cases, the yards of calico that would turn into Mark Five seat spring-case coverings and the red moquette that would form part of the interior trim! People often used to ask: How do Jaguar do it for the price? One of the answers lay in the golden rule; 'Don't spend money if you can improvise instead'. Rankin often proved himself capable of working wonders with little or no budget.

What occupied Rankin next was a new Jaguar Super Sports car (to give it its initial designation), and at a preview in Grosvenor House on the Friday before the show opened, members of the press were given their first sight of one of the most beautiful sports cars the world has ever seen; and if there *was* a hint of 1940 Mille Miglia BMW in the car—how much more precisely-sculptured were its lines, and how many had ever seen that particular BMW anyway? The XK 120 had arrived—and so, it seemed, had the XK 100; that was due to be powered by the four-cylinder engine which was always a little rough and, as mentioned earlier in this chapter, was never put on sale.

Not only did the new Jaguars make news; they virtually stole the show from everyone else. Company secretary Ted Huckvale was using the escalator between Earls Court tube station and the exhibition hall, where Nelson advertising had obtained a complete monopoly of poster frames, when he overhead someone remark: 'Looks as if Jaguar has the only ruddy car in the show!'

No wonder the works Christmas functions were happy ones. At the 27th annual staff dinner—prepared, of course, by Mrs Thompson and the canteen staff—John Silver was master of ceremonies and, after short speeches from Harry Teather and William Lyons, the revelry began. Among the many winners that evening was Alice Fenton who took the mysterious 'Musical Knees' novelty prize. John Silver always promoted the social side of factory life, and he acted as master-of-ceremonies again for the second annual works Christmas party at Coventry's Rialto Casino. It went well, too—until 1 am, when the bus for Bedworth and Nuneaton failed to turn up because the bus company proprietor had booked the wrong night.

Late 1948 saw more Transatlantic activity than ever, with Bruce Smith from the Service Department joining Hoffman to look after the Jaguar service operation in New York. A small export administration section had already been set up in Coventry; Sam Hird, with experience of working in the USA, was superintendent and he was assisted by Eric Barnes. In the new year, an Export Sales Manager was appointed—Ben Mason who had been at Singer for five years after leaving the Standard Motor Company, where he had been export manager throughout the growth of SS Cars Ltd, and had been of great help to William Lyons when the company was taking its first exploratory steps abroad. Born in Walsall in 1889, Ben Mason had left school at the age of 12 to become a carpenter; he began clerical work when he was 20 and, seeing a great future in overseas trade, acquired a vast knowledge of many foreign languages. This remarkable and humane man had many interests outside the company, from music to community work, from the theatre to golf. This did not seem an anachronism even in the dedicated world of Jaguar, however, for he was respected by all who knew him. He was to lead the Jaguar export drive until his retirement at the age of 74.

Early in 1949, Jaguar was represented at the New York show by Lofty England and Ernest Rankin, where Hoffman was introducing the new cars. Jaguar's new XK 120 was a sensation wherever it was seen, but how well did it perform? The XK engine, though refined in its behaviour, had not been intended for racing; but its performance and its further 'tunability' were beyond question. Nevertheless, that spring Ron ('Soapy') Sutton and fitter Jack Lea slipped quietly across the Channel to Belgium with one of the new cars. A former racing driver and tester, Sutton had been around the motor industry, with spells at Rolls-Royce, Lea-Francis, Morris, and Daimler. He had joined the Jaguar experimental department early in 1948. Jack Lea had been Ron Sutton's riding mechanic in the 1930 Ards Tourist Trophy race.

Leaving Hassan at home with 'flu', Sutton and Lea made for the Belgian motorway and quickly established that the XK 120 could easily exceed the maximum speed its name implied. Rankin chartered a Douglas DC3 in which Lyons and Heynes brought 20-odd members of the press to Belgium in late May. Joska Bourgeois, the Brussels distributor, arranged road closure and Belgian press coverage. Even though Hassan was now fit, he insisted that Sutton should still make the public demonstration. In several runs, speeds of over 130 mph were reached and, although the XK 120 was not yet in regular production, the publicity for Jaguar was enormous. Ian Appleyard could not get an entry for the new car in the Alpine Rally but, while everyone else flew home Wally Hassan took Tommy 'Whizzbang' (as Hassan refers to Wisdom) for a reconnaissance of Alpine Rally territory. After the white car (HKV 500) came home it was converted from left to right hand drive and prepared for the XK 120's first race.

When the *Daily Express* announced that there would be a one-hour race at the big

Silverstone Meeting in August, it was as if the idea had been tailor-made to persuade Jaguar to take an interest in motor-racing. A test session with England and Hassan at Silverstone—only an hour or so's drive from the works—convinced Lyons that his new cars could hardly fail to win such a race. Lofty England was given the job of choosing the drivers for the three cars entered. His experience with the Royal Thai racing team made Prince Birabongse his first choice as 'B. Bira', as he was known, was still a superb driver of Grand Prix cars. He would drive the production prototype XK 120, painted blue and registered HKV 455. The other two drivers selected were Peter Walker and Leslie Johnson. Walker, whose driving England had admired for a long time, was to drive the unregistered red car whilst the white car (HKV 500) was for Johnson. Heynes and England both knew Leslie Johnson well, as a BMW driver. Indeed, he had loaned Heynes his 328 cylinder head for examination during the war. (The company had acquired a four-door BMW, too, and even installed an experimental Jaguar engine in it.) England, in particular, recalled racing against Johnson at Brussels only three years earlier, and so that choice was not difficult either.

As the first post-war production-car race got under way, Len Potter's Allard led from a 'Le Mans' start but 'Bira' moved ahead almost at once followed by Johnson and Walker. From then on, the Jaguars had it all their own way, apart from Walker being harried at first by Norman Culpan's very fast Frazer Nash. 'Bira' spun out of the lead at Woodcote corner at two-thirds distance and Rankin's report blamed it on a rear tyre bursting rather than driver error—*not* vice-versa as is sometimes suggested. The rear wing was bent by a straw bale, but although the car was otherwise undamaged it was forced to retire when Bira's wheelchanging attempt came to nought because the jack dug-in to the grass. After a

Mark Fives and XK 120s on the line, in the 'Manchester' factory, Coventry.

front-wing altercation while lapping Tommy Wise's Jowett Javelin, Johnson took the 'Jabbeke' car to victory, ahead of Walker who had moved well clear of the embarassingly-fast Culpan. The two Jaguars and the Frazer Nash had lapped every other competing car at least once.

Employees who had travelled in three coaches and paid 16 shillings per head (including admission) went home delighted. Besides the great 1-2 victory for Jaguar, older hands had been impressed by the way Cyril Mann's aged SS Jaguar 100 had managed to take 15th place out of 26 finishers—in spite of a pit-stop. The great era of racing Jaguars had begun.

Earls Court that year was again a hive of industry. By that winter, however, XK 120 deliveries had still only just begun, and it was soon clear that something must be done to boost production. The original decision to make only a limited quantity of sports cars was causing headaches, and a prime source of dollar-earning looked as if it might evaporate. Aluminium panels from Cooke's of Nottingham—suppliers of the lovely old '100' wings, too—were being mounted over wooden framework fabricated at Swallow Road. Lyons did the quickest mind-change he could, but it was well into 1950 before steel body panels began to flow in from the Pressed Steel works at Oxford. Before that, 240 'handbuilt' cars were made. The ultimate XK 120 production figure would exceed 12,000 in three different body styles!

To keep American appetites whetted, Leslie Johnson went to the USA in January 1950 to take part in what was to be the XK 120's first-ever race abroad. The Sports Car Club of America (SCCA) in effect replaced the Automobile Racing Club of America (ARCA). Founded in 1944, the SCCA had been intended as an historic vehicle preservation group. However, the ARCA was not re-formed, and the SCCA started making its own plans for road racing. This began at Watkins Glen in October 1948 when Frank Griswold (Alfa Romeo)—winner of the last ARCA race in 1940—was victorious again. There were more SCCA races in 1949, but it was not until the 'round the houses' road race at Palm Beach Shores, Florida on January 3 1950 that the XK 120 appeared; in fact, three took part and another was used as pace car.

Fiercest car in a strong field was the Duesenberg-Ford of George Huntoon who had competed in ARCA events with an MG Magnette, and had driven an Alfa Romeo to victory in the first SCCA Bridgehampton 100-mile race on Long Island, in 1949. Basically this machine was the Duesenberg-Hartz with which Fred Frame had taken second place in the 1931 Indianapolis 500-mile. 'Frame had won 'Indy' a year later in a Hartz-assisted Miller.) The car was now owned by I.J. Brundage of Miami and had a much modified Ford-Mercury V8 engine with Winfield camshaft. The 1950 Palm Beach race started in dry weather and, after the usual early *melée*, Leslie Johnson moved his Jaguar up into second place behind the flying Huntoon. Then came the rain and the high winds, and Johnson made his pit-stop—it had been decreed everybody should make one—which dropped him to an eventual fourth place.

The final order reads rather like a small 'Who's Who' of American Sports car racing. Huntoon covered the 50 laps in rather less than two hours. He was followed by Briggs Cunningham (Healey), George Rand (Ferrari), Leslie Johnson (Jaguar), Phil Walters (Healey), Miles Collier (Riley-Ford V8) and Tom Cole (Allard-Cadillac). The former SS100 driver Cole was awarded the booby prize (according to *Palm Beach Post-Times* associate editor, Tom Penick) 'for pulling the best boner for telling how a spectator helped him out of the sand, which was against the rules'. Sam Collier—who was killed at that year's Watkins Glen race in a Ferrari—finished 8th in one Jaguar XK 120 while Bill Spear ran out of brakes with the other.

Brundage said afterwards that his special could have gone a little faster, and Huntoon kept a steady 40-second lead. Leslie Johnson drove 'a nice race', but told Brundage that the Jaguar's brakes needed 'improving'. In the years prior to Jaguar fitting disc brakes, many a driver would make that comment—usually more strongly-worded! Cunningham having had a Cadillac engine shoehorned into his Healey—a pre-Le Mans experiment that did not please General Motors—meant that Johnson's Jaguar won the Healey Trophy (best production car) and the Hoffman Trophy (best British car). Although not an outright win, it was a good début for the new Jaguar with the 'boulevard ride' and the quiet exhaust note. Full advantage was taken by Max Hoffman to publicise the Jaguar's dual character at the New York show that spring.

Sports car racing was coming to life in the western United States, too, and the first recorded XK 120 result occurred in the California Sports Car Club's Sandberg Ranch speed hill-climb on April 2 1950, when J. Robbins (Jaguar) took second place in 44.8 seconds. The winner was G.T. Darwin's Mercury V8 special in 43.4 seconds. Circuit racing came to California a fortnight later at Palm Springs, where the main event was really a contest between Tom Frisby (Allard), Sterling Edwards (Edwards), Roger Barlow (Jaguar), and Bill Pollack (MG). Frisby led initially, but soon retired in the searing heat. Edwards's original V8 sports car then battled for the lead with Jaguar-dealer Barlow's XK 120; but the Jaguar retired among the sagebrush with a severe case of brake fade and a jammed throttle—caused, perhaps, by sand? The Edwards thus became the only car to cover all 40 laps. In the same month Clemente Biondetti briefly led Sicily's Targa Florio in a works XK 120 which Jack Lea had brought to Italy from Coventry, but such a tough event could only serve to highlight the very special character of car needed to withstand harsh, if expert, driving on badly-made roads. The Jaguar did not finish.

As a result of the 1949 Silverstone success, in 1950 Jaguar had actually prepared five cars, for the use of Biondetti, Johnson, Walker, Wisdom and motor trader, Nick Haines. All but Walker took part in the 1950 Mille Miglia. Johnson's XK 120 reached the finish in a well-earned fifth place. This kind of racing was never to be Jaguar's *forte* but, to quote Lofty England, these early attempts to come to grips with all kinds of racing conditions 'proved of considerable value to us, both for future competition successes and for our production cars, quickly showing up faults that might never occur at all in normal use'. A good example of this was Biondetti's Targa Florio retirement, caused when a connecting rod broke; from then on, every rod was crack-tested. His main Mille Miglia problem was rear-spring breakage—the combined result of heavy fuel loads and hump-backed bridges—but the Italian drove like a demon to salvage eighth place.

The honour of being the first person to win an overseas race in an XK 120 must go to Alfonso Gomez Mena. He acquired his car from Jaguar's new Havana agent, Frank Seiglie, just in time to compete in the unlimited production car race run by the national club of Cuba on February 24 1950. As may be imagined, though, the opposition was not very strong!

Early 1950 saw the departure from Swallow Road of Chief Development Engineer Walter Hassan—for the second time! His predecessor Laurie Hathaway, who had recently left Coventry Climax to become a freelance consultant (for Jaguar Cars, among others), told him that Coventry Climax boss, Leonard Lee, was looking for a chief engineer. Fork lift trucks and fire pump engines inspired Hassan less than the actual position he was being offered. He was soon to discover that he would become involved with motor racing once again—and, one day, with Jaguar, too!

As Hassan's 'opposite number' on engines, Claude Baily part-filled the gap along with tuning expert Jack Emerson, who had been a great motorcyclist in his day, occasionally using Swallow sidecars. Now Emerson was responsible for the performance and the reliability of Jaguar engines in long-distance events. His record speaks for itself. An

Stirling Moss and William Lyons meet in the pits at Dundrod in 1950, prior to Moss' first great TT victory with the XK 120. That is his father on the right.

experimental workshop superintendent was now urgently needed, too, and Phil Weaver left the service department and moved from London to Coventry to do the job. The London service manager's job went to a quiet and highly thought-of Scott called Lindsay Kay, who was to spend many years smoothing the path between Jaguar Cars, Henlys, and the customer.

More lessons were learned when three of the works-loaned XK 120s were taken to Le Mans—this time the lesson was: here was a race uniquely suited to the calculated kind of victory any financially-minded manufacturer would prefer. Two cars finished in mid-field, just behind Briggs Cunningham's amazing Cadillacs. With Bert Hadley as co-driver, however, Leslie Johnson drove another fast and canny race, reaching second position shortly after half distance. Preserving the brakes—which were as troublesome as ever on all three cars—by use of the gearbox was to prove too great a strain, and in the 22nd hour the clutch centre pulled out. Le Mans lesson: remove standard Borgalite driven plate, and use solid clutch plate henceforth. Jaguars were never to become in-famous for clutch failure again. Heynes and England were already working on plans for the *next* Le Mans while they were still in France.

Shortly afterwards, in another part of France Ian Appleyard, navigated by the former Patricia Lyons whom he had married in the spring, took his new XK 120 to victory in the Alpine Trial. It was works-prepared, but even with new sales department assistant, Donald Alan Currie, in the vicinity of the rally on Jaguar's behalf, they both came to feel that rallying was being regarded very much as the 'poor relation' of motor racing. One anxious moment occurred when Appleyard's sister, Margot, who was staying on the Continent at the time, waved cheerily from a mountain side into which the Jaguar ran while its driver was recovering from surprise and waving back. It was a rare mistake in a rally career with more results to show for it than most.

The factory decision to go motor racing was made absolute by the famous victory of young Stirling Moss in the Tourist Trophy in September. Driving the Tommy Wisdom XK 120 (JWK 988), he beat all-comers in pouring rain on the fast, tricky and narrow Dundrod circuit in the hills between Belfast and Lough Neagh. Soon afterwards, Moss drove with Leslie Johnson for 24 hours round the banked Montlhéry circuit near Paris in the latter's regular car (JWK 651). In the USA the first full competition season for Jaguar was rounded-off nicely when a young man from International Motors, the Jaguar people in Hollywood, returned from a spell of training at Jaguar works and started winning in his own XK 120. 'I prepared it with the help of Richie Ginther. It was bored out to 3.8 litres in 1950. We lightened the car considerably, too, but it ended up front-heavy.' That did not stop a future world champion named Phil Hill from becoming the first Jaguar driver to win a noteworthy North American race—at Pebble Beach, California, in November 1950.

At about the same time, in New York's Waldorf Astoria Hotel—the address used by SS 'importer' Richard Taylor back in 1935!—North America was being introduced to the car towards which everybody at 'The Jaguar' had been working since the post-war programme had begun. Big *and* beautiful, certainly *not* a copy-cat, the Jaguar Mark Seven was the realisation of a dream. In October 1950 William Lyons, now President of the SMMT, had been delighted when *The Autocar* dubbed the new car the 'Prima Ballerina' of the London show. Now he and his employees had to get down to coping with world demand that quickly saturated the factory's potential capacity. Every corner of the higgledy-piggledy Jaguar factory that had grown up at Swallow Road over a period of 22 years was now in use; but already a solution had been found.

William Lyons (far left) and members of the press watch Ron Sutton demonstrate the top gear flexibility of the XK 120 in Belgium, immediately after its 130 mph-plus runs, in 1949.

12: Great cars and great victories
(1950 to 1957)

The next decade was to be so full and exciting that for many Jaguar people it would seem to pass in half the time. The front page headlines in the final 1950 edition of Rankin's *Jaguar Journal*, now in newspaper format, were full of enthusiasm for the new Mark Seven saloon. One of them reported upon how company secretary Edward Huckvale had implemented William Lyons' snap decision to invite all employees to Earls Court in 1950 to witness public reaction to the new Jaguar saloon. This news item ended by pointing out that Lyons had made the gesture because he felt that the importance of the occasion warranted it; it was not meant to create a precedent for an annual motor show trip. An adjacent lead story was the dramatic one. It referred to the fact that the whole manufacture of Jaguar cars was to be transferred to another factory—two miles away in Browns Lane, between the suburban villages of Allesley and Brownshill Green.

In 1928, Swallow had arrived in Coventry with the use of some 40,000 square feet of floor space. Expansion on the site had reached 600,000 square feet by 1950, when Lyons had applied to the ministry to add a further 50 per cent to the working area. There was indeed plenty of open space which had been acquired between the existing factory and Beake Avenue but Lyons could not obtain permission to build there. He was aware of the

RAC Rally winner in 1951 and 1953, and runner-up in 1952 and 1956, the Jaguar XK series was remarkably successful in British rallying as well as racing. Not a regular competitor, John Lyons (William Lyons' son) nevertheless finished sixth in the hotly-contested 'XK' class of the 1952 Morecambe Rally. He is seen here in the final test. His sister, Pat, won the Ladies' Prize but for once his brother-in-law, Ian Appleyard, was not present to walk off with the top prizes; he was away on reserve 'call-up' that weekend (The Motor).

ever-decreasing use to which the large 'Number Two Shadow Factory' of Daimler was being put, and eventually Sir Archibald Rowland, permanent secretary to the Ministry of Supply, was able to work out a scheme enabling Jaguar Cars to obtain a lease on those million square foot Browns Lane premises. The deal was that Jaguar would supplement Rover's work on the Rolls-Royce Merlin-based tank engine known as the 'Meteor', and tool-up for its manufacture. (This was done well ahead of target, but Lyons was pleased when this contract ended, enabling Jaguar to return to its prime objective.)

The unique 'military operation' of moving the complete facilities without loss of amenity *or* production was masterminded by John Silver. He had the co-operation of each departmental head, of course; but, as with the last 'big' move 23 years earlier, it was Harry Teather's co-ordinating work on materials for *all* departments that enabled the plan to go through as smoothly as it did. One name to be mentioned in this connection is that of Ernest Holmes, a 'one-man band' then, but the only contractor prepared to give Silver a firm estimate for the move. At weekends he would round-up lorries from around the Midlands, and by this means transferred whole departments between Friday night and Monday morning. Basically the machine shop was moved first. When the power supply was in, and a position marked for it on the factory floor at Browns Lane, a machine would be moved—complete with its operator and sufficient material to be going-on with!—and in action again within hours. By autumn 1951 the tool room, machine shop and road-test departments were installed and the last vestiges of Daimler activity were being shooed back to their main factory nearer the centre of Coventry. A year later, with the arrival of the paint shop, the move was complete; and on November 28 1952 Lyons called together a convention of distributors, dealers, suppliers and press, to show them the new facilities, and to re-establish contact; for during the company's growth many of the old personal relationships had lapsed, and the lack of cars for the home market had meant that goodwill had often been sorely taxed.

Exports had risen (said Lyons to his guests) from less than ten per cent in 1938 to 84 per cent in 1951; but if the company had failed to export, the low steel allocation would have reduced output to 'a completely uneconomic level'. Lyons also acknowledged the good value that his products represented and warned of the danger of losing competitiveness through over-pricing. He was asking his suppliers to co-operate on prices, although he knew that Arthur Whittaker would always strike a hard bargain anyway.

1951 had been a great year for racing. The new competition car had been created very quickly, with a body by Malcolm Sayer a learned, quiet, charming ex-Bristol aero-dynamics expert. Bob Knight played a big part in the chassis design. Early testing was done by 'Soapy' Sutton, but then he left to test military vehicles for Alvis, having had similar experience previously with Daimler. Lofty England, therefore, did much of the XK 120C test-driving himself. As well as being service manager, he slipped naturally into the new job of racing team chief. As recorded in the opening chapter, two of the cars at Le Mans retired after oil-pipe flange fractures (due to vibration) had resulted in loss of pressure and consequent engine damage. Peter Whitehead and Peter Walker won the 24 hour classic easily and at record speed, however. Their victory in the sole surviving C-type was to be backed-up by countless others at home and abroad, and the XK 120 also had a good year in rallying.

1952 was less successful, mainly because the Jaguar attack upon Le Mans failed. This stemmed from the Mille Miglia, in which Stirling Moss drove a lone works C-type, equipped with Dunlop disc brakes. The new Mercedes Benz 300 SLs were taking part and afterwards Moss sent a telegram to Lyons asking for more power at Le Mans, based on his experience. A last-minute decision to give the C-types longer, more streamlined nose and tail sections for Le Mans meant modifying the coolant system. In doing so, some new water pipe routes and diameters were incorporated. This led to severe overheating, and the whole team was out of the race within a very few laps. As it turned out, a car to the previous year's specification (modified only to prevent oil pipe breakage) could have won again—but this rare opportunity for Jaguar to beat Mercedes-Benz was lost.

The Mille Miglia had not been a good race to compare the British and German cars. The latter had spent many weeks practising, and experience and memory alone enabled them to be driven through the mountains in poised fashion. Even the great Stirling Moss was to improvise when corners came at him unexpectedly, for he had seen only a small part of the route beforehand; and the occasion when Mercedes acceleration had really impressed him was after he had put two of the Jaguar's wheels over the edge momentarily and was still sorting himself out! England was suitably annoyed when Norman Dewis told him this story. Dewis' first job as chief experimental test driver (having left Lea-Francis for Jaguar to replace Ron Sutton) had been to ride with Moss in that 1952 Mille Miglia.

The 1953 Le Mans 24 hour race was the most satisfying of all for Jaguar. Against top-class opposition, the C-types returned to France and finished first, second and fourth—the result of more experience, more power, and disc brakes. Without serious planning, Jaguar very nearly found themselves winners of the World Sports Car (race) *and* the European Touring Car (rally) championships. With help from the young *Ecurie Ecosse* team from Edinburgh, Jaguar was the runner-up *marque* in the former; Ian and Pat Appleyard very nearly won the latter, but had to be content with second place too. The Appleyards announced that they would give up rallying at the end of the 1953 season, although despite pressure of business Ian Appleyard did in fact continue to take part in the occasional event for several more seasons. Lyons' (then) son-in-law was undoubtedly Britain's greatest rally driver of the 1940s and early 1950s.

All over the world, Jaguar drivers were earning laurels for Coventry and for Britain—particularly in the USA, where most production versions of the racing model were sold from mid-1952. As with the XK 120, it was Phil Hill who gave the C-type its first transatlantic win, when he beat Phil Walters (2.6 Ferrari) in a hundred-mile race on the old 'round the pond' circuit at Elkhart Lake, Wisconsin, in September 1952. In another race he was third behind two Cunninghams ('after having been nearly asphyxiated by a burnt-through exhaust system') with the car, owned by 'Chuck' Hornburg. Later that month John Fitch driving Max Hoffman's new C-type defeated F. White in the 'Old Grey Mare' Ladd Special with ease, to come first in the Seneca Cup *Formule Libre* race at Watkins Glen. Later in that meeting street racing in the small upstate New York township came to an end when a child was killed by an Allard that had not actually gone far off course. This must have been one of the SCCA's hardest-learned lessons about crowd-control; circuit safety was improved after that.

There was a works connection for those first C-types in America, because R. Graham Reid kept in close touch with the factory on matters of race preparation. Reid had lost a hand in the war, and had taken a clerical position in the Jaguar service department afterwards. He and Lofty England had a similar brand of humour. At one service department Christmas party they decided to bundle Bill Norbury into a crate when he was singing 'I ain't got nobody'; Norbury was still singing as the crate was borne off-stage. 'Jock' Reid was now working in New York as Max Hoffman's general service manager, having taken over from Bruce Smith.

Not many drivers were capable of getting the best out of the C-type. One exception was Masten Gregory who had his first of many race wins in this model at San Francisco in 1953. Several events later (at Floyd Bennett Field, New York) a practice spin into a marker drum led to a fire. Gregory bought another C-type on the spot, and the wreck of the first was acquired by Tage Hansen and Sherwood Johnston, who was already a distinguished driver of Jaguars having won the 1952 SCCA national championship with an XK 120. During the rebuild in Hansen's Boston workshop Johnston took the car, still bodyless, to the 1954 Mount Washington hill-climb and broke his own record with a time of ten minutes and 44.8 seconds for the course which was still as loose and rough as it had been in pre-war days.

Jaguars and their engines were finding their way into all kinds of vehicle by the mid-50s. The Unsers, uncrowned Kings of Colorado, used a Jaguar powered single-seater to record best time up Pike's Peak—America's most famous hill-climb of all. Rising to over 14,000 feet this road was to be used in the early 1970s during Jaguar's XJ12 test programme. In Britain, Manchester solicitor Norman Buckley was much the most successful of the few men who used the XK engines for water speed record breaking; Jerseyman Frank Le Gallais became the first man to make a rear-engined Jaguar special; H.W.M., Cooper, Lister, and Tojeiro all built sports-racing car chassis for the Jaguar power-unit; Sydney Allard came to an arrangement at one stage to offer XK engines, although only a few Allard-Jaguars were ever made.

By 1952, 20 British constabularies were operating Jaguars as police cars. Police mechanics were now regular visitors to the service school which had been open since 1949 to provide essential training for the widening world sales and service network. The school was run for many years by George Dewbury, one of the original service men to join SS from Standard back in 1934.

Having achieved the position of highest dollar-earner among all importers to the USA, Jaguar introduced automatic transmission for the Mark Seven at the 1953 New York Show. Just before, Lyons announced the appointment of Johannes Eerdmans as Jaguar's chief executive for the United States. On one of his rare holidays, at Woolacombe some years earlier, Lyons had met and been impressed by the Dutchman, and when he read that Jo Eerdmans had resigned his directorship of the Delarue company he offered him the new job and they crossed the Atlantic together on the *Isle de France* (all air-services being grounded by snow at the time they wanted to go). Neither Hornburg nor Hoffman was pleased, but Hoffman had already upset Lyons by his high-handed attitude at a meeting,

The 1951 works Le Mans C-types lined up at Swallow Road.

when he had virtually told his agents (and Lyons) that they could like or lump his hire-and-fire policy for dealers who were not happy with the numbers of Volkswagens, as opposed to Jaguars, that he might foist upon them. The Hoffman relationship was to dwindle quickly to nil; the Hornburg one continued to flourish. To me, this is a fascinating instance of how the Jaguar 'caught on' quickly, whereas the Volkswagen did not. Early in 1954 the Jaguar Cars North America Corporation was formed officially, although it had already been operating for some time in Park Avenue, with Eerdmans as its president. Jaguar continued to lead all the dollar-earning imports.

In May 1954, Edward Huckvale, secretary for over 25 years, was made a member of the Jaguar Cars Ltd board. An improved competition car was announced, but not named, just before Le Mans. Its nickname in the Browns Lane competition shop was 'D-type', and that name was to be picked up and used for it officially, although there was no logical reason for naming it thus. (Its predecessor's initial letter stood for 'Competition'.) Beautifully streamlined to Malcolm Sayer's figures, the D-type Jaguar was all set for victory at Le Mans against strong Ferrari opposition, but blocked fuel-filter elements and other maladies afflicted the team. 1953 winners Duncan Hamilton and Tony Rolt put on a wonderful display, experiencing wheelspin in the wet at about 170 mph on the long Mulsanne Straight. They failed by 105 seconds to catch the winning 4.9-litre Ferrari of Froilan Gonzalez and Maurice Trintignant after one of the closest-ever 24 hour races. While coming second was not the same as winning, the new car had impressed everyone who realised what a basically reliable, safe, fast purpose-built Le Mans car the D-type Jaguar was—as it was to prove by winning Le Mans for the next three years. In July 1954, however, the Jaguar team gave the car its second outing, winning the Reims 12-hour race without any difficulty at all. The drivers were Ken Wharton (a driver of known versatility) and Peter Whitehead—the careful and reliable farmer who had given the C-type its début win, too.

That autumn, the XK 120 was succeeded by the XK 140—more refined mechanically, and still very beautiful to look at, although the sensibly-big bumpers were clumsy in appearance, compared with the XK 120's small neat ones. The Mark Seven was improved too, and Jaguar's five shilling ordinary shares rocketed at motor show time from around 50 shillings to 70 shillings, in the wake of the new models and rumours of a Chrysler takeover! ('We are very pleased that people are still showing such great interest in our products', responded the even-tempered Arthur Whittaker to the *Coventry Evening Telegraph*, 'and consider that it is a very good sign.') With the exception of Volkswagen, Jaguar was still the top USA import, and Lyons set off for America at the New Year to consolidate his company's position there. The remarkable growth of Jaguar was largely attributable to his ability to create around his products an aura that captivated Americans, and brought them flocking to the showrooms.

At home, a rumpus was coming to a head on the question of team drivers. For the first time, a driver-selection test session was held at Silverstone. Mike Hawthorn had already been selected. Although almost in the 'veteran' class, Duncan Hamilton and Tony Rolt were retained for their superb Le Mans record. Peter Whitehead, very much the gentleman driver, who raced various other cars on his own anyway, went to Australia in the knowledge that he was unlikely to be picked for a fifth season. Peter Walker had refused to take part in the Silverstone session and joined the Aston Martin team; and Ken Wharton had become competition manager of Daimler (who were making quite a good attempt at racing and rallying with their Conquest Century model) without advising anyone at Jaguar, where it was 'assumed he would realise he would not be nominated'. To make the team up to six regular drivers, Donald Beauman, Jimmy Stewart, and Desmond Titterington were nominated. Jackie Stewart's elder brother had an accident early in the

A new type of Jaguar—the compact 2.4. Bill Heynes took this one to France prior to the 1955 announcement. Note the high sidelamps and built-in foglamps which were altered for production (E. Adlington).

season, however, and decided to give up racing altogether having damaged an arm that had been broken less than a year earlier. The Scot's place was taken by Ivor Bueb.

Ecurie Ecosse continued to do very well with Jaguars in British events and, as Lyons returned to Britain, it was announced that a team of Jaguars would be run in the USA. This followed winter tests at Sebring by Phil Walters, Bill Spear, Bill Lloyd, and Briggs Cunningham, the American millionaire who had given up racing his own make of cars in favour of sponsoring others. Cunningham's Ferrari was tried, too, and its performance did not match the Jaguar's—one good reason for Cunningham's decision. Walters took the car to Daytona Beach and recorded over 164 mph in the annual speed trials there, before returning to Sebring for the twelve-hour race. The car—last of six 1954 works machines—was being looked after by Len Hayden. He had come to Jaguar as a racing mechanic for the 1953 season, whereas everyone in the factory team before him was always 'borrowed' for racing from another job in the engineering or service department.

In a close finish Mike Hawthorn and Phil Walters won that important Sebring race. It was galling, to say the least, when there was an argument over the lap-scoring, and victory could not be confirmed for more than a week. Everything had been going so well, that the successive tragedies of the summer of 1955 were all the harder to comprehend. First, on a preliminary trip to France in connection with the forthcoming Le Mans race, a works Mark Seven twitched on the cambered road south of Cherbourg and hit an American army lorry head-on. William Lyons' only son, John, was dead. Then came the carnage of Le Mans itself, when Mercedes driver Pierre 'Levegh' and many spectators were killed; what had begun as a great duel between Jaguar and Mercedes ended in a worthy yet hollow victory for Coventry. The final straw was a pair of accidents in the Tourist Trophy race at Dundrod in September that claimed three drivers' lives. Although not affected directly by the crashes, another Jaguar versus Mercedes-Benz battle came to nought, when the engine of the single works-entered Jaguar, driven by Hawthorn and Tit-

Three of the finest of all Jaguar rally drivers—Ronald Adams, Cecil Vard, and Ian Appleyard—seen with their Mark Sevens after winning the 1955 Monte Carlo Rally team prize. Adams drove PWK 700 again in 1956 to win the Monte outright for Jaguar.

terington, broke on the last lap but one. They would have been third in today's terms, but at the time were not classified.

Leader from the very start of that was an ex-works D-type owned by Jack Broadhead and driven by Bob Berry. Although employed at the Jaguar works, Berry raced as a private individual and was regarded as one of Britain's up and coming drivers; he had been racing his own much-modified XK 120—with one of the three works lightweight bodies that had been built in 1951 in case the C-type was not ready—very quickly during the previous season. He had been a student at Cambridge before joining Ernest Rankin in the Jaguar publicity office in 1951. In August 1955, he had competed in the Goodwood nine-hour race finishing fifth, Norman Dewis making a rare race appearance as his partner. In Ulster, Berry's lead was shortlived, but he was going strongly in third place at the end of lap one. On lap two (Berry takes up the story) 'unfortunately I clipped a bank at Tornagrough, which is a double "S" bend and very tight. The blow was not very great—it did not even deflect the car—but it was sufficient to damage the front offside tyre which started to deflate. Three quarters of a mile later I slowed right down as the car was handling most peculiarly and, entering the left-hand Quarry bend, the tyre deflated completely. Virtually unsteerable, the car mounted the grass bank on the right and slid easily over the top and down into the field beyond. The only difficulty was that the field was about twelve feet below, a fact that nearly gave me heart failure. However the car remained upright and the rest of the race was observed from the pits. The most unfortunate person in this episode was poor Ninian Sanderson who did not get a drive'.

Berry was to have a much more serious accident at Goodwood the following Whitsun. He had won one race and was on top of his form, leading another, when the Jaguar escaped from under him, depositing him badly injured on the grass whence he could hear 'the never-to-be forgotten sound of the D-type pounding itself to destruction', as he described it for the *Jaguar Apprentices Magazine*. Car and driver proved fully repairable and they raced again, although never really seriously—and anyway, Lyons had made it clear that Berry could not be spared from the office for Friday practice sessions in future, let alone two-month spells in hospital and convalescence!

Late 1955 saw Cunningham's D-type Jaguars race 'at home' for the first time—Sherwood Johnston finishing a close second on the completely new 'Road America' circuit at

Soon to be appointed Home Sales Director of Jaguar Cars, Alice Fenton poses at the 2.4 convention, at Browns Lane in September 1955. (Miss N. Fenton).

Elkhart Lake after a huge dust-up with Phil Hill's Ferrari, the Californian taking the honours when Johnston 'opened the door' for him on the last lap. Johnston then took the Jaguar to victory in the sports car *Grand Prix* at Watkins Glen, where C-type driver 'Doc' Wyllie won the supporting Seneca Cup race. Johnston proceeded to win the President Eisenhower Trophy at Hagerstown, Maryland, where the D-type beat Hill's Ferrari in another close and exciting race. Charles Wallace's XK 140 scored a superb 'production' victory over Paul O'Shea's Mercedes-Benz 300 SL at the same meeting. 'Chuck' Wallace was declared SCCA class 'C production' national champion for the second year running, driving XK 120 and XK 140 cars, and was to earn several D-type drives with Cunningham's team in consequence. Johnston was 1955 'class C-modified' champion, having gained his early-season points with a Ferrari. Although Johnston's D-type was shoved out of the lead by the fiery Spaniard 'Fon' de Portago's Ferrari at the winter meeting in the Bahamas, 1955 was generally one of the best racing years for the Jaguar *marque* in America.

Back in Coventry, Bill Heynes and the Jaguar engineering team had been spending no more time than they could help on sports-racing car design, after creating the C-type and the D-type. What were race victories for, if not to win confidence in the Jaguar name and therefore more sales of *series* production models? The Mark Seven and the XK 140 were doing well, but were due for major face-lifts soon. The D-type was being built on a real (though not moving) production line. Taking this 'limited-run' car into the main assembly hall presented many labour problems, and there were dismissals. Some people were reinstated next day, but it took several of the old D-type 'gang'—notably Les Latham and Eric Titcumb—nearly a quarter of a century to establish that this did not count as a 'break in service'! During 1955, too, a much more modern production line had been installed by John Silver's men; and this one did not have the familiar 'body-meets-chassis' look about it.

For several years, virtually since the phasing-out of the old four-cylinder saloons in 1949, Lyons and Heynes had been working-up the idea of a compact, unit-construction saloon with a short-stroke version of the six-cylinder XK engine. (The four-cylinder XK had been shelved altogether, never having achieved the required level of smoothness.) In September 1955, a second big convention was held at Browns Lane to launch the Jaguar 2.4-litre saloon. Once again Lyons hit the market with the right product at the right price.

The new car could be purchased for under £1,300 including tax, and no other Jaguar car yet approached £2,000—apart from the somewhat 'academic' D-type, listed at £3,663. After several years with production static at around 10,000 cars annually, output over the next four years was to double. With the introduction of the '2.4', employment at Jaguar was shooting up, too, towards the 4,000 mark.

Browns Lane remained the company's only site. Although it was large, it would not be large enough for ever. There were two ways of expanding temporarily, though. The original shadow factory office block, at the south end of the works, had been retained for the use of the General Electric Company, who needed the space for secret projects. Jaguar, the new leaseholders, had therefore been permitted in 1951-2 to build their own offices on to the front of the works canteen and social facilities block. This incorporated a ball-room which Lyons was determined to retain as a company showroom. For years he had lacked entrance and reception areas that he felt were worthy of Jaguar, but at the same time had not felt justified in spending money on such a luxury. The move to Browns Lane had provided the opportunity. (When Jaguar had vacated Swallow Road, the Dunlop Wheel and Rim Company had moved in. Several years on, the Ministry of Supply agreed to sell the Browns Lane factory to Jaguar.) When the 'GEC block' was eventually vacated it would become Jaguar's engineering headquarters. The other (unexpected) expansion at Browns Lane was to be triggered-off in February 1957, when the northern third of the works would be gutted by fire and new buildings built very quickly.

Recognition of his remarkable achievements, particularly in building the export business and the company itself, came to Lyons in the 1956 New Years Honours List, when he was made a Knight Bachelor. New Year's Day saw an important development when Briggs Cunningham formed a new company, to become associated with Jaguar's already-thriving North American operation, and a fine new Jaguar showroom and offices were opened on East 57th Street, New York City. The service and parts organisation was to benefit too, from Cunningham's interest in the Momo Corporation. Alfred Momo had left Italy in 1920 and, apart from a short period back there, spent his working life in America—first at the Rolls-Royce Springfield works and ultimately with his own precision engineering shop in Queens, New York, where he looked after Cunningham's racing activities.

Television launch for the 2.4 at the RAC's country club, with help from the Jaguar racing team. Left to right: Lofty England, Bob Berry, Duncan Hamilton, Ivor Bueb, Mike Hawthorn and Raymond Baxter. Far right, studying script, is Macdonald Hobley.

Royal visit, 1956. Her Majesty the Queen talks to Sir William about the Le Mans-winning D-type. Behind her, Prince Philip is chatting with Bill Heynes, Arthur Whittaker and John Silver.

Jaguar was selected by the readers of *Road & Track* and *Popular Mechanics* as the most popular sports car, with Porsche and MG second and third in each poll. In March, Sir William and Lady Lyons and the Jaguar board greeted Her Majesty the Queen and Prince Philip, who toured the Browns Lane factory. They were introduced to at least three of the other former Blackpool men, too—Jack Beardsley (machine shop manager), Bernard Hartshorn (assembly tracks manager) and Harry Teather (purchasing manager). They also met the newest apprentice, 15-year-old John Deakin—now a principal engineer on the body side. The Royal couple were told of a production rate of 380 cars a week, with a target of 500 soon to be met; 60 million dollars had been earned for Britain since the export drive began; full time and overtime were being worked. Reading the facts as dispensed on that memorable day, only one statistic sounded a warning note for the long-term future: the average age of board members and other senior executives was 51 years.

There was strength and continuity of management for the time being, though. Just after the Royal visit, four of the loyalest of Lyons' senior executives were appointed directors. They were worthy appointments and everyone was delighted that Miss Alice Fenton, who had been with the company for over 30 years, was made Home Sales Director. She was devoted to the company, very popular and vivacious, yet firm in her many dealings with her colleagues in the company, and with members of the trade. John Silver and Ted Orr became production and works directors. Unfortunately, it would not be long before Orr and Lyons had a monumental row over a matter of principle concerning wage negotiations in the factory; Orr left and joined Armstrong Siddeley. (One of his sons, Michael, was to establish Japanese Colt cars in the UK in the 1970s.) The fourth appointment was that of Lofty England, as service director. The four promotions were not actually to board directorship, but this probably did not make too much difference, for there was still absolutely no doubt as to who was chief executive or took the decisions that counted.

Although the works team ran into big problems at Le Mans, it was still a Jaguar victory. 1956 was a fairly quiet season in terms of numbers of events, for the aftermath of the Le Mans tragedy had resulted in some cancellations. Jaguar became the first marque to win the world's two most famous motoring competitions—Le Mans and the 'Monte'—in the same year. After nearly managing it on several previous occasions, a factory-loaned Mark Seven saloon finally won the Monte Carlo Rally outright, manned by Ronald Adams, Frank

One of the most successful works Jaguar drivers, Ivor Bueb, seen in the winning long-nose D-type (XKD 605) in the 1956 Reims 12-hour race (The Motor).

Bigger, and Derek Johnston. The new 2.4 saloon gained its first victory in May, when the Belgian engineer, writer and driver Paul Frère, won his own country's major saloon car race on the fast Spa-Francorchamps circuit in the Ardennes. The Cunningham team had a good season of racing in the USA again (although it was to be even better in 1957). Embarrassed by his performance against them with a D-type owned by Hansen's of Boston, Cunningham and Momo acquired the services of Walter Hansgen who took the class 'C' modified title in 1956 and 1957—being declared the SCCA's 'Driver of the Year' on the second occasion.

The Suez crisis finally caught up with Jaguar in November 1956 when, for the first time, a four-day working week was brought in. Everything was fine in America, but petrol restrictions had taken a heavy toll on demand in Britain and Europe. Happily, within two months, a full five-day working week was restored.

On January 21 1957, a 'new' sports-racing model was announced. Any plans there may have been to make more than a very few of these XKSS models were dispelled on the evening of February 12 when fire ripped through that part of the factory where the first few were being made. (The cars were being constructed from near-complete D-types that had been in store, and it might not have been very easy to make any more, once the small supply had run out, anyway.) There followed an amazing clearing-up operation, encouraged by owners, agents, suppliers and rivals; within two days, car production was under way again. 1957 was still going to be a record year. Ten days later it was declared that all the 'hundreds' of offers from metal dealers had been declined. 'Not only are bodies being cut up piece-meal with oxy-acetylene torch cutters, but engines, gearboxes, axles, springs and other components are being cut through and then hammered into a condition rendering them useless for anything but scrap.' This reassurance to the public was welcome and necessary. Shortly after the fire, when all apprentices were assigned to the devasted area, I had stepped into a saloon surrounded by burned-out shells but protected from total destruction because it had been passing through a small insulated booth at the time of the fire; the engine fired and I *drove* the blistered car out into the yard to join the hulks that were being dragged and carried there.

Right *An early model for the E-type with Malcolm Sayer (centre) and Derrick White (in jacket). The latter, a fine chassis engineer, was responsible for much development work including the 'lightweight' E-type and the XJ13 mid-engined project.*

Below *February 1957: Burnt-out Jaguars are pushed and carried from the main assembly hall the morning after the great fire. 'We'll do the job . . . the fire makes it a little harder, that's all', Sir William told Harold Hastings of* The Motor, *who reported that the first cars to come off the shortened production lines* (**overleaf**) *did so by mid-day, 36 hours after the fire!*

What mattered was clearing a space, so those 270 fire-damaged cars could be replaced as soon as possible.

Almost defiantly, on February 26, Jaguar announced *another* new model, the '3.4'—their first 120 mph saloon. It had already been declared that, although competition car development would not be dropped altogether, Jaguar Cars Ltd would suspend racing as a works team, and so most of the latest 'long-nose' D-types were sold to *Ecurie Ecosse* and Cunningham. (One of these cars was, in fact, returned from the USA and then loaned by Jaguar to Turin's excellent Biscaretti Museum.) Engineering effort could now be directed at Jaguar road-cars of the future.

Like those of Briggs Cunningham, David Murray's *Ecurie Ecosse* cars enjoyed a splendid year in 1957, winning at Le Mans for the second time, to give the D-type its hat-trick and make Jaguar the most successful marque in the history of the famous French endurance test. From 1958, the regulations for Le Mans decreed a top engine capacity limit of three litres. Designed as a 3½-litre, and obsolete after four seasons of racing, the Jaguar D-type stood little chance from now on. Several teams tried three-litre versions of the XK engine, but these were not a success. For events where capacity was not limited, the Americans and the Scots turned to Brian Lister's small engineering company in Cambridge. Lister's own Jaguar-engined sports-car had already astounded established entrants by its speed, with Archie Scott-Brown at the wheel. With 3.8-litre engines available, the Lister-Jaguar was to be competitive for three seasons at international level. In America, Walt Hansgen won his SCCA national class again in 1958 and 1959.

Introduction of the 3.4 Litre saloon gave Jaguar a new interest in racing and rallying. Although the competitions department, as such, was dispersed within the experimental engineering area, there had always been considerable help and preparation work in the service department. The competitiveness of the new 'small', powerful Jaguar encouraged the company to continue to provide assistance, and Coventry was to dominate the touring car racing scene for a long time to come.

13: Sir William creates the Jaguar Group (1957 to 1966)

Although it eased some of the pressures of Jaguar's hard-pressed engineers, withdrawal from motor racing did mean that competition car manufacture would no longer play an integral part in the company's activities. There *would* be several projects in the 1960s—but they were desultory by comparison with a commitment to year-in-year-out winning of the 24-hour race at Le Mans in the days when the regulations had been clear and fairly consistent. Long after that great and memorable period, Bill Heynes told Philip Turner of *Motor*: 'Far from being relieved when we pulled out of motor-racing I was more than sorry to abandon competition cars. Not only had we achieved success on the track but it had helped me build up a team of engineers, in the design office and on the shop floor, second to none in the industry. The enthusiasm which spread through the whole factory, I'm sure, made a great contribution to Jaguar success in production and in the world markets. The competition and development men on the shop floor must take credit for the many extra hours and meticulous care they put in on the cars, but it was the support of the whole factory that made the racing venture possible'. Heynes (who had himself received several accolades) singled out his top men, Baily, Hassan, Knight, Sayer, Jones, and Emerson for special mention. He also paid tribute to the suppliers of services and components, especially Harry Weslake for his work on valve port and cylinder head design and Joe Wright of Dunlop 'who developed the disc brake in 1952, and insisted on the production of a racing tyre by his company which could last the length of a Le Mans race'.

Jaguar had become a household word, helping British prestige everywhere; now the experience gained in racing began to show. In its third major 'face-lift', in 1957, the XK series of sports-cars was rejuvenated largely by the inclusion of disc brakes for the 'special equipment' XK 150. As only a very few if any 'standard' models were made, it is true to call the XK 150 the first car to be made in thousands as opposed to hundreds with four-wheel disc brakes. (Of course, all the Jaguar D-types from 1954 had had discs all-round; so had the rare 1955 Austin-Healey 100S and a version of the Jensen 541 from 1956. The Triumph TR 3 had also been earlier than the XK with disc-type braking, but to the front wheels only.) The 2.4 and 3.4 soon acquired the option of disc brakes; then the third manifestation of the large 'twin-cam' Jaguar saloon range—the Mark Nine—appeared with discs, too, as well as the larger (3.8-litre) engine capacity and power-assisted steering.

Late in 1959, the compact saloons were given a much-improved appearance, and were launched with a choice of three engines and disc brakes with everything. This was the Mark Two, so the previous 2.4 and 3.4 were immediately dubbed 'Mark One'. The Jaguar Mark Two was a sensible compromise between family car and businessman's express. For more than three years it dominated saloon car racing, culminating in the first (1963) European touring car race championship, won by Peter Nöcker driving a 3.8-litre model entered by Jaguar's very enterprising young German importer, Peter Lindner. The Mark Two also gained a fine reputation in France, particularly as a result of Bernard Consten's driving in

Forty years on from the first Swallow sidecars—the main board of Jaguar Cars Ltd in 1961. From left: F.R.W. England, E.F. Huckvale, A. Whittaker, Sir W. Lyons, W.M. Heynes, J. Silver, and R.W. Grice (Coventry Evening Telegraph).

the *Tour de France Automobile*—a marathon mixture of rally and race conditions. Between them, the Jaguar Mark Two and the cars that it inspired (the S-type and the 420) remained in production for nearly ten years.

As another decade passed, however, the sports cars and the large saloons were showing their age; and the first signs of radical change came in 1960. At the 1959 London show, Jo Eerdmans discussed the new sports car with Sir William Lyons and the matter was followed up that December with a letter from Eerdmans's publicity chief Everett Taylor Martin to Ernest Rankin. Jaguar Cars Inc (as the North American subsidiary was now called) wanted to show the car at New York in April 1960. A small light-green alloy-bodied sports car of quite striking similarity in general appearance to the D-type had been a familiar sight, at the MIRA test track near Nuneaton and on country roads from Warwickshire to Wales, for many, many months. By mid-1958 Christopher Jennings, editor of *The Motor* and his wife—formerly Margaret Allan, one of the original SS 'works' rally drivers—had tried the car and found it 'a potential world beater' even with a short-stroke 2½-litre XK engine fitted. Registered VKV 752, this car was identified as E1A and was, naturally enough, known as the 'E' type by those involved with it.

In December 1959, Everett Martin was asking Rankin for particular types of photograph, so that literature could be printed; the heat was taken out of the situation when Rankin was able to confirm with Sir William that there was no question of making any announcements yet. Rankin advised Martin, and put the correspondence away in a file marked 'XK 160 Announcement'! A false alarm of a different kind came just afterwards, when it was announced that Jaguar Cars Inc would market Leyland commercial vehicles in the United States. Leyland Motors (USA) Inc, did not work out; Eerdmans got the orders but, says Sir William Lyons, the vehicles gave trouble. Soon Jaguar would make its own way in the commercial vehicle world, anyway!

1960 began sadly from the company's point of view. On March 21 Sir William Lyons wrote to all distributors and dealers: 'It is with the greatest of regret I have to inform you of the death on Saturday night of Miss Alice Fenton, a loyal and devoted servant of this Company for over thirty-five years'. In a statement to the press he added that 'her loyalty and enthusiasm for the company's progress were invaluable . . . I have lost a colleague and a friend'. Alice Fenton had had treatment for what was thought to be Bell's Palsy. She enjoyed motoring. Her Mark Nine-engined Mark Eight gave her a lot of pleasure, as did fresh air, and *she* had an idea that the open sunshine roof may have been the cause of the loss of control she was beginning to note in the nerves on one side of her face in 1959. The auburn-haired Lancashire lass had been feeling much better when, at barely 50 years of age, she suffered a fatal cerebral haemorrhage.

Alice Fenton had been engaged but never married; the idea of it did not appeal to her. That was during the war, when her job held little interest. As peace came, so did her enthusiasm to move ahead with Jaguar and she turned down the offer of a 'Whitehall' post to do so. Her ultimate responsibility as Director of Home Sales, and the respect she commanded as First Lady of Britain's motor industry, were evident by the turnout for her funeral. She had been with the company for 35 years. Had she lived, who knows what further heights she might have attained?

In the spring the rumours of an 'E' type were becoming more numerous. Briggs Cunningham's 1960 Le Mans entry of a Jaguar for Dan Gurney and Walter Hansgen was adding weight to them, even though there was nothing new at the Geneva or New York shows. Rankin issued a strong denial of a Jaguar return to racing: 'The close liaison existing between Jaguar Cars Ltd. and Mr. Cunningham, coupled with his renewed desire to compete in this year's Le Mans race, resulted in an agreement by which Jaguar were to prepare a 3-litre car for use by Mr. Cunningham . . . The car itself is not an entirely new design, but is a development based on the D-type . . . it incorporates certain features which have not been previously employed by Jaguar'. First seen during the April practice session at Le Mans (and bearing the registration number VKV 752!) this car was larger than the first running prototype. It had a full race fuel-injection XK engine, and was second fastest, lapping at over 120 mph. For the race itself, 'E2A' (as it was numbered) was fastest in practice, but after a brief spell in third place spent a long time in the pits, eventually retiring in the early hours of the morning. More than 20 years would pass before Jaguar's next victory in any major 24-hour race. 'E2A' went back to Coventry where it lost its Le Mans fin (*à la* D-type) and gained a hump in the bonnet to accommodate a well-tried 3.8-litre engine. It spent the rest of the year in America where Hansgen gained a win at Bridgehampton and a third at 'Road America'. It had no other success and, once again, Cunningham returned it to Coventry, where news was being made once more.

Introduction of the 'compact' saloons had meant more production lines, and the machine shop and engine assembly and test facilities were being pushed into a much smaller area than was reasonable. The tracks themselves were somewhat cramped, too, and the relief provided by the new buildings—erected so quickly after the 1957 fire—was only temporary. Not wishing to move to a 'development' area, Lyons was unenthusiastic when he sent teams to different parts of the British Isles to inspect possible sites. In the end, Lyons did the job himself—and in Coventry, too! A preliminary announcement, on May 26 1960, told the world that the Jaguar empire was about to double in size.

The story of Daimler in Coventry is not as old as that of Gottlieb Daimler himself. Indeed the use of his name for that of a British company and its products can be regarded only as a desire to honour the great German pioneer; unless, of course, one is uncharitable enough to think that it might have been part of the attempt by Harry Lawson to create some kind of national monopoly for motor car patents. In fact the name was first adopted in Britain by Frederick Simms, who fitted 'Daimler' engines to boats in London from 1893. The first British motor-car factory—that is to say, for *volume* production—was between Sandy Lane and the Coventry Canal. Built as a cotton mill, it was converted for car manufacture in 1896 and the first Coventry Daimler cars began to appear in 1897.

Since the turn of the century, Daimler had become *the* Royal *marque* as well as a distinguished maker of bus and coach chassis and armoured vehicles. Acquired by the Birmingham Small Arms Company in 1910, Daimler had done great work in both world wars and suffered much damage in the second. Lanchester, noted for originality and excellence of design, had been associated with Daimler since 1931, but had been dropped as a marque in 1956. In 1908, Daimler had acquired a site at nearby Radford. It became the main factory and in 1937 the original cotton mill was abandoned altogether. It was the Daimler name and business, with the Radford factory, that Jaguar purchased from BSA for £3,400,000, formally concluding proceedings at 11 am on June 18 1960. Of his negotiations with BSA chairman Jack Sangster, Sir William Lyons said later 'I do not recall a more amicable deal with anyone'. This feeling was undoubtedly helped when they tossed a coin over £10,000 (Sangster had forgotten about some owed pensions). Lyons won.

Rankin was quick to ensure that Jaguar's move into the relatively hallowed halls of 'The Daimler' would be seen in the best possible light. The second statement (June 18) ended: 'Jaguar Cars Ltd. wish to deny unfounded rumours to the effect that sweeping changes, including even the extinction of the Daimler marque, are to be expected. Whilst one of the most obvious and immediate benefits accruing to Jaguar as a result of their purchase is the availability of much needed additional production facilities for Jaguar cars, the Company's long term view envisages not merely the retention of the Daimler marque, but the expansion of its markets at home and overseas.'

Once again, it was Jack Silver who took charge of factory re-organisation, together with Bob Grice who had followed Ted Orr as works director. (An Austin man, Grice had in fact worked at Jaguar for a period previously, in charge of the production road-test shop.) The basic plan was to retain commercial and military vehicles at Radford, but to move all car production to Browns Lane. All Jaguar machining and engine construction would, in turn, be moved to Radford. These actions would be taken in stages, to prevent hindrance of production at either plant. Acquisition of Daimler also meant an approximate doubling of the total work-force to nearly 8,000. One of the most practical and diplomatic actions was to build a new company clubhouse—which Jaguar had needed, as a social asset, ever since the move to Browns Lane—on the Radford works sportsfield. A Daimler man, John Young, was appointed full-time social secretary. All the same, and quite naturally, it still took many Daimler people a long time to adapt to the new order. On the other hand, their company had been ruled by a bigger one for 50 years already, so no one was unused to the experience.

The Daimler car range was interesting but hardly practical; and the volume was too low. The Daimler company had anticipated being sold, and some pretty rapidly-conceived ideas were evident. Daimler had already given up the idea of making a small car based on the Dyna-Panhard, and (later) a medium-sized one with the small V8 engine and, of all things, a Vauxhall body; but a glass-fibre sports-car *was* being made. This was called the SP 250, and it was to remain in production until 1964, by which time over 2,600 would be built. Its 90-degree V8 2.5-litre engine gave it a fine performance, but its Triumph TR-inspired chassis did not give it the very best of road behaviour—although sometimes it went remarkably well in production sports car racing, especially in Australia and in North America where Duncan Black won the SCCA national Class 'C' production car championship. David Ogle had nearly finished designing a coupé body of his own for the SP 250 chassis when he was killed in a car accident in 1962. The job was completed by Tom Karen and after making a handful of SX 250s, the Ogle company sold the body design to Reliant for their Scimitar. Jaguar was not involved in this or the strange Hooper razor-edge body that appeared once and never again, but did make a couple of good-looking open bodies with a view to replacing the distinctive but distinctly weird shape of the production models. It was calculated that the price difference between it and the Jaguar E-type would be insufficient to make the 'Jaguarised' SP 250 a practical proposition. The engine, however, was used until 1969 in a Jaguar Mark Two-based Daimler saloon, and in marine applications.

When Jaguar acquired Daimler, the big six-cylinder Majestic saloon was approaching the

Acquisition No 1: In purchasing Daimler from BSA in 1960, Jaguar entered the passenger vehicle chassis business just as the rear-engined 'Fleetline' was to be launched, and within a few years Daimler was the biggest producer of double-deck bus chassis. Here Fleetlines mingle with traditional front-engined Daimlers in Broadgate, the centre of Coventry (T.W. Moore),

end of its short life; but the similar-looking 4.5-litre V8 engined Daimler Majestic Major—a real wolf, in traditional Daimler clothing—was about to go into production. That fine 120 mph disc-braked machine would out-perform the bigger Jaguar saloons, and the road behaviour was as good if not as smooth as theirs. It seemed a great pity when the excellent 2½ and 4½-litre V8 engines (designed by the BSA group's motor-cycle power unit man, Edward Turner) were not adopted for the Jaguars and Daimlers of the 1970s—although there were very good reasons. Jaguar engineers were in fact already working on a V8; but it was a 60-degree unit and never smooth enough for Jaguar, so was discarded. Tooling for the 4½-litre V8 would not have made commercial sense. Having paid for its tooling costs many times, the XK engine continues to serve a valuable role, in the mid-1980s.

Daimler's contract for the military Ferret was taken on by Jaguar. When replaced by the Jaguar-engined Fox (manufactured elsewhere) Ferret production ceased in the early 1970s. On the passenger vehicle side, Daimler were ready to prove their viability with a new double-deck chassis. Its general concept, in particular its transversely-mounted rear engine, was a straight 'crib' from the new Leyland Atlantean; but the new Daimler had several advantages, including that old favourite of municipal transport managers— the ubiquitous Gardner diesel engine. It also had right-angle drive (with input and output shafts at the same end of the gearbox) and a dropped-centre axle giving it a basic advantage over the Leyland in terms of flat floors and a low step.

Cyril Simpson, who had been with Daimler since 1918, stayed on as chief engineer well beyond the normal retirement age to see the bus into production. The Daimler Fleetline was introduced at the 1960 commercial vehicle show, and was a great success. Thanks to Bob Crouch—son of the famous early Coventry car-maker—his small sales team, and the vehicle's intrinsic qualities, the Fleetline soon outsold the Atlantean and, after several years, Daimler could claim to be the largest producer of double-deck bus chassis. Production eventually reached nearly 30 Fleetline chassis a week. This was boosted by a decade of steady, if small, sales of front-engined chassis, mainly for use in Kowloon.

Most interesting yet least-known of the projects relating to Daimler shortly after Jaguar bought it, was the one to which Clifford Elliott was assigned. Its interest lies in the proof it provides of Sir William Lyons' determination not only to have adequate car making resources but to move into the commercial vehicle field seriously. Cliff Elliott, a noted engineer of Dodge Trucks, was brought in by Lyons, and given the task of designing a Daimler truck. This job had not left the drawing boards at Radford, however, when Lyons purchased the remnants of Guy Motors—so the project was shelved, and the first Daimler truck to be designed for over 30 years became the last, too. (It should be recorded, however, that Atkinsons very nearly did a deal, around 1948, to make a truck with Daimler's 8.6-litre diesel engine coupled to a David Brown gearbox.)

The extra responsibilities of Jaguar's top men were given recognition in March 1961, when Arthur Whittaker became Deputy Chairman and Bill Heynes Vice-Chairman (Engineering). Edward Huckvale continud to serve on the board as Company secretary. New board members were John Silver and Robert Grice, retaining their production and works directorships; and Raymond (Lofty) England whose appointment as Assistant Managing Director was especially significant. As a former Daimler apprentice, he took a particular interest in maintaining that *marque*'s identity. Following England's promotion, Geoffrey Pindar was made general service manager with Bill Norbury manager of the repair workshops. Ken Bowen (who had spent the war as a member of the SS fire brigade, and on ARP duties with Eric Warren and Cyril Maslin) was officially appointed as overseas service representative soon afterwards.

Preparations for new Jaguars were now in evidence, and the production specialists—

Acquisition No 2: Jaguar bought Guy Motors of Wolverhampton when it was in liquidation, in 1961. The Guy marque was revived by the introduction of a new range of trucks and tractor units which ran for 15 years, from 1964 to 1979. Here a Guy Big J (Big Jaguar)—driven by Commercial Motor *technical editor, Tony Wilding—passes a works Jaguar 240 on the steep ascent of Shap, in the days before the M6 transformed winter driving on the main road between England and Scotland.*

Horace Barnes, Bill Hudson, Ted Barber, John Witherall, Bert Langley, Cyril Kirk, and many more—were having to work flat-out. The reason for all the drama was two-fold. Jaguar was about to announce two of its most important new models—both in the same year!

If any car ever achieved 'legend' status in its lifetime, the E-type Jaguar did. Looking very like the competition prototype 'E2A', seen a year earlier at Le Mans, the E-type (not the XK 160!) was launched by Sir William Lyons in person at the 1961 Geneva show. Somehow, Malcolm Sayer's superb streamlining and Lyons' eye for detail had combined to produce a new concept in road-going sports-cars. Admittedly, two of the new cars were provided to customers in sufficient time for them to finish first and third in a quite-important race against Aston Martins and Ferraris at Oulton Park in April, shortly after the announcement; and several works-devised competition models were made subsequently. It was, however, as a grand *touring* car that the E-type Jaguar was conceived and built. In round terms, 30,000 XK 120, XK 140 and XK 150 sports cars had been made in 12 years. In only a slightly longer period, more than 70,000 E-types would be made.

While the E-type was making its initial impact on the public, Jaguar engineers were thoroughly testing two heavily-disguised and rather large saloons for eight weeks in south-west France. From the experimental department went fitters Barrie Wood and Ted Wildman, who were relieved by Harry Hawkins and Frank Lees at 'half time'. Norman Dewis organised the test schedule, with Graham Burrows, Clive Martin, Frederick Merrill and Alan Palmer sharing the driving. One car was written-off against a tree, although the driver, Fred Merrill, was fortunately not badly hurt. The second car continued the remorseless routine with only one major incident when Clive Martin forgot a level crossing and saw the barriers only after being momentarily dazzled by a car waiting on the other side. He managed to bring the big car to a halt astride the track and quickly moved it off again. Then he parked to examine the (slight!) damage the barrier had done. 'As I was doing so', recalled Martin, 'the weekly diesel express thundered through the crossing . . . .'

The car continued to be thrashed around the route until it had completed nearly 40,000 miles. It was the first time that a full continental test programme had been undertaken by Jaguar. Even so, many of the niggling faults that came to light on that mission could be dealt with only after the car had been in production for some time. If not the best Jaguar of all time, the new Mark Ten was certainly the most sophisticated, and it soon developed into a very fine car indeed. At the Browns Lane convention Sir William Lyons rightly praised the Jaguar engineering staff on what they had achieved 'undaunted by the high standards set'. Bertie Henly replied by wishing Sir William as much success with Daimler and Guy as he was having with Jaguar. He said he could not find adjectives to describe the Mark Ten, and asked the prize-winning Jaguar works band to lay 'Happy Days Are Here Again' instead. As with the E-type, the Mark Ten generated 'rave notices' in the press and on television. The concept of those great new cars of 1961 has changed little in the intervening years . . . yet the behaviour and looks of today's Jaguars and Daimlers are still comparable with any car in the world.

Modernisation of both factories was part of the integration programme at the Jaguar and Daimler factories, but not without the usual eye to economy. When a 'new' body-finishing and painting plant was installed, for example, it was in fact a 're-assembly' from Mulliner's Birmingham works where Standard and Triumph bodies had previously been treated.

A look at Lotus as a possible purchase around this time did not result in action by Lyons; but the ultimate example of Lyons economy resulted in the purchase, after long negotiations with the receiver, of Guy Motors. 'I made it clear', wrote Sir William years later, with a perfectly straight pen, 'that whilst I appreciated it was a low offer it was the maximum to which I was prepared to go'. The sum that the receiver put to the bank was £800,000. Sir Donald Stokes was one man who had looked at Guy and gone away again.

Sydney Guy had resigned as works manager of Sunbeam at the end of 1913 and set up in business nearby, in the Fallings Park district of Wolverhampton. Guy trucks and passenger vehicles gained a good reputation quickly. The company even made cars for a few years. Guy made trolleybuses, too, and in 1947—ten years before Sydney Guy's retirement—acquired the Sunbeam Trolleybus Company. The trolleybus market was dead when Sir William Lyons came along in 1961, but it was ironic that Jaguar now owned a company called 'Sunbeam' in view of his pre-war experience. The vehicles were good but the balance sheets were not; Guy had been losing nearly £300,000 a year. Arthur Jones, formerly general manager, was made Managing Director of the new Guy organisation. Elliot was transferred from Daimler to be responsible for engineering, ably assisted by Ernest Clarke. Soon James Johnson, an ex-Foden man who would get the top job later, was brought in to run sales; he was assisted by David Griffiths. Guy Motors was revitalised, and a new truck and tractor unit range was ready for the 1964 commercial show. It was called the Big J—the 'Big Jaguar'—and produced for nearly 15 years. Although disguised as 'Leylands', Guy truck and bus chassis were still being made for export in the 1980s, though not at Wolverhampton.

Early in 1962 there had been warnings from Sir William Lyons and from the Chancellor of the Exchequer, Selwyn Lloyd, about the effects of wage demands and inflation on industry.

Acquisition No 3: Fire pump engines and fork-lift trucks may have been the bread and butter of Coventry Climax but, when Jaguar took it over in early 1963, the small but famous firm had already won two Grand Prix World Championships, thanks to the cars of John Cooper and the driving of Jack Brabham. Coventry Climax were to stay in racing for three more seasons, during which Jimmy Clark was to win the Championship twice, in Lotus cars. Left to right: Leonard Lee, whose father had founded the company soon after the turn of the century, Jim Clark, Colin Chapman of Lotus, and Walter Hassan who, as a result of this merger, effectively 'returned' to Jaguar for the third time in his career! The engine is the highly-successful 1½-litre V8 Coventry Climax GP engine, designated FWMV ('feather weight marine vee').

One of many experimental projects carried out by Jaguar Engineering was the mid-engined XJ13, with Sayer body made up (as a 'one-off' only) by Abbey Panels of Coventry. Engineers most involved in the project and its development were George Buck (power units) and Michael Kimberley who went on to become Managing Director of Lotus. It was never raced, but it made the Guinness Book of Records *after lapping the motor industry test track (MIRA) at over 161 mph in 1967—still the highest recorded lap speed for an enclosed circuit in Britain. The V12 engine was a 5-litre 4 ohc unit (code-named 'XJ6'!) producing over 500 bhp; a road-going version was tested in a Mk X, but never produced commercially.*

'This rat race must stop if we are going to continue as an important part of the industrial world', said Sir William, at the annual apprentices prize-giving ceremony. 'If it does not, then our competitive position collapses and our expanded facilities become superfluous if not redundant.' As Jaguar continued to grow, chief accountant Arthur Thurstans was given a place on the board. S.E. Aston from Daimler had effectively taken over as company secretary from E.F. Huckvale whose death in 1962 was a particular loss to Lyons; Huckvale was 73 and had been ill for some time.

On March 7 1963 Sir William Lyons and Leonard Lee announced to their respective employees that Coventry Climax Engines Ltd would become part of the Jaguar Group—with Lee remaining Managing Director and deputy chairman under Lyons. His father, H. Pelham Lee, had begun the family business with a partner in 1903; and Leonard Lee had developed the fire pump and fork-lift truck businesses which had become the company's main products. His enthusiasm had led to the design and construction of racing engines from 1954, and these had powered Jack Brabham's works Cooper cars to victory in the 1959 and 1960 Grand Prix world Championships. (They were to do so again for Jim Clark and Lotus in 1963 and 1965. With 96 wins to their credit, Coventry Climax engines still rate third only to Cosworth and Ferrari in Formula One racing history.) With Coventry Climax came an excellent technical team, led by Walter Hassan, who had become a member of Lee's board. Like the members of both boards, Hassan had not been consulted; he had read about the merger in the *Coventry Evening Telegraph*. Only afterwards did Lee tell him that he had been looking for a

Above *The XJ13, photographed at MIRA, driven by Norman Dewis. Did it inspire the American-built XJR-5? It was, after all, the only Coventry-made Jaguar with its engine in the middle.*

Serious consideration was given to creating a mid-engined road car, following the XJ13 exercise. An early 'rough' (below) led to this interesting Malcolm Sayer model (left) which had alternative tail treatments. American alloy craftsman and foreman of Jaguar's styling workshop, Bob Blake, is seen showing what it might have been, at a New York seminar in 1976. In the end, it was the XJ-S that went into production.

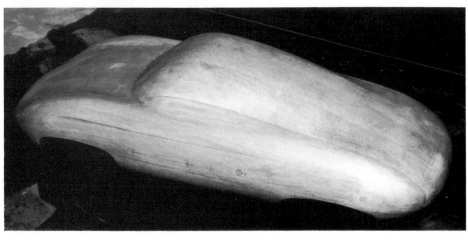

chance 'for some time' to combine continuity of Coventry Climax business with new owner-ship. Of all the companies acquired by Jaguar in the 1960s, 'The Climax' remains by far the most identifiable unit to this day. It was 'freed' from BL in 1982 and, under former Henly-Lansing-Bagnall man Stephen Grey's direction, Climax fork trucks are being produced independently once again.

Many of the Jaguar pioneers reached the end of their careers in the mid-60s. Eric Warren and Ben Mason retired as home and export sales managers, to be followed respectively by Alan Currie and John Morgan who already had eight years overseas experience with Rootes. Ernest (often called 'Bill') Rankin, was succeeded as public relations manager by Bob Berry, with John Rogers from Guy Motors looking after advertising and Fred Webber exhibitions. It did not seem so very long since Rankin had been doing all three jobs himself! Several new posts were created, one being industrial relations manager; senior sheet metalworkers' representative Harry Adey successfully crossed this 'fence'.

Record after record was broken as the Jaguar Group grew. Not every decision proved ad-vantageous, however. The purchase of Henry Meadows Ltd, Guy Motors' next door neigh-bours, late in 1964 was to prove pointless when Jaguar-Cummins Ltd—a link with the Columbus, Indiana, diesel engine makers—failed to materialise. The truck sales company, Richardson's of Oldbury, bought the site but did not use it. 'Jaguar-Cummins' reached the formation stage in April 1965, but soon afterwards it was realised that the Cummins VIM(V6) and VINE(V8) engines were not going to be suitable for the Guy Big J trucks or the Daimler Roadliner single-deck bus for which they were intended, and a plan to build the engines in Britain was dropped. Fortunately there were several alternative 'straight-six' diesels in the Big J range already, but despite attempts to revive it with a Perkins V8 power-unit, the Roadliner was to be dropped before long.

The motor-car business was progressing well, and—as the Coventry Climax racing programme ended—Wally Hassan returned to Jaguar as director in charge of power units. In 1964 he was instrumental in bringing in a former colleague Harry Mundy (who had been technical editor of *The Autocar* for eight years) as chief development engineer for Jaguar power units. Another Coventry Climax man, Peter Windsor-Smith, went to Daimler as chief bus engineer, following Cyril Simpson's retirement; his senior assistants were Frank Everitt and 'George' Fabel. With Claude Baily still very active as chief designer at Browns Lane, working mainly on V12 engines, the 'Jaguar Daimler Climax' organisation could claim to have the strongest team of engineers in the motor industry.

Sir William Lyons and his fellow directors were not getting any younger, yet it would not have been in anyone's nature to ask them what plans there were for Jaguar's future. Only Lyons, holder of 260,000 out of 480,000 voting shares, would have any idea; but there were no family ties now, with anyone he or his board might wish to nominate as his successor for personal reasons. To let the company grow bigger still, and yet to stay autonomous; these seem to have been the thoughts uppermost in Lyons' mind as, over the years, several of the great motor moguls came knocking at his door—not the least frequent of his callers being from a bus and truck factory situated not a million miles from where he had set out upon his own career. One thing was certain; Jaguar was beginning to make too many models. The E-type was doing very well, thank you, exceeding 200 units a week at the peak of its appeal. The saloon range, however, needed slimming down. Interim models were brought in to bridge the gap between the Mark Two and the Mark Ten, but they would soon be supplemented and/or succeeded by Lyons' ultimate Jaguar motor car. This was intended to be the car with the world's quietest and most refined riding qualities, bar none, and retain Jaguar's famous attributes of performance, controllability, comfort, and value for money.

The Jaguar XJ saloon would live up to all these requirements, and it does so today. Sir William Lyons knew it was going to be all right when, on July 11 1966, he and Sir George

Harriman made their joint statement: Jaguar Cars Ltd and the British Motor Corporation Ltd would merge. The irrevocable step had been taken.

The following is a list of directors of Jaguar Cars Ltd as it stood in the summer of 1966, immediately before the merger with the British Motor Corporation: *Chairman and Managing Director:* Sir William Lyons; *Deputy Chairman:* Arthur Whittaker; *Vice-Chairman (Engineering):* William Heynes; *Deputy Managing Directors:* Raymond England and Robert Grice; *Board Directors:* Leonard Lee, R. Lockwood, Alan Newsome, and Arthur Thurstans; and *'Executive' Directors:* Geoffrey Ball (work study), Claude Baily (power unit design), Jack Beardsley (Radford factory), Norman Benfield (Browns Lane factory), Robert Berry (press and public relations), Albert Brown (production), Alan Currie (home sales), Jack Earl (quality, Group), Walter Hassan (power unit engineering), Robert Knight (vehicle engineering), Bert Langley (planning), John McMillan (supplies, Group), John Morgan (export sales, nominally a separate company), Geoffrey Pindar (service), Harry Teather (purchasing), and William Thornton (body engineering).

The Jaguar group of companies consisted of the following, in 1966, at the time of the merger with the British Motor Corporation: Jaguar Export Sales Ltd; Jaguar-Cummins Ltd (50 per cent); SS Cars Ltd; The Daimler Company Ltd; The Lanchester Motor Company Ltd; Daimler Transport Vehicles Ltd; Barker and Co (Coachbuilders) Ltd; Hooper and Co (Coachbuilders) Ltd; Guy Motors Ltd; The Sunbeam Trolleybus Co Ltd; Coventry Climax Engines Ltd; Coventry Climax Electrics Ltd; Coventry Diesel Engines Ltd; Henry Meadows Ltd; Newtherm Oil Burners Ltd; and Badalini Transmissions Ltd (50 per cent). *Overseas:* Jaguar Cars Inc; Jaguar of New York Inc; Jaguar-Daimler Distributors Inc; Jaguar Cars (Canada) Ltd; and Coventry Climax Engines (Australia) Pty Ltd.

From the compact 2.4 of 1955 came the Mark Two, S-type and 420 Jaguars, all popular as high performance police cars. These S-types date from the mid 1960s.

14: The coming together
(1966 to 1972)

As well as having the continued helmsmanship of Sir William Lyons, Jaguar Cars Ltd was in a position of added strength during the early post-merger days by virtue of its strong future-model programme. Four months before the merger, 'with a view to co-ordinating manufacturing and general administration', Lyons had appointed England and Grice as joint deputy managing directors. At the same time Coventry Climax chief, Leonard Lee, and (ex-officio) R. Lockwood—who did auditing work for Lyons in Blackpool, following Mather's death—were nominated Jaguar board members, to be joined soon afterwards, in June 1966, by Alan Newsome, the solicitor. At the same time as those first two appointments, however, 16 senior men (see opposite) were officially appointed 'executive directors', in charge of specific functions within Jaguar Cars Ltd, and in several cases covering the whole Jaguar Group.

Awareness of the rapidity of Jaguar's growth, particularly during the previous decade, had resulted in developments designed to improve efficiency, especially on the international service side. Direct supply of parts from Coventry to distributors throughout the USA was one important step. Another was the formation of a new company (Jaguar Export Sales Ltd) with John Morgan as its director based at the works.

A traditional Jaguar policy was to come into its own before 1966 was through. As indicated in the previous chapter there would be a complicated 'pre-XJ' period in which Jaguar was to offer four six-cylinder engine sizes, four Jaguar saloon body types and three sports-car body types—quite apart from several Daimler equivalents—all at the same time. That policy was, simply to create desire through scarcity. This began by allocating distributors more cars than they were likely to get. Of course, this would 'stretch' company/trade relationships on occasions, for distributors would be taking a great risk if they 'cried wolf' by not having sufficient orders to meet their allocation. Close personal contact with the factory sales and service departments went a long way towards maintaining the distributors' goodwill.

In former years, Eric Warren had acted as the company's ambassador, keeping the wheels of UK trade oiled. His speciality was to get warring distributors together on 'neutral ground' to resolve territorial or other differences, and he was usually successful. In 1966 Alan Currie was in charge of home sales department, with William Benton and Anthony Cochrane as Northern and Southern managers. Cochrane, who now runs his own transport consultancy, is convinced that the key to Jaguar's consistent sales success lay in the Lyons edict—that no distributor or dealer should advertise any Jaguar product for 'immediate' or even 'early' delivery. If a distributor or dealer had a large stock of Jaguars for any reason, it was his duty to make sure that not more than one example of any model went into his showroom. Alice Fenton used to recount how the boss had once ticked her off, after hearing her happily confirm to a customer that his choice of SS car was available at once. 'You should have promised to *try* and help, then 'phoned him back an hour later, saying you'd been successful in finding a car to his specification', Lyons had told her. Such sales tactics may seem

unsophisticated now but they definitely worked and went on working. While the company expected great effort and loyalty from its distributors and dealers, it also took trouble to avoid telling them how to run their businesses. 'The tendency was to ask them what *Jaguar* could do, to help *them* sell more cars', says Cochrane, '*and* they would tell us.' The confidence and mutual respect were considerable. Even in the winter of 1966-7, with all those different models to sell and financial constraints everywhere, the Lyons marketing policy was maintained—naturally helped by the product's good value, in relation to the potential opposition—not that there was ever as much Jaguar or Daimler advertising as they would have liked.

The 1960s was a period of 'getting together' in many spheres. Large groups were being formed in the motor trade, and some well-known names disappeared as others became more prominent. Nelson Advertising was acquired by Benton and Bowles who made good use of the experience of Bob Bett and Eric Colbon; when they retired, 'B & B' retained the Jaguar UK business. (They would lose out to the John French Agency, finally, in 1983, by which time Dorlands would be handling Jaguar's overseas advertising other than in North America.)

At New Year, 1968, Sir William Lyons relinquished his title of Managing Director of the Jaguar Group; but he remained Chairman *and* Chief Executive. England and Grice now became joint managing directors. Arthur Whittaker was not well, and beginning to hand over responsibility for group supplies to John McMillan, whom he had brought from Wilmot Breeden to be his personal assistant in 1961; now McMillan joined the Jaguar board. Soon afterwards Louis Rosenthal, who had been managing director of Meadows, was put in charge of manufacturing at Jaguar and became a board-member, too. It was also in January 1968 that the British Leyland bombshell came. It was not what Sir William Lyons had wanted. He had hoped that the merger between Jaguar and BMC would provide the ideal answer for his company; but the snowball was already rolling on, and gaining momentum. He still felt that a united British motor industry would be the strongest one, however, for throughout his career he had shown his awareness of the threat from foreign competition; and in only one year (1940, following the purchase of Motor Panels) had his own company

Far left *Importer Charles Delecroix, Sir William Lyons and export director John Morgan introduce French President Charles de Gaulle to the XJ6 at the Paris motor show.*

Left *Arriving at Palm Springs to 'launch' the V12 E-type in 1971, Sir William is followed off the 'plane by retiring Jaguar man Johannes Eerdmans and, between them, Graham Whitehead, head of Jaguar Cars Inc today.*

Right *A 70th birthday portrait of Sir William, with Lady Lyons at Wappenbury in 1971, with their Norwich terriers.*

ever shown anything other than a good profit. On the other hand, Jaguar's new 'equal-status' partner, BMC, had just made a huge loss. Thus BMH was in a poor bargaining position during 1967, when Sir William Lyons spent much of his time trying to support Sir George Harriman *and* maintain autonomy for Jaguar. (*The Leyland Papers* by Graham Turner recorded the formation of British Leyland in a most dramatic way.)

In his message to everyone at Jaguar on January 19, 1968, (during the Brussels Motor Show, from which the British press rushed home, for no one in Belgium had the full story), Sir William Lyons stated that 'both BMH and Leyland are convinced that the merger is in the best interests of the country, the companies and all their employees'. He also stressed 'that Jaguar will be able to pursue its own course within the overall policy of the new corporation' and that he would (as a member of its board) 'promote our interests at the highest level'.

The British Leyland Motor Corporation became operational on May 14 1968, and on June 11 its first new model was announced. It was the new Daimler Limousine. Soon this massive vehicle would be offered to coachbuilders as a 'drive-away' chassis—for the specific use of undertakers . . . Despite the formation of British Leyland, plans for the XJ6 announcement were far enough advanced for this to be very much a 'Jaguar' occasion. Announced on September 26 1968, the car really *was* the culmination of all the ambitions Sir William Lyons had for the company he had founded; and the applause he received at London's Royal Lancaster Hotel, when the spotlight was switched on to him and his new creation, was spontaneous.

One interesting comment at the time of the XJ6's announcement that 'within the next two years it is intended to introduce new and additional power units' and indeed V12 and V8 engines were already in cars and on test—but only the V12 ever reached the production line, although the new machine tools were set-up to take either type. The XJ6 soon began winning accolades keeping Jaguar's name strong in all parts of the world. Among its most important successes was its nomination as 'Car of the Year 1969' by a *Car* magazine jury, and it won the 'Don' Safety Award soon afterwards. (The 'Don' panel also highly commen-

Leading lights of British Motor Holdings (1966-68): **Left to right** *BMC directors Lester Suffield, Ron Lucas, Joe Edwards (Managing), and Sir George Harriman (Chairman); then Sir William Lyons, the Morris Minor and Mini creator Alec Issigonis, and Pressed Steel-Fisher boss J.L. Lutyens. The linking of Britain's major body suppliers under BMC in 1965 had been influential in Lyons' agreement to the merger of BMC with Jaguar in 1966.*

ded the new Dennis ambulance with Jaguar 2.8-litre engine, but that Guildford product never got beyond the prototype stage.)

Towards the end of 1968, Arthur Whittaker went into full retirement. He had helped build the body for Walmsley's Austro-Daimler, he had been Swallow's first sales rep and he had become Deputy Chairman of the Jaguar Group. He was known throughout the industry for his business skill and fairness. Sir William Lyons described his contribution to the company as 'immeasurable'. Lofty England now became deputy chairman.

During the XJ6's early days, when production was taking time to get under way, a Series Two version of the E-type continued to sell well, helping to keep up export volumes. In 1969 Daimler was brought into line, with a 'fluted grille' XJ6; and 1970 saw the saloon range suddenly reduced to one shape—the XJ shape—as 420G production ended. By this time, Bill Heynes—now a CBE-holder among his many other achievements—had retired (mid-1969) after guiding Jaguar engineering so wisely for over 34 years. He was succeeded on the Jaguar board jointly, by Wally Hassan on the engine side and Bob Knight in charge of vehicle engineering. Walter Hassan, OBE, stayed on until he was 67, to see the arrival of the new Jaguar V12 engine. It had been very much 'his baby' and he was only sorry that it could not have had fuel injection from the outset; that was to come in 1975. Wally Hassan and Bob Grice retired on the same day, May 1 1972; The retirement of Arthur Thurstans, the financial chief, had happened ten months earlier. Lyons himself went (accompanied by Harry Mundy) to the American launch of the V12 E-type which also marked the virtual bowing-out of Jo Eerdmans in favour of Graham Whitehead, the English boss of BL's North American subsidiary.

1972 was, of course, jubilee year for the company and in conjunction with the Coventry authorities, the city's main art gallery was 'taken over' from spring to autumn by a comprehensive exhibition of Lyons' life and work, with rare vehicles loaned from far afield. It was to be the best-attended exhibition in the art gallery's history. Sir William and Lady Lyons opened this, and another 'Swallow anniversary' exhibition in Blackpool later in the year. Sir William was, after all, able to give some more time to such happenings now—for he himself had handed over the reins of office. He was well into his 71st year, and it was over 50 years since he and Walmsley had begun working together.

The 'official' anniversary was, of course, on September 4 1972. It must have come as no surprise to him, yet it still seems ironic that, within a month, 'Jaguar Cars Ltd' ceased to exist as a separate company. From October 1 1972, British Leyland's corporate policies and politics did at least still permit 'Jaguar' an identity, and an identifiable top man . . . but not for very long.

15: BL but unbowed! (1972 to 1980)

Of the few top men left at Jaguar, Lofty England was the natural successor to Sir William Lyons as Chairman and Chief Executive. Yet the 'youngster' of the Jaguar boardroom, was already 60 years of age. He knew that for Jaguar to retain any of the autonomy originally intended for it, a long-term successor for *him* must be found. England's start was not easy. Almost as soon as he had committed the company to a July launch for the latest Jaguar car, a strike was called. The longest previous strike had been an unofficial one of about five weeks during 1965 (over payment for door-window frame preparation); and as it had been unofficial, Lyons had followed his policy of 'no production, no discussion'. On the whole, Jaguar's labour relations record was above average.

The strike of 1972 was declared official, however, and it stopped Jaguar for over ten weeks in the middle of the year. Negotiation procedures had been exhausted, and the haggling over wages—related to the changeover from piecework to a flat rate pay scheme—dragged on and on. In the week prior to the company's 'official' 50th birthday, Sir William Lyons, in a statement to the *Coventry Evening Telegraph*, felt moved to spell-out his 'deep concern' about the company's prospects. An accompanying editorial described it as 'a masterly exposition of the fundamentals of industrial economics . . . it sets out in faultless logic everything that needs to be said about prices and wages. Anyone in Coventry who does not now understand does not want to'. Inflation and British Leyland were to conspire to dull such understanding for many years to come.

After things returned to normal, England was able to get down to a year of business con-

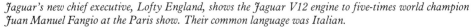

Jaguar's new chief executive, Lofty England, shows the Jaguar V12 engine to five-times world champion Juan Manuel Fangio at the Paris show. Their common language was Italian.

solidation for the XJ range; and, as if in tribute to Bob Knight, his two leading engineers Harry Mundy and Jim Randle, and the whole engineering team, the Jaguar XJ 12 was declared 'Car of the Year'. Thinking back to his Daimler apprenticeship, Lofty England chose a special name to identify the XJ 12 in Daimler form; Daimler had made a V12 before, like the one he had driven in the 1932 RAC Rally. It had been called the 'Double-Six' and that was the name England now revived. He also cherished the link forged with Vanden Plas in the BMH days, when the new limousine was being created. Now the co-operation of Roland Fox (who had succeeded his father as boss of the British Vanden Plas company) and his chief lieutenants—Harry Beshaw on engineering and Fred Onslow on production and sales—led to the introduction of a special luxury Daimler saloon for top businessmen and women not wishing to go as far as a Rolls-Royce in terms of price. (This may be badge-engineering, but no more so than Bentley and Rolls-Royce. If ever Jaguar presented too 'sporty' an aura for Britain's Prime Minister, the name 'Daimler', apparently, does not.)

Despite frequent interruptions and problems in the progress of his empire, Lord Stokes found time to come to Browns Lane to present the prizes at the annual apprentice day in April 1973. 'Jaguar is top of the British Leyland range and is going to stay there', he said. 'Jaguar Cars has tremendous opportunities for the future, at home and abroad . . . Jaguar needs British Leyland, but clearly British Leyland needs Jaguar and we intend to develop the company to its utmost.'

By this time, the most belligerent of Leyland's three deputies, South African and international specialist Jack Plane (whose London flat had been the scene of Sir George Harriman's final and apparently inevitable capitulation to Stokes in autumn 1968) had departed from the corporation—and was already sniping at it! This left former Ford and AEI man, and BL finance director since 1968, John Barber, vying with 'local boy' George Turnbull (who was doing what he could, to sort out the Austin Morris Group) for the job of 'next in line'. Meantime Lofty England, who believed in continuity and therefore 'overlapping succession', was trying to line up possible candidates who were already running car companies themselves. Not unnaturally, they told him they were happy where they were.

With another major BL shake-up in the offing, Stokes rang England at rather short notice

The last of the line!—this E-type has been kept for posterity by Jaguar. With it (left to right) are Peter Craig and Jack Randle, plant directors of Browns Lane and Radford respectively, sales director, Alan Currie, and chief executive, Geoffrey Robinson. The XK 120 is from the Jaguar collection, too. This picture was taken early in 1975.

Above left *Retirement has enabled Sir William to take a closer interest in his farms. Here he examines his 1977 championship-winning flock of Suffolk sheep.* **Above right** *George Lee and Harry Teather retired in 1976 and 1973 respectively. Both worked for Swallow in Blackpool. Between them they served the company for one hundred years.*

asking him to be chairman of Jaguar and for his agreement to bring in Geoffrey Robinson as Managing Director, although no date was fixed. That shake-up became public knowledge on September 7 1973, when it was announced that George Turnbull would leave the corporation 'by mutual consent', and the ripples went down the line—but Barber was now BL Managing Director under Stokes. The announcement included Geoffrey Robinson's appointment; it came shortly after Lofty England's return from Ellon, in Aberdeenshire, where the updated (Series Two) XJ models had been given their press previews. He was actually spending a few days in the Isle of Man, and received the news on the start line of one of the Manx Grand Prix races. Over the telephone he told the *Coventry Evening Telegraph*: 'I don't see any reason why I can't make Mr. Robinson into an 'England' man', and pointed out that his successor would have three years to be moulded into the Jaguar tradition. All this was overshadowed nationally by Turnbull's departure. His creation of a Korean car, the Hyundai, would keep Turnbull in the industry's headlines, however.

Geoffrey George Robinson—born in Sheffield in 1939 and therefore only 34 years old—was already Managing Director of Innocenti, then British Leyland's Milan factory. After national service in the Intelligence Corps, he had gained a BA in Russian and German at Cambridge and an Economics MA at Yale. Impressed by American politics in general and the Kennedy family in particular, he returned from the USA in 1963 and worked for the Labour Party until 1967. Then he joined the Industrial Reorganisation Corporation which had been formed with government backing to assist and promote mergers; thus Robinson obtained an extremely good view of British Leyland taking shape. The Conservatives were returned to Government in 1970, and soon wound up the IRC; John Barber had already offered him a job at British Leyland though, and in a very short time Robinson was made finance controller of British Leyland. May 1972, however, saw Robinson on his way to Italy, to run the Innocenti business—and teach himself another language! In the autumn of 1973, Stokes called him back to run Jaguar.

It did not take Lofty England long to realise that his 'three-year' plan was not going to work. He *had* expected the new man to come in *as* boss; after all, this is what Robinson had been in Italy. On the other hand he had accepted 'non-executive' Chairmanship of Jaguar in the belief that the newcomer would 'play his way in' and take advice. 'I am an old man', England had told the *Evening Telegraph* in his rather tongue-in-cheek way. 'We need to have a successor. It is no good walking out of the door on my last day to start looking for a new man.'

On October 25 1973, Geoffrey Robinson was telling Keith Read and Edward Townsend—*The Coventry Evening Telegraph*'s motor industry men—that his aims were to continue to pay good wages, to improve facilities, and generate the profits to pay for them. 'As chief executive, all executive responsibility is invested in me. Lofty and I have an excellent working relationship and there are many areas where his advice and experience are necessary.' The story concluded: 'My aim is to stay longer at Jaguar than the corporation has let me stay so far in other jobs. I cannot think yet of a better place to spend my working life. I have a good group of colleagues and all the employees have a genuine interest and pride in the company'.

The first 'fuel crisis' was already beginning to bite when, in December, Robinson addressed a meeting in Coventry, at which he spoke of a £60-million investment plan to raise Jaguar output from 30,000 to 60,000 cars a year by the end of 1975 *and* build in 'flexibility' to increase that to 90,000 'if necessary' at a later date. As it involved plans to expand into a green belt—the 'wedge' of land between Browns Lane (Allesley) and Coundon—the meeting was public and reported nationally. Robinson devoted himself to work, basing himself just a mile from the factory in the Post House Hotel. When not dealing with Jaguar matters he was continuing to handle Innocenti problems or discussing the future of the local Triumph motorcycle works, the demise of which he would be instrumental in postponing.

In January 1974, Lofty England announced that he would retire. 'It must be done; it makes sense', he told Keith Read, who asked him if he felt that five months (it had been even less!) had been sufficient time for Robinson to settle-in. 'Yes, he has been chief executive

Sir William and Lady Lyons with Jaguar craftsmen Bill Burke, Frank Burrell, Robin Coleman and Roy Mitchell at Jaguar's woodwork and trim display—part of the 1978 Town and Country Festival at Stoneleigh.

Wappenbury Hall, Sir William's home since 1937. The car is the Series Three XJ6, launched in 1979.

before', answered England. 'He has the ability and energy to do the job at Jaguar'. What he did not say was that he felt Robinson was trying to 'achieve the impossible in five minutes' and had probably been told to do so.

While England set off on a final tour of overseas agencies, Robinson completed his management re-shuffle at Browns Lane. Only two Jaguar men—Alan Currie (who had joined the board 18 months earlier, just before Jaguar had ceased to be a 'real' company) and Bob Knight—were nominated for Robinson's seven-man 'management board'. This is how George Pritchard reported the changes in the *Coventry Evening Telegraph* on February 27 1974:

'Three former senior executives with the Ford Motor Company are now part of the top management at Jaguar Cars. And two of the three are members of the seven-man management board led by Mr. Geoffrey Robinson.

'Their moves to the Coventry company are part of a considerable shake-up in higher management which has taken place since Mr. Robinson's arrival in October as Jaguar's managing director and chief executive.

'The men from Ford are Mr. R. Lindsay who has been appointed manufacturing director, Mr. I. Forster, purchase director; and Mr. S. Keyworth, staff director for production planning and control.

'With the creation of a new management team completed at Jaguar, the Coventry company are geared up for modernisation and expansion, says Mr. Robinson.

'And, he adds, there is within the company a spirit of co-operation and contentment, with interest evident all round as plans are made to increase production substantially when conditions again permit.

'Along with Mr. England, Mr. L.W. Rosenthal (who was manufacturing director), Mr. J. Butterworth (purchase director) and Mr. J. Ashworth (plant director, Radford) have retired since October 1, 1973.

'All were near or over 60 years of age, Mr. Robinson points out.'

Like Rosenthal, Ashworth was a former Meadows man; he had been in charge of the Radford works since Jack Beardsley's retirement in 1969. Jim Butterworth had succeeded Harry Teather only a few months earlier, for Teather had reached 65 in the summer of 1973 when he retired as Executive Director, Purchasing. He had served Jaguar longer than anyone: and it was a sad effect of the changes in Jaguar that he, of all people, was happy to be leaving. Of his own departure early in 1974 England says: 'I was no longer enjoying my work which had always been so rewarding in the past'. Other notable departures included those of Jack Earl (Charles Newcombe's successor in charge of quality), and finance chief David Jenkins, who had succeeded Arthur Thurstans. They were given 'corporate' jobs. 'Jaguar was already a successful company. I did not come with any preconceived ideas of reorganisation. But I do believe that one of my skills is that I am not bad at leading people', Robinson told David Dunckley of the *Birmingham Post* soon afterwards. Indeed, on paper, 1974 *was* a year of high output, despite the oil crisis and the three-day week—but it was achieved without the promised improvement in quality; and later, a team of fitters was sent to America to 'update' the stockpile. The two-door XJ models were not hurried on to the production lines; their wide doors and complex window-winding and sealing had taken a lot of engineering and production development, and they were not as straight-forward to build as the four-door XJs.

It is not possible to assess what might have happened if the Robinson regime had been allowed to continue. His was an energetic team and some of his plans did begin to bear fruit; however, the planned investment, even short term, far exceeded any sum a private 'Jaguar-sized' company could expect to have available at any one time for expansion. Even today, there seem to be people who work on the principle that a bottomless pit is still there to be drawn from, somewhere on BL's barren wastes.

Robinson pressed ahead with his massive expansion plan, and in October 1974 it looked as if the Coventry and West Midland planners would approve it. Then the whole programme was 'frozen' while Sir Don Ryder's investigation team (appointed on December 18 by Anthony Wedgewood Benn, after it had been discovered that BL already had net liabilities of £43 million) explored the tottering empire prior to making its fateful recommendations. Ironically, it was Robinson's manufacturing director, Robert Lindsay, who was reported in the *Coventry Evening Telegraph* on January 23 1975 as saying '. . . we would be far better off on our own. This is a profitable company, and it will remain so'. As a former Ford man, he must have been frustrated at recognising the names of some of Ryder's advisers.

Soon, John Barber had resigned and Lord Stokes was no longer in charge. Having already upset them by jumping the gun on some of his projects, Robinson now found himself thoroughly thwarted. The Ryder report, parts of which were published on April 23 1975, made it clear that Jaguar would not continue as an entity. The job of 'chief executive of Jaguar' was not, therefore, part of the Ryder plan, either—nor was a Jaguar 'management board'. This was contrary to Robinson's strongly-voiced aspirations for Jaguar. The 'board' had to disband, and Robinson resigned. Later, following the death of Maurice Edelman, MP, Geoffrey Robinson was elected Labour Member of Parliament for Coventry North-West. How could the young man fail? His shop-floor popularity had been considerable, *and* the two main Jaguar plants were in what is still his constituency.

At this point Leyland Cars was formed and Jaguar ran the risk of losing its way altogether. A Jaguar 'operating committee' was announced by new car chief Derek Whittaker, with Cowley manufacturing man Tony Thompson 'in the chair'. Unfortunately circumstances and politics conspired to prevent that 'committee' from 'operating', especially as the Radford and Browns Lane factories were now being managed from different corporate centres. Somehow, several Jaguar cornerstones managed to avoid being totally wrecked by the swinging ball of destruction; but, for the first time, Jaguar and Daimler did not have their

Masters of the power game—Harry Mundy, who retired in 1980, with his former colleague, Walter Hassan.

own motor show stands, and the brand new XJ-S (so nearly misnamed 'XK-F') was bunged in with BL's other Earls Court offerings.

One man who fought long and hard to keep enthusiasm and *marque* pride going at Jaguar was Browns Lane plant director, Peter Craig. Apprenticed as a coachmaker in Scotland, Craig came south and, after a brief period at Standard, joined SS cars in 1941 and worked on 'Stirling' bomber wings. After several years at war, he returned to what was now Jaguar, and began to work his way 'up the tree'. After Robinson's departure he used diplomacy as well as persistence to keep a Jaguar aura at 'his' factory and undoubtedly succeeded. Against all 'corporate' thinking, he even re-introduced a small works newspaper, called *Jaguar Topics*. The saddest aspect of it was his own obituary in the first edition. Derek Whittaker had come to know him well. When Peter Craig died after what had been hoped would be a simple operation in February 1977, Whittaker wrote: 'He worked tirelessly to promote the image of Jaguar—an image of which he was so rightly proud'. There were many other tributes, too. Also recorded in the new newspaper was the retirement of George Lee (in 1976), superintendent of the sawmill and last 'Blackpool man' of all to leave.

While whole departments, such as sales and service, had disappeared into the amorphous corridors of BL power, one had remained aloof—Jaguar Engineering. Since Wally Hassan's retirement in 1972, Bob Knight had been in command and remained a board director (whenever there *was* a Jaguar board). Geoffrey Robinson had called him his 'right hand'. When Robinson had gone, Knight insisted upon reporting direct to Derek Whittaker. In the period of general acceptance of the Ryder team's recommendations, maintaining this arrangement took up a great deal of Knight's time, but it ensured a very positive identity for his department, and therefore for the Jaguar motor car itself. A quiet man and a profound thinker, Bob Knight has great resilience, commands loyalty, and usually keeps his puckish sense of humour just below the surface. The story of the BL 'headshrinker' who placed 'Quick Decision-Making' high on the list of his attributes is one that Knight often tells against himself. His achievements did bring their rewards, with a CBE in January 1977 and, a year later, the post of Managing Director—of Jaguar Cars.

Recognition of the term 'Jaguar Cars' was something new. Indeed a new broom *was* sweeping through the corporation. Derek Whittaker and Lord Stokes's successor, Alex Park, soon left the impossible tasks imposed upon them by the now-discredited 'Ryder Plan' when Michael Edwardes became the new man at the top towards the end of 1977. Not only was the long battle for Jaguar engineering integrity won but, in due course, Knight was able to rescue the essential and essentially personal customer service function and bring it back from Oxford to Coventry, to be run by Neville Neal. On the manufacturing side, Knight was ably backed by Peter Craig's young successor, Michael Beasley.

There was still no single head man at Jaguar, however. The difficulty could have been foreseen back at New Year 1978, when Michael Edwardes—so soon to be granted knighthood—announced his 'recovery plan' for the nationalised corporation. From then on, the word 'Leyland' would mean 'commercial vehicles' once more, car marque names *would* be cherished after all, and the company would seek a kind of anonymity for itself as a whole behind the letters BL. That was the overall plan.

The detail was less simple. There were to be two bosses of the car-making business. Ray Horrocks and Pratt Thompson were the new men, replacing Derek Whittaker. Horrocks was to run Austin Morris, while the quiet American, William Pratt Thompson, set up his headquarters at Browns Lane with the intention of making his ragged-edged conglomeration work—as Jaguar Rover Triumph Ltd. Sadly but inevitably the attempt to combine the so-called 'specialist' marques was doomed, neat though the idea might look 'on paper'. The JRT plan was dropped within two years of its formation, and Thompson moved to a BL international post in London without getting to know Jaguar people at all. Once again, the 'front offices' of Jaguar were empty, and the winter of 1979-80 saw nominal chairmanship of Jaguar (among various other functions) fall to Percy Plant, best known at that period for his skill at closing factories down. Jaguar needed bucking-up more than ever. A full-time chairman must be found, and Plant was as anxious as the next man to appoint one.

Jaguar employees' feeling of 'detachment' came to a head when assembly workers went on strike over grading and pay on April 9 1980. Shortly afterwards they heard Sir Michael Edwardes's ultimatum: return to work or lose your jobs. With rumours of Jaguar assembly being moved to Solihull or even stopping, morale at Jaguar over Easter 1980 was as low as it had been when Ryder published his plan five years before.

*   *   *

Like Browns Lane, the Banner Lane factory, just west of Coventry, was built as a 'shadow' factory. Standard-Triumph sold it to Massey-Harris Ferguson in 1959. Subsequently an imposing tower block was built in front of the works, overlooking acres of school playing-field. From his office high above, John Egan could see a cross-section of the youth of Coventry, traditional home of Britain's proud motor industry. He had been educated there himself, at the famous Bablake School, and felt a strong attachment to the city. He had qualified well—as a petroleum engineer with Shell *and* gaining a master's degree in business studies. As an engineer and as a businessman, he had grown in stature

Below far left *Technical Director, later Managing Director of Jaguar Cars, Bob Knight, who retired in 1980.* **Below left** *James Randle, Director of Product Engineering, seen with the Group 44 racing team, 1984* (James J. Ellis).

Right *Jaguar's first full-time chief executive for five years, John Egan, came from parts directorship of Massey Ferguson Construction & Machinery Division in April 1980 at the age of 40. He was educated in Lancashire, in Coventry and at London University. He began as a petroleum engineer with Shell, then gained an MSc at the London Business School. Later he was General Manager of AC-Delco (GM) UK parts division before joining BL in its early days. After making his name as the force behind 'Unipart', he went to Massey Ferguson in 1976. In his first few weeks at Browns Lane it seemed there was a new hum in the air . . . an optimistic hum! His first 'quote' was: 'One cannot have better ground to build on'.*

with GM's AC-Delco organisation and gone on to create 'Unipart' for British Leyland. In the bleak mid-70s he moved on again. Now it was spring 1980, and he had become older and wiser as a globe-trotting top executive for Massey-Ferguson. He was happy, too, but the offer in his pocket was tempting him, against his better judgement . . . . He watched the children at play across the fields. A month or so later he was talking to Keith Read of the *Coventry Evening Telegraph:* 'I thought: "What are these kids going to have if someone doesn't do something about the motor industry? They can't all go on the dole".'

Forty-year-old John Egan had spent four months making up his mind about becoming top man at Jaguar. Thoughts of Coventry's future, as well as his own, helped him reach his decision. He moved into Sir William's office at Browns Lane quietly. He spent the whole of Saturday and Sunday, April 26 and 27 with shop stewards, union officials and managers and, after those two long days of persuasion, a small majority vote set the production lines in motion. What Egan had done was, simply, to declare his personal commitment to Jaguar. He had no other business interests, either in BL or elsewhere. 'I know the underlying dedication, loyalty, and enthusiasm of the Jaguar workforce', he said, making them no promises, but asking for time; for he had found himself in sympathy with the strikers' sentiments if not their actions.

Later, Egan told the *Evening Telegraph* that he would 'certainly not leave before getting results . . . I'm not interested in any other job'. The statements had a faintly familiar ring to them; but there was nothing wild in Egan's ambition. His persistence and dedication have proved infectious. The final chapter is a happy one . . .

16: The new beginning (1980 to 1985)

John Egan's sheer enthusiasm was effective at once, and his presence as a full-time 'Mr Jaguar' was soon reflected in morale and productivity. He was clearly proud to be following in the steps of Sir William Lyons and Lofty England. In a letter to the *Coventry Evening Telegraph* in 1976, England had written from retirement in Austria at a time when he felt a reminder of Sir William's achievements was badly needed. Since his arrival in Coventry, Lyons had (he wrote) 'steadily built up its production and activities when other companies were failing, was personally responsible for the concept of the cars Jaguar produced, gave employment to many thousands of people in Coventry, and was largely responsible for the company's export achievements . . . .'

On his arrival at Jaguar, John Egan was quick to say that his difficulties would not be as great as those Sir William Lyons had faced. Very soon he was following the famous practice of taking a new car home at night, picking it at random and reporting on it next day; and he was encouraging his new team to share his enthusiasm. One of the first jobs he tackled was the all-important one of controlling body manufacture and paint quality—a bigger priority than ever, following an unsatisfactory changeover to a new paint-shop and thermo-plastic acrylic paint in 1979. All the while, Egan realised the urgent psychological need for a 'father figure' at Jaguar and did not shirk the role. Initially, he never reached his far destinations within the factory; he made time to stop and talk to people and listen to what they had to tell him.

It was to be over a year before the most dangerous threat—that of Jaguar's total closure—went away.

Well received at its Torquay launch in 1979, the Series Three—its 'Sir William' contours enhanced by a new, crisp, Italian-inspired roofline—met universal praise. Things were different in the showroom, however. A limited colour range drew attention to the big problem—that of painting bodies at the Castle Bromwich (Birmingham) factory, well away from Jaguar's traditional Browns Lane headquarters. What colours there were lacked sparkle—quite literally—and the finish was not always consistent either. However, Jaguar was permitted control of the factory (formerly part of Fisher & Ludlow, then Pressed Steel Fisher) and, after completion of the latest Triumph TR7 sports-car bodies, Castle Bromwich became a Jaguar-only operation. The low-bake technique was discarded, and in due course the Browns Lane body paint 'hospital' would be closed down altogether. Transportation damage problems were overcome, and a computer-controlled body storage system was installed at Browns Lane. In its hour of most need, Jaguar was beginning to acquire responsibilities more akin to an independent company than to a division of a corporation.

Still shouldering these responsibilities, Manufacturing Director Michael Beasley reckons that the successful integration of Castle Bromwich into the Jaguar system, under the management of Gerard ('Gerry') Lawlor, was essential to the marque's survival.

Lawlor's 'opposite numbers' at Browns Lane and Radford respectively are Walter Turner and Eynon Thomas, the latter having taken on the job in the summer of 1985, succeeding Jack Randle who had completed 50 years with the company—apart from a brief break in his service between 1939 and 1940. Other senior production men to have worked through from 1940 are Raymond Barradell, Cyril Burdett, Thomas Harman, and William Stanton. Quality Manager Bill Stanton was 14-years-old when he joined Daimler in 1937. He and many of his colleagues could see the unreality of *Quality '77* and its successors—campaigns aimed at achieving identical quality standards throughout British Leyland. The communicative Japanese-style discussion groups introduced in 1980 have been much more effective in co-ordinating the Jaguar quality programme.

Stan Parkes, head of production purchasing—another essential 'quality control' area, now overseen by Patrick Audrain—was also 14 when he arrived at SS Cars Ltd in 1938. 1940 starters include Fire Chief Officer Alf Baker and Group Chief Vehicle Engineer Tom Jones, who still remembers his first job on the Swallow sidecar drawing board. Mid-1980 saw the retirement of enigmatic Robert Knight. It is difficult to imagine anyone else achieving what he had achieved, for he had preserved a Jaguar engineering core throughout the late 1970s against the gigantic corporate pressures. Without him, it may be that Jaguar would not have come through the holocaust, as it has done, in a manner that is unique in the industry. For that work, as much as for his engineering capabilities, Bob Knight holds a special place in the history of this great British car. Earlier when Knight took on the less-familiar role of Managing Director, Jim Randle became his natural successor in charge of vehicle engineering.

Jim Randle (47 in 1985) had been a Rover apprentice, moving to Jaguar in 1965 when it was still an independent company—so he has seen every phase of BL's development while playing his part in ensuring that no BL insignia were ever allowed to appear on production Jaguars. Long service is a feature of every department. Board director in charge of vehicle quality, David Fielden, was an apprentice with the company in the 1950s—as was Trevor Crisp who took over power unit engineering when the legendary Harry Mundy retired in late 1980.

Broadening the scope of Jaguar's engineering resources has led to the creation of a number of new functions; and by the mid-1980s there was a resident engineering team in North America where so much product test work takes place.

Where John Egan found long experience he put it to good use, and this was emphasised by the continuity of management after his first five years in office. When he arrived in April 1980, however, there were some key functions over which he was not given immediate control. He had to prove himself. The most significant of these areas were those of sales and marketing, which remained within a complex BL structure. There were, however, two men from the 1960s' Jaguar team who could be nominated for return to the fold almost immediately. Bob Berry, once tipped as the man most likely to run Jaguar, returned from Austin-Morris and BL International marketing; but it was not a satisfactory situation for him, to have one foot in BL's camp and one in Jaguar's. He was head-hunted successfully by Alfa Romeo however and, by late 1980, was seen to be putting his characteristic gusto into selling the famous but flawed Italian marque to sporting Britishers—not the easiest of jobs. In 1982 he moved into the retail motor trade.

The other Jaguar front-man to 'come home' (and he has stayed) was John Morgan whose diplomatic powers are backed by a wealth of practical experience around the world. His return from BL in Japan to lead the redevelopment of Jaguar markets in Europe was a positive move which helped the mood of growing confidence. Further 1980 appointments included Kenneth Edwards—the only member of Geoffrey Robinson's 1974 Jaguar hierarchy to return to Browns Lane—as Company Secretary and Personnel Director; and the unrelated John Edwards with whom Egan had worked at Massey-Ferguson's European parts operation. Then only 31, John Edwards was made Finance Director and pitched in at the deep end. Very deep it was too. For the first time in five years, some figures had to be produced and they were not a pretty sight. Just how the next five years' figures would change the face of Jaguar will be found towards the end of this chapter.

It was not just the quality drive that changed the face of Jaguar. The energy crisis of the 1970s had led to a number of dubious assumptions. One such assumption was that the V12 engine would be phased-out by the early '80s. (There was even a scheme to 'tide-over' the XJ-S by installing an XK engine.) Possibly the most important single false premise, thankfully erased, was one pointed out to me by Nigel Heslop, staff director in charge of product planning, who came to Jaguar from Rover in 1978: there was a feeling that every new BL model had to be an *all*-new model, from a clean sheet of paper. Jaguar, he believes, has proved that a whole range can be re-vitalised and remain modern with relatively few tangible alterations. The age old theory of progress through evolution holds good today, and as strongly as it ever did.

This does not necessarily apply in the racing world. The one place where Jaguar was able to capitalise on racing success in the 1970s was North America, and this was achieved through Group 44, a team created in the early 1960s to race Triumph TR sports cars. From 1974, V12 E-types prepared by Group 44 (and to a lesser degree by Huffaker of California) proved capable of defeating the Corvettes then dominating SCCA national events. Group 44 founder Robert Tullius, having won a championship in 1975, began a serious XJ-S development project which led to further victories and titles; this helped Jaguar sales when BL's reputation in the USA was approaching rock-bottom. As BL's import company ran out of models to sell, support for Bob Tullius had to be curtailed. In 1980, Group 44 was on the point of being wound-up and Tullius was thinking in terms of some new kind of specialisation. Then, through the two Englishmen, Graham Whitehead and Michael Dale—who had served BL's interests so energetically from their Leonia, New Jersey base for so long—Tullius and Egan met. Soon a new competition car was being created by the Tullius team, with Jaguar finance and the special skills of designer Lee Dykstra.

The result was an American-built Jaguar V12-powered car, well-suited to the IMSA category of GT prototype racing. It was named the XJR-5 and, although American, treated as a Jaguar car—and why not? Its aura, its inspiration, and its engine were related directly to the Coventry product as propounded in the exciting but unproved XJ 13 of an earlier time. (See photographs on pages 159, 160, 240 and 244.)

In August 1982 the XJR-5 was third on its debut at Elkhart Lake, Wisconsin, where Phil Hill had given the C-type *its* first American outing with a first *and* a third place exactly thirty years earlier. In 1983 Group 44 won four races and many more high placings and Bob Tullius finished the season as runner-up in the IMSA GT championship. More success followed in 1984. There was an underplayed (but, inevitably, much-publicised) 'return' to Le Mans where two XJR-5s performed with great credit—but a minor crash and a 'lost' gear prevented either making it all the way to the finish. The XJR-5 has done much to rekindle the spirit and rebuild the image of Jaguar at home and abroad, even though no production-model concept of the foreseeable future is likely to bear any relationship to it—except, perhaps, in fuel economy, a significant aspect of today's racing.

The European scene was changing as rapidly as the American one. While Tullius was racing the E-type and XJ-S in the USA and Canada, Jaguar made sure that the XJ-S would not be eligible for Group Two in Europe—although it *could* have been done, no doubt. The reason was that Jaguar engineers wanted no part of BL's touring car racing plans. At a time when the market-losing corporation was in need of any favourable publicity it could get, however, tuner-engineer Ralph Broad (who had often declared that he could make the V12 Jaguar a race winner) persuaded the directors of BL Cars to put the XJ 12 into Group Two. Hundreds of thousands of pounds were spent in 1976-77, but the car won no races and was withdrawn. If Jaguar's engineers had thought that BL would consider homologating the XJ 12 for competition, it is logical to suppose they would have found a way of preventing that, too.

Only after Egan's arrival did a European race plan begin to make sense again. The co-incidence was the introduction of Group A for 1982, by which time the Scots businessman and racing driver Tom Walkinshaw had been given tentative factory approval to race the XJ-S in European Touring Car Championship events. Group A brought car specifications somewhat nearer to standard than those of previous international touring car formulae. It was Walkinshaw who convinced John Egan and Jim Randle that, despite severe fuel-capacity and weight handicaps (in relation to engine size), the XJ-S could be competitive in European Touring Car Championship races. With sponsorship from Motul Oil and, later, from Jaguar itself, the TWR-prepared XJ-S cars won an ever-increasing number of events. Third in 1982 and a close runner-up the following year, Walkinshaw finally broke the BMW stranglehold by becoming European Touring Champion of 1984—the first Jaguar driver to take the title for 21 years.

Thirty years earlier, racing could influence road car design. The Jaguar-Dunlop disc brake was a classic example, and so was the E-type—a direct descendant of the D-type, three times a Le Mans winner. Nowadays the main purpose of racing is purely to promote sales. When the XJR-5 and the Group A XJ-S were being conceived, back in 1981, sales were needed—desperately—or Jaguar might yet be closed down. The catalyst for confidence proved to be a 1981 visit by North American dealers. The new internal communicating system throughout the works helped to ensure that all cynicism was met with an air of enthusiasm and optimism and by the end of their stay the US traders had assured John Egan that they would take virtually twice as many cars the following year. The great 'turnaround', as it is generally called, had happened. (See pages 241 and 244.)

Things did not improve quite so rapidly on the home front. I had the fascinating experience of visiting most of the main UK agents in 1981 (in connection with the first edition of this book). Then, the contrast between those who behaved as if there was a future for Jaguar and those who did not was probably at its most marked.

In December 1981, Egan was permitted to appoint a full-time sales and marketing director—Neil Johnson, formerly of BL International. At his first BL dealer council meeting as a Jaguar man, in March 1982, he startled delegates by announcing Jaguar's new policy: there would be a drastic reduction in the number of dealers. Respect for history *might* play a part in deciding who would stay, but no dealer had an automatic right to the Jaguar franchise—he must earn it by meeting special standards applicable to all. These standards would be judged by one of six regional managers then being appointed to work under a new UK sales operations director, Roger Putnam, who came over from Lotus in July 1982.

There was no respect for groups. If Bloggs Motors was good enough in one town but not in another, the bad branch would lose its Jaguar and Daimler franchises. Some have proved able to renew their own faith in Jaguar and been, as Neil Johnson puts it, 'born again'. Others have gone; and all the time, the idea of the Jaguar car as something special is developing once more. A big question mark hung over one company—Henlys, the firm without which Jaguar Cars may never have existed at all—for it came under new ownership in late 1984 and the form of its own development was still not clear when this edition went to press. Meanwhile, a franchise development fund was introduced. By ploughing back 3½ percent (of dealers' 18½ percent) discount into the best parts of the network, Jaguar found dealers' standards continuing to improve—things had moved a long way from the days when high-cost pre-delivery and service work had discouraged some agents from retaining their Jaguar franchise at all.

In other parts of the world, the same kind of specialisation was taking place. In some countries it was possible to return to a previous situation. In the USA, the old name 'Jaguar Cars Inc' came out of cold storage, to operate from the existing BL premises in New Jersey, just across the Hudson River from New York City. Graham Whitehead, Michael Dale, and their team could concentrate upon Jaguar matters, while also fulfilling the obvious residual obligations for such famous marques (defunct in North America) as MG and Triumph. Whitehead, once a Wolseley apprentice and today a director of Jaguar plc, is also responsible for Jaguar Canada Inc which, in its BL guise, had taken on the distribution of Saab cars and parts.

The process of providing specialised representation around the world continues, and when this edition went to press there were still many fluid situations. One country—West Germany—deserves special mention because it produces Jaguar's main rival products and has by far the biggest potential for vehicles in Jaguar's sector of the European market. Yet, under BL rule, Jaguar was in greater disarray there than almost anywhere, with a reputation for poor service and un-caring representation. Drastic action was taken in 1983, with the formation of Jaguar Deutschland GmbH as a joint company between Jaguar and Walter Frey Holding AG. (As recorded earlier, Walter Frey's father, Emil, was the first person to represent Swallow abroad.) The early indications were that Germany was becoming one of Jaguar's biggest growth markets and Neil Johnson had a target of ten percent of its luxury car market—something over five thousand cars a year—by 1990. (Further details of Jaguar's export market development can be found in Appendix XXII.)

The new AJ6 3.6-litre engine was announced in Autumn 1983. Other major investments included a collaboration agreement on the use of Dainichi Kiko robot technology for long-term new-model programmes. In an editorial on October 25 1983, the *Coventry Evening Telegraph* referred to robotics: 'It's the way industry has to go if it intends to compete for the customer's money. "Without it," as John Egan so incisively put it, "there would be no tomorrow." Encouragingly, Jaguar's faith in its future is backed by the assurance of Government cash, supporting MP John Butcher's promises of last week. So much for former Jaguar boss and MP Geoffrey Robinson's scornful dismissal of the government's intention as so much baloney.'

Unintentionally echoing a Porsche slogan, Jaguar had been campaigning the 'Pursuit of Perfection' throughout the build-up of a new sales and marketing department at Browns Lane. Prior to launching the six-cylinder AJ6 engine for the XJ-S, several advertising agencies were invited to tender for Jaguar's business—including Benton & Bowles. As a result, they relinquished the Jaguar-Daimler account to the F. John French agency which won the contract for a new theme ('The Legend Grows') and for their successful handling of some awkward model name changes, including transferring the 'Sovereign' name from Daimler to Jaguar, which seemed an uncharacteristic move.

Amongst John Egan's many accolades in 1983 was Midlander of the Year. Although his later school education *was* at Bablake in Coventry, his original home had in fact been in Rossendale, Lancashire. Egan's father was a Ford dealer at Lea Brook Garage; the Egan family home was 189 Burnley Road, Rawtenstall. John Egan and his elder brother James—now a gynaecologist and long-time Jaguar enthusiast based in California—were sent to boarding school in Manchester but not for very long. (A strange co-incidence, perhaps—that William Lyons, another Lancashire man, should have left Manchester before completing *his* course there?) John Egan moved to the local Bacup and Rawtenstall

Above *The Jaguar versus BMW battle was fought on the European Touring Car Championship race circuits from 1982, when 'Group A' regulations gave the Coventry marque a chance of success. The XJ-S got better and better, culminating in a great victory in the 1984 Spa-Francorchamps 24-hour race by this car, driven by Hans Heyer, Win Percy, and team chief Tom Walkinshaw who went on to become European champion for Jaguar.*

Below *Still under wraps when this edition went to press, the new generation of Jaguar saloons was still code-named 'XJ40'. This one was seen by Dave Warren of the* Sunday Mercury, Birmingham, *as it swept along the M6, past the familiar sight of Fort Dunlop . . . or is it now Fort Sumitomo?*

Grammar School as a fourth former, taking seven O-levels before being whisked away to Coventry when his father took over a garage in the Foleshill Road there. In October 1983, Geoffrey Rumney of the *Lancashire Evening Post* sought out former Rawtenstall headmaster, William Copley, who had no difficulty in remembering young Egan: 'Always a very able boy—shrewd, a good lad obviously with plenty of potential. But then Rossendale's full of successful businessmen.' For the same story, Egan told Rumney:

'I just hope that my ambitions for the company will be realised—and I have no ambition other than Jaguar.' He also told of 'explosive' management meetings in his early Jaguar days and how he had lived on a knife-edge for months as the productivity war waged: 'If we had failed, Michael Edwardes would have closed us down.' On independence he was less forthcoming. Egan repeated to Rumney his predominant basic thought: 'That's a matter for the BL board and I'm not on the BL board,' he said.

On December 1 1983, a Conservative body, the Centre for Policy Studies, published *BL Changing Gear,* the well-used title for a report which urged Trade & Industry Secretary Norman Tebbit to speed up the total separation of the profitable sections—notably Jaguar and Egan's earlier 'baby', Unipart—from BL, for sale to private ownership. Within a fortnight, Tebbit confirmed that Jaguar would be sold-off during 1984. That would be a year in which Jaguar rarely left the headlines.

In January came confirmation of record sales in the USA—over 15,000 cars in 1983—a positive result of the 1981 dealer exercise. Acceptance in North America always has been and always will be crucial to the very existence of a true Jaguar motor car.

History repeated itself in February 1984. In 1956, Her Majesty the Queen and Prince Philip had toured Jaguar on the eve of its best-ever decade, in which output would double. Now her son, Prince Charles, and Lady Diana charmed the people of Jaguar with as informal a visit as could be imagined. The euphoria had begun. Speculation was rife but brief; General Motors were almost fatherly in their concern—which virtually assured Jaguar of British ownership. BMW, Ford, and Mercedes-Benz let it be known that they, too, felt that Jaguar was about to come alive. In the Spring came new commitments to quality, and more headlines about cats leaping or roaring.

The structure of the new organisation became clearer by May 1984 when it was announced that John Egan would maintain his role as chief executive of the Jaguar Group meaning that he would remain Chairman and Managing Director of Jaguar Cars Ltd—the operating company—and Chairman of Jaguar Cars Inc, which handles the marque's biggest export market. There would also be a new 'umbrella' company—Jaguar plc—on whose board Egan would be joined by Beasley, the Edwards and Graham Whitehead. (See page 7 for details of 1985 Jaguar Cars Ltd board members.) Hamish Orr-Ewing, one of the men behind the 1960s' marketing success of the Ford Cortina, Chairman of Rank Xerox, was appointed by BL to chair it during the formative period until early 1985 when that task would be assigned to John Egan. (He is pictured on page 235.) BL director Raymond Horrocks, another former Ford man and a guiding light in the detaching of Jaguar, would be a non-executive Jaguar plc director; so would Edward Bond—the Beecham Group Finance Director and, perhaps more significantly, a member of the panel on takeovers and mergers, representing the CBI, since 1977. From the outset, then, Jaguar was going to show, in no uncertain terms, that having regained its freedom there was no intention of relinquishing it—whatever the external pressures.

May, June and July 1984 were climactic months for the Jaguar management, as the famous name was prepared for sale. Finance Director John Edwards and his unrelated colleague, Company Secretary Kenneth Edwards, were the leading midnight oil burners, spurred on by the encouraging picture which they were painting for the punters. Back in 1980, for example, productivity had dropped to 1.4 cars per employee. From close on ten

Right *Jaguar Day at the London Stock Exchange, 1984.*

thousand employees, by a 'painful' programme of redundancies, John Egan and his team had pulled the numbers down to about 7,200 in 1982—by which time the company was responding strongly to its new-found self-sufficiency. By the end of 1983, despite a strong recruitment drive, the productivity figure had risen to 3.4 cars per employee for the year.

During the late 1970s, Jaguar was too deeply enmeshed in British Leyland for separate trading information to be extracted subsequently. From 1980, however, it was possible to give an indication of Jaguar's recovery pattern. Pre-tax losses of £47.3 and £31.7 million from respective 1980 and 1981 turnover figures of £166.4 and £195.2 million had preceded a most important 1982 profit figure of £9.6 million from £305.6 million in turnover. The fully monitored figures for 1983 were just as dramatic: Before taxation, the year's turnover of £472.6 million had produced profits of just £50 million.

Then, as the Offer for Sale was about to be published, it was indicated that the first six months of 1984 would yield profits in excess of £40 million. The scene was set for the greatest moment in modern Jaguar history . . .

The long hot spring and summer of 1984 reached their climax on July 29. Brian James put it in a nutshell for the *Daily Mail* two days later: 'It's hard to compete for sporting headlines on the day 84 grand pianos playing Gershwin heralded the opening of the Los Angeles Olympic Games. So you can be forgiven, amid all the clamour from Los Angeles, for not knowing why the men who make Jaguar cars were tap-dancing around their jigs and lathes yesterday. Down there in the eye-straining small print it was just recorded that a Scot named Tom Walkinshaw had led home a team of three Jaguar drivers to win the 24-hour race at Spa Francorchamps in Belgium . . . the timing is perfect: This week, after years of drab anonymity in the motoring massif of British Leyland, Jaguar are going private—putting shares worth nearly £300 million on to a suddenly eager market.'

Tales of 'stags' and stampedes for shares had been reported nearly fifty years earlier, when SS Cars Ltd was floated. Now Sir William Lyons himself was among the buyers as Hill Samuel & Co Ltd (on behalf of BLMC Ltd) lit the blue touch-paper consisting of 177,880,000 ordinary shares of 25p each. With a price of 165p per share, the scene at Barclays Bank in London's Farringdon Street resembled 'the start of a sale at Harrod's china department', reported the *Financial Times*' Alison Hogan on August 4. As she was told by one policeman: 'It's like an upper class bookies.'

By pure coincidence August 5-12 1984 was the Jaguar Drivers' Club's International Jaguar Week—a week in which devotees came from around the world to share their enthusiasm, to see Jaguar, and to meet its people. Most of today's top people took part, including John Egan and Hamish Orr-Ewing—and so did many of the foundation-layers, including Blackpool apprentice George Lee who was seen to pause by the 1928 Swallow sidecar on display. It was a genuine honour for owners from as far away as California and Malaysia to be invited to meet Sir William and Lady Lyons, and Bill and 'Dutch' Heynes, at their own homes. The respect was, clearly, mutual. (That had been a piece of typically spontaneous organisation by Lofty England—perhaps the most dyed-in-the-wool 'Sir William' man of all?)

1985 dawned brightly, and it was clear that Jaguar had entered a period of true stability. Under Michael Beasley's guidance the company had manufactured an all-time record of over 33,000 Jaguars and Daimlers in 1984, with well over half of them destined for the USA (see appendices on pages 241 and 244). Despite more and more examples of 1987-model Jaguars, coded 'XJ40', being photographed and commented upon by a speculative press, the mood remained confident. The existing 6- and 12-cylinder XJ models were achieving regular quality standards to match the unique character and refinement which had been their hallmarks ever since Sir William Lyons launched the original XJ6.

Only with such an exceptional product could the people of Jaguar have hoped to see their company pull through, from near-extinction. Jaguar people, it is clear, do not give up—and their reward on this occasion was a new feeling of job satisfaction, while the XJ series sold better than ever before. In early 1985, as the first Jaguar plc Annual General Meeting approached, Jaguar's 10,000 employees could afford to feel secure but not complacent—for staying at the top is as hard a job as getting there. The news was that 1984 had seen a continuation of high productivity (3.6 cars per person, or thereabouts). It was expected that pre-tax profits of at least £90 million would accrue from a turnover of more than £600 million, and each employee was due to receive over £400-worth of shares (subject to four years' retention). This was the second such opportunity since the company returned to the private sector.

Fifty years earlier (see page 87), 33-year-old William Lyons had set in motion the floating of SS Cars Ltd (an event which, incidentally, the *Financial Times* alighted upon for *déja vu* comment at the time of the 1984 share issue). In October 1935, at SS's first AGM, shortly after offering a ten per cent dividend on ordinary shares and announcing a brand-new SS range called 'Jaguar', he spoke of the previous year's trading profit which 'cannot be considered unsatisfactory at £32,135'. (This had represented £24,209 net—see page 105.)

As Jaguar's Honorary President, Sir William Lyons—whose influence undoubtedly will continue to play a part in future Jaguars—was able to express his pleasure more effusively in 1985. There is no doubt that the very high regard Sir William, John Egan, and everyone at Jaguar held for one another was a sound foundation for keeping the marque British—*and* truly great.

PART 2, THE PRODUCTS

Introduction

In describing and illustrating the company's products, I have tried to bear in mind what the enthusiast knows already *and* what the newcomer to the subject will want to learn. Having decided to concentrate on the early and rare models in the tables, my intention has been to provide reference material for the historian and perhaps some passing interest for every other reader. Jaguars sales records, started by Alice Fenton and Alec Blythe, have provided me with many hours of enjoyable research-time. I regret not having been able to find official figures prior to 1931.

In interpreting the information available in the production records, the avid reader will discover several slight discrepancies; but these *are* always slight, and probably occurred because different people recorded different information. The two main sources have been the chassis records ledgers and the new car deliveries files. Each has generally corroborated the other's information, and most of the slight variations (all of which would take hundreds of hours of further research to interpret in detail) can be explained by: chassis numbers within a sequence being missed out, although this is rare, *or* the effect of factory cars being broken-up or sold second-hand, therefore not counting as 'new car' deliveries (eg experimental or competition cars, cars retained during the war, etc), *or* the effect of vehicles being transferred from one 'model-year' to another—fairly frequent pre-war.

Readers wishing to see Jaguar's achievements 'in a nutshell' are recommended to turn to the two general tables at the end of the book. Anyone wishing to discover more about an early SS, Jaguar or Daimler car should write, giving chassis number and reason for enquiry, to the author (care of the publisher) and he will do his best to help, especially if a black and white photograph of the car is enclosed! If any reader has difficulty in locating his or her local Jaguar or Daimler club, the author will be happy to advise, too, on receipt of a stamped addressed envelope. There are clubs in many parts of the world.

I. The Swallow sidecars

Swallow sidecar identification was by Model Number. The 'Model 1'—described as the 'Coupé Sports De Luxe'—was based upon William Walmsley's £28 octagonal 'Stockport Zeppelin' design, with aluminium panels and painted mouldings. It was still being listed in 1927 but, unlike the other styles in that year's catalogue, not priced. It was available only on the heavier-duty chassis. Weather protection was very good, but when it was in place the passenger could hardly see out.

The Model 2, or 'Light Weight De Luxe' was stubby-tailed, like the Model 1, being five feet ten inches long; but it was pentagonal and weighed less—about 100 lbs, including the twin-axle chassis. It was also of much simpler construction, which also made production easier. When fitted to the lightweight chassis (as used in the 1924 TT) the Model 2 sidecar came down to about 80 lbs in weight. In 1927 there was a difference of 30 shillings between the two versions, the lighter one (for 2¾ to 4 hp motor cycles) being the cheaper at £22 10s. The Model 3 was shortlived, and probably an uprated Model 2 for use with more powerful motorcycles.

Most popular of all the Blackpool-built Swallow sidecars was the Model 4—the Super Sports. It was virtually a Model 2, but had a dashing pointed tail that increased the length to seven feet one inch. For this extra bit of style, the asking price was only £1 more than for the equivalent Model 2. For a further £3, a soft coupé top (with reasonably sized 'windows'!) was available. This sidecar had a hammock-type seat to ensure 'luxurious comfort and the desired depth in the body'.

The 'streamline' theme was developed in the Model 5, described simply as 'Sports Model'. It reverted to octagonal panelling, and not even the mouldings were painted; the whole being finished in 'frosted' or polished aluminium. It had a curving celluloid wind-screen, probably for the first time on a Swallow production model, although a similar one was shown on a Model 4 in a 1928 illustration. Like the Model 4, it was priced at £23 10s (or £25 with the twin-axle chassis); but, although probably the most dramatic-looking of all Swallow sidecars, the Model 5 does not seem to have been made in great numbers.

Although other models *were* used for racing, the first competition sidecar as such was the one known at Swallows as the 'Scrapper'. Designated the Model 6, it was very light and cost £15 in 1927. Almost as cheap at £16 16s (with light chassis, but without screen or extras) was the Model 7, otherwise called the 'Semi-Sports'. The Models 6 and 7 were the first Swallows to feature the more orthodox upward-curving nose and one-piece side-panels, and in 1928 the Model 7 was being advertised as the cheapest Swallow at £12 12s. The combined effect of the 1926 move to the Cocker Street works and the 1927 introduction of the Model 7 enabled

Swallow's first half-page advertisement appeared in The Motor Cycle *on November 23 1922, after a last-minute space allocation at the London show.*

Swallow Model 4 advertisement (one-eighth page) from a 1928 edition of The Motor Cycle. *Sidecar prices had been slashed. (Note the new address.)*

The Motor Cycle and Cycle Trader to say: 'During the past four years the production of this concern has shown an average annual increase of 375 per cent, while since they introduced, in October of last year, a semi-sports model No 7, retailing at £12 12s, production, up to the end of April last, was seven and a half times greater than it was in the corresponding period of 1927. From the fact that the majority of the Swallow sidecars are of the sports or semi-sports type, it would seem that at any rate, so far as this class of trade is concerned, there is no risk of the sidecar waning in popularity'.

The Model 7 was listed until 1936, by which time the word 'utility' was being used to describe it; polished aluminium bodywork had long-since given way to fabric covering, and the price (on the cheapest chassis) still pegged at £12 12s. There were not many extras, but a door could be specified for 15 shillings more. A Model 7A (the Syston Sports) with more streamlined nose and tail continued in production right up to the end of civilian sidecar production.

Probably the only 'Zeppelin'-theme sidecar to be made after the move to Coventry was the Model 4, and *it* disappeared from the catalogue in the early 1930s. However new types of Swallow sidecar were produced right up to a Model 15.

The Model 8 was a 'touring' design. Variations included the 8A 'Hurlingham' which had a dickey seat (the first Swallow two-seater sidecar) and was introduced in about 1934. Later came the 8D 'Kenilworth', a two-seater 'saloon'.

Following the same general lines as the 7 and 8, the Model 9 series of 'De Luxe Touring' sidecars could be identified by top panels which were (to quote the 1935 catalogue) 'deeply louvred, sweeping with distinctive grace from nose to the toe'—in other words, fluting *à-la*-Vauxhall. Some versions, funnily enough, acquired the model-name 'Bedford'.

Models 10 and 11 respectively were the 'standard' and 'De Luxe' launch-type, with swept-up 'prow' and mahogany 'deck'. They were later called the 'Severn' and the 'Avon'—obvious to call them after local rivers, perhaps, but less so to use the name of a rival coach-builder! The Model 11's specification included chromium-plated rails which added to the

Swallow 'Bedford Tourer de Luxe', with Vauxhall-like fluting (Model 9A).

impression that it was designed for a paddle round the Serpentine. By 1939, incidentally, all Swallow sidecars, apart from the Syston (7A) had some kind of door.

The 'Godiva' Coupé (Model 11A) was introduced in 1939 'to make a special appeal to the fair sex' as the catalogue put it so chauvinistically; and it was certainly attractive, getting away from the rather vulgar 'launch' shape. It had the neat look of a Model 8 or 9 without the usual plainness, and possessed such practical features as a hinged bootlid and a proper windscreen. (This was not the first '11A' however, for there had been an 'Aero Launch Coupé' with the same model number in 1937! It was the kind of duplication that is baffling only to the historian, however, and probably passed unnoticed at the time.) The final range in the 'launch' configuration was the Model 12 series of 'Sun Saloons' finishing up in 1939 with the name 'Marlow'. The first ones (1934-5) were single-seaters, but later a child's dickey seat was offered as an extra.

Swallow avoided introducing a 'Model 13'. A neat little streamlined model—flat side-panelled but in the sporty spirit of the first Swallows—was designated the Model 14. In 1935 it featured sharply cut-away cockpit sides and a strong-looking grab-handle; it was called the 'Donington Special'. By 1939 it had become the longer and less-purposeful 'Shelsley Sports Tourer', and it was not now specifically recommended for competitions! This 'New Model 14' seems to have been the pride of the range, however, as it was selected for the 1939 catalogue cover artwork.

1936 saw the arrival of the last new sidecar range, the Model 15, evolved as a result of Swallow's desire to provide a coachbuilt saloon that would be 'a fit companion for the most expensive machines produced', as the catalogue put it. It was fitted to a new Universal chassis with 'car-type' (quarter-elliptic) springing; this replaced the three different chassis frames previously offered. The Model 15 'Ranelagh Saloon' was the most expensive Swallow sidecar ever offered and, at £31 10s, did not last more than two or three seasons; but it was very sleek and distinctive. By 1939 it was replaced by the New Model 15 two-seater 'Ascot' saloon—better value at £25 10s, but pretty ordinary to look at. The Swallow slogan 'Car Comfort at Sidecar Cost', was well-justified, however.

There are insufficient records to give accurate production figures for sidecars in the 1920s and 30s. At least *I* have not traced them, except for some very late pre-war information. During the war, however, over 9,000 Swallow sidecars were made for various purposes. The passenger-carrying ones were based on the Model 8/9 style, but do not appear to have had any simple designation. Details of all war-time output are included on page 215. The business was sold with every indication that post-war production of sidecars at Swallow Road had not been considered at all.

II.   The Austin-Swallow

There is little doubt that the first Austin Seven Swallow two-seater bore some relation to an open Talbot that William Lyons' former employers, Jackson Brothers passed to Swallow Coachbuilding late in 1926, for re-bodying after a racing accident—generally supposed to have occurred at Southport. Between acquisition of their first Austin Seven chassis from Parker's early in 1927, and the announcement in *The Autocar* of May 20 that year, Lyons and Walmsley used the inventiveness and skilled labour (ie: Cyril Holland) to make their first neat little Austin-Swallow, registered FR 7995.

The original photographs of it were returned from *The Autocar* to the Blackpool works, but they do not appear to have survived. (Very little material exists relating to the Blackpool operation, except a few catalogues and photographs, and the memories of those who worked there. However, a fellow apprentice from my own early Jaguar days, Tim Loakes—who was responsible for so many of the instruction book illustrations—has kindly brought the first official Austin Swallow picture to life again, for this book; see page 39.)

The car had a rather drooping, long, vulnerable tail, domed cycle-type front mudguards and, already, the characteristic rounded radiator cowl with the headlamps mounted on either side—not on the scuttle, as was still the case with standard Austin Sevens. The wire-mesh radiator guard bore the Austin 'scroll', on its own. There was a hole near the bottom of the guard which took the starting handle—the standard Austin handle, painstakingly hacksawn-through and an extension piece welded-in! The 'bench' seat seems to have been a feature of this first car, and a mahogany instrument panel *certainly* was; upholstery was real leather, and the hard-top had a Bedford cord lining. The optional hard-top—which brought the price from £175 to £185—had an oval celluloid rear window, and hinged at the rear decking; but that did not prove a practical arrangement. It is thought that several were built but that none survives.

At the time of the May 1927 announcement, it was stated that Swallows would 'fit chassis supplied by any Austin agent'. In October 1927, the first full-page Swallow advertisement appeared in *The Autocar* showing the Austin and Morris two-seaters, and advising the reader to 'consult your dealer' or Brown and Mallalieu (Blackpool) or Parkers (Manchester or Bolton). The interesting thing about the two Austin illustrations is the number of major changes in appearance that had taken place since the Austin Swallow had been announced;

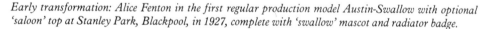

Early transformation: Alice Fenton in the first regular production model Austin-Swallow with optional 'saloon' top at Stanley Park, Blackpool, in 1927, complete with 'swallow' mascot and radiator badge.

and it is my opinion that very few weeks can have passed before the modifications had been brought-in unannounced—probably in August 1927. The problem of the cycle-wings breaking-off had been too serious to ignore.

Those 1927 advertisement photographs (with Alice Fenton 'modelling') were re-touched and used for an editorial announcement of the changes in *The Autocar* of February 3 1928. Here weight is given to the theory that the cycle-winged model would have been made only in very small numbers, since *no* mention was made in the text of the most obvious development—swept-down wings joined by running-boards. The windscreen looked more 'professional' now, too, curved-in at the base rather than straight-sided; the tail was as bulbous as before, but seemed to 'droop' less. A 'swallow' flew from the top of the cowl, which had a flatter-based aperture. The scroll now incorporated the words 'Austin-Swallow'. Here is the main part of *The Autocar's* description of the first definitive Austin-Swallow two-seater production models:

'The latest model has a neat fixed head in place of the hinged head previously fitted, and a good deal more head room has been provided by giving the roof a more pronounced dome, thus doing away with the necessity for hinging the head in order to facilitate entry to the car. More leg room has been provided, and the car gives ample seating capacity for two people without any cramping. The V screen may have, at slight extra cost, a two-panel portion on the driver's side, so that it can be opened if required when driving in fog or for ventilation purposes. In addition there is a hinged ventilator in the roof, and an adjustable roof light is also provided.

'Whereas formerly the car was available in one finish only, cream and crimson lake, an alternative finish is now available, the new colours being a very attractive suede grey with green wings, chassis and top. Real leather upholstery and cord cloth roof lining are provided in the appropriate shade of red or green.' [This was prepared by Percy Birch, the company's first full-time trimmer.]

'Although the coupé top is no longer hinged, it is very simply fixed to the body by two bolts at the rear and by snap fittings on top of the windscreen. It can thus be removed in a matter of a few minutes, and a folding sports type hood can be substituted, converting the car into an open sports model for summer use.'

A second photographic session took place beside a golf course on The Fylde in the spring

Austin Swallow two-seater, with 'saloon' top; class winner at the 1929 Southport concours d'elegance. Holding the trophy is Stanley Parker, the original Swallow distributor, who had surreptitiously supplied William Lyons with his first Austin Seven chassis in January 1927. With Parker is George Cundy, who became his Manchester depot manager.

Note the grille on this 1930 Coventry-made Austin-Swallow saloon, now with vertically-sliding windows in longer doors, and more room inside. Note also the fashionable ship-type ventilators. (The prototype is illustrated on page 42.) (C. Tanner).

or summer of 1928. Two cars were present—a third version of the Austin-Swallow two-seater and the first of a new line in coachwork—the Austin Seven Swallow saloon. Both cars had a new cowl, and imitation dumb-irons—an idea that was to be copied frequently. The saloon does not seem to have been shown in public until Henlys entered one for the big September *concours* at Southport. (Parkers' took an Austin-Swallow two-seater with 'saloon-coupé top to the same event.)

Throughout 1929, both types of Austin-Swallow began to become a familiar yet distinctive sight on Britain's roads. One particular 'package' dreamed-up at Henlys that summer was the combination of an open Austin-Swallow and Dunelt trailer complete with snazzy outboard motor boat for £280. It must have been a power-to-weight nightmare, however, and one can see why the saloon version was not selected as the towing vehicle!

The Swallow-bodied Austin Sevens were much more luxurious and individual than other coachbuilders' offerings. (One exception was the O.H. Special of 1929, made to the specification of former Van den Plas designer Captain H. O'Hagan. This beautifully-proportioned little coupé had a lowered chassis however, and was modified to the extent of 18 extra inches in the wheelbase! Probably a 'one-off' anyway, it was made by Cadogan Motors.) Almost from the outset, the Swallow saloon's specification included a Houbigant Ladies Companion Set in the nearside glove-compartment lid. The prototype's horizontally-sliding windows were replaced for production by counterbalanced ones that slid down into the doors. As *The Autocar* found in its 'Used Cars on the Road' series early in 1934, however, the glass tended not to rise squarely in its channels. On the whole they found the 1931 car had lasted well, though. Each car did improve in mechanical specification, too, as time passed—although, of course, several weeks after the introduction of a chassis-maker's new feature might go by before the Swallow-bodied version appeared with the same thing.

Late in 1929 came yet another change in the radiator cowl, and one of the first customers for the saloon in this form was HH the Sultan of Perak, whose car was painted in his royal colours of purple and black. An improvement around this time was a change from flat wooden floorboards to metal wells—virtually essential for rear seat comfort. Coventry production methods permitted a reduction in the amount of raised beading used externally.

A fifth and final radiator cowl was brought in for the fifth and penultimate Austin-Swallow selling season! This was the change to what has become known in the Swallow Register as the 'Mark Two', and was introduced in time for the 1930 motor show. It is quickly-identified by the broader grille with a bar down the middle and the 'Austin-Swallow scroll' offset; the number plate was now mounted well ahead of the radiator cowl, either on the front of a new louvred tray or on the bumper which was now offered.

The Austin-Swallow continued in regular production until early 1932, finally tailing-off that summer. The best guide to quantities comes from recent research carried out by Gil Mond of the Austin Swallow Register, based on the few surviving cars with a readable body number. This was chalked or painted inside the door panel. The indications are that rather more than 800 two-seaters and 1,700 saloons were built in all, making a total of well over 2,500 Austin-Swallows. This seems a realistic figure, even if production did reach 40 Austins a week very occasionally in the 1929-30 period. It is known that there were some very lean periods too—and Blackpool production (1927-28) was always very restricted anyway. Perhaps, one day, a complete production record may be found; meantime, it is fortunate that Jaguar's records from mid-1931 are so nearly complete. For that, we have Alice Fenton, Alec Blythe, and their successors to thank for some of the best-noted sales information in the industry.

Austin Swallow prices	**February 1928**	(Chassis only)	£99
		Open Sports	*£175*
		Detachable coupé	*£185*
		(soft and hard tops)	*£190*
	February 1929	*Open Sports*	*£170 10s*
		Detachable coupé	*£180 10s*
		(Soft and hard tops)	*£185 10s*
		Saloon	*£187 10s*

Swallow reduced their two-seater prices by £5 10s for 1931 but held the saloon price right through to the final (1932) selling season; then Swallow's prices were down to: Open sports £150; Detachable coupé £160; Saloon £165. These prices apparently included Wilmot Breeden double bumper-bars, quoted at 60 shillings per pair, so value-for-money during that national slump period was clearly at a premium.

The earliest surviving sales record book indicates that 109 Austin Seven Swallow 1932 models were made as follows: 89 Saloons, 16 Two-seaters, three Coupés (hard-top) and one Special van. Here are the last significant entries from the ledger:

Chassis No	Car No	Despatched	Notes
147672	B5-972	Feb 1932 to Bolton area	Last coupé delivered
149835	B5-5135	June 1932 to Cape Town	Last export (two-seater)
153794	B5-7095	July 1932 to London area	Last saloon delivered
154889	B5-7252	Aug 1932 to Surrey	Last delivery but two (two-seater)
148499	—	Aug 1932 (Clarke Bros)	Last delivery but one (special van)
150295	B5-3595	Oct 1932 to Norfolk	Last delivery (two-seater)

Note: There is no indication as to why the very last Austin Swallow delivery was so late in the year. The van (148499) was specified as follows: 'Special van, painted to represent accumulator . . . two doors with sliding lights . . . one bucket seat . . . no partition behind driver'. (Oh, for a photograph—the author would pay handsomely.)

III.   The Morris-Swallow

Nearly a page of *The Autocar* for August 19 1927 was taken up with the story of 'An Inexpensive Sports Car', and this is part of that story:

'Recently we described and illustrated an attractive type of sports body for the Austin Seven chassis which was produced by the Swallow Sidecar and Coachbuilding Co., Cocker Street, Blackpool, and the same firm has now in production a sports two-seater body for the Morris-Cowley chassis. This body is considerably lower than the standard coachwork, and embodies a longer scuttle in which the lines of the bonnet follow through to the tops of the two doors. A two-panel sloping V screen is fitted, while below the scuttle is a polished mahogany instrument board, on which the standard dials and controls are well arrranged.

'The seats give a reclining driving position, and the steering wheel is dropped about six inches. This enhances the driver's comfort considerably, and the position is all that could be desired for a tall or medium-height driver, while the undivided screen gives unobstructed vision over a very wide angle.

'In general appearance the car is most attractive, for its low lines are enhanced by long D-section wings, which carry sports type wing lamps, and also by the fitting of Ace wheel discs. The space between the rear dumb-irons is filled in by a metal shield across the back of the car. Behind the driving seat is a large, fully upholstered, disappearing dickey seat, and leg room for the passengers in this is provided by sunk wells in the floor boards. A simple hood and rigid, metal-framed side-screens complete the equipment.

'Panelled in aluminium, the body is coach finished in cream and crimson lake, the latter colour being applied to the top of the bonnet, scuttle, and dickey seat covers, and extending slightly down the sides; a black line divides the crimson from the cream. Polished wood garnish strips cap the doors and the instrument board mouldings. Chassis, wheels, wings, head lamps, and all exposed mechanical details are also painted crimson lake, while real leather of the same colour is used for the upholstery.'

Morris Cowley-Swallow, brightly painted in cream and crimson, with elegantly curving tail but an incongruously-high bonnet line. A hood was fitted, but how it stayed up is not clear. Henlys' advertisements showed the windscreen as being flat-topped, probably because the artist could not see where the glass ended in the photograph. (Here, the real glass line has been emphasised, but otherwise this picture is virtually unretouched). Alice Fenton is the diminutive model; the gates are those of Stanley Park, Blackpool (Miss N. Fenton).

For some reason, the Swallow body seems to fit lower and more snugly on the Morris Minor chassis than the Austin. This 'one-off' was on show at Henlys in Euston Road in the autumn of 1930, and was probably a result of the discord between William Lyons and Sir Herbert Austin over the supply of chassis. The original Morris radiator cowl was retained, and this did not lend itself to a 'pen-nib' colour-divider which, sensibly, was not attempted (The Autocar).

There were two photographs, one with and one without a spare wheel mounted on the off-side front wing. The car was illustrated again in the previously-mentioned October 1927 *Autocar* Swallow advertisement with Alice Fenton at the wheel, although she did not in fact learn to drive for another 20 years or so!

In 1928, Henlys advertised the Morris Cowley-Swallow briefly, pricing it at £220 (announcement price had been £210) for the 'cape-hood' model, £230 with 'saloon-coupé' top, or £235 with both. The car does not ever appear to have been fitted with either soft or hard tops for photography. The original pictures show it to have had a strange, high windscreen, without a top rim. Probably because they could not see it, artists tended to draw-in a flat-topped screen; and because Alice Fenton had sat so low in the car Henlys re-drew the driver, who became a passable prototype of Hitler.

The accompanying list shows that there were relatively few Morris Cowley and Oxford 'specials'. Although the price was right, the Cowley-Swallow was very slow and the Oxford-MG would have shown it up very badly. In any case, as has been seen, Lyons and Walmsley were ready to build on virtually any chassis that came their way. By the time they were set to move to Coventry, it was clear that the Cowley-Swallow need not be included in the range; it was therefore made in Blackpool only—and in a *very* limited way. One example is thought to exist but even that is not certain.

This was not quite the only Morris connection. Not even given a price, and therefore almost definitely a 'one-off', was the Morris Minor-Swallow which Henlys put on display at Euston Road in autumn 1930. It looked lower and better-proportioned than the Austin-Swallow saloon from which it was derived. The normal Morris Minor radiator cowl was used, and that gave the car a squarish bonnet—so, although the car did get the usual Swallow two-tone treatment, it was *not* given the 'pen-nib' nose.

By this time, Morris had already added two cylinders to the Morris Minor for an additional model called the Wolseley Hornet. Soon William Lyons would be able to obtain *that* chassis, and make something a little different once again. Perhaps this was one of his reasons for not proceeding with a Morris Minor-Swallow?

The first of Swallow's larger saloon bodies to go into production was this one on the FIAT 509A chassis, some, if not all, of which arrived at Swallow Road with 'artillery' wheels which were normally discarded for wire-spoked ones (J. Ritchie).

IV. The FIAT-Swallow

It is known that design of the Swallow saloon 'shape' was well under way in the winter of 1927-8, and the first Austin Sevens to have it were made in Blackpool. The first 'big' version of this style was built on an Alvis 12/50 chassis by Cyril Holland in Blackpool in 1928. It was not until the company had begun to find its feet in Coventry, however, that a larger Swallow saloon body actually appeared on the market.

William Lyons' contact with James Ritchie, the Glasgow FIAT agent, led to Swallow obtaining some obsolescent FIAT 509A chassis, and the transformation was announced in *The Motor* and *The Autocar* in the first week of July 1929—by Henlys, who claimed to have 'arranged for Swallow bodywork to be fitted to the 9 h.p. FIAT chassis'! In the same issue of *The Autocar* was a road-test report on an upright Weymann-bodied six-light FIAT 509A saloon, which was found to be well-finished but suffered from drumming: 'With the 9 h.p.

FIAT 509 Berlina, still being offered in 1929, shows why the British FIAT man, D'Arcy Baker, included the Swallow version in his catalogue alongside! This was listed at £225, compared with £260 for the FIAT-Swallow, none of which survives today (C. Cole/FIAT Centro Storico).

Left 1931-model Swift-Swallow is identifiable by vertical central strip on radiator. This picture shows the owners of the only survivor, Mr and Mrs Bill Duff, winning the 'ensemble' prize at the Gaydon concours in 1969.

Right Biggest of all the Swallows was the elongated six-cylinder saloon, described as '15' or '16', of which a few only were made for one season (1931-2) on the bigger Standard chassis while the SS was still in the preparation stage. This one has been with the Childs family in Dorset since new—Mrs Childs is in the background in this 1930s shot—and must be the only survivor of its type (M. Childs).

FIAT one knows that there is an engine at work the whole time'—and the engine was described as 'diminutive but willing'.

The flow of FIAT chassis through the Swallow Road works was quite efficient during their short production period—probably entirely in 1929. In Italy, the FIAT 514 had already been introduced that September and it seems likely that the FIAT-Swallows were made in one batch from stockpiled chassis. The 509A was the only FIAT type to receive Swallow coachwork. Probably 50 to 100 were so treated.

Compared with the very old-fashioned FIAT saloons, Swallow's version was a delight to look at, despite or because of the bold radiator cowl. The few available pictures show it as having wire wheels. That ever-helpful historian, the late Michael Sedgwick, could remember two post-war survivors, one of which had the standard artillery wheels. No FIAT-Swallow is known to exist now.

V.   The Swift-Swallow

Still not quite ready for production, Swallow-bodied Standard Nine and Swift Ten saloons did appear on Swallow's stand at the 1929 Olympia motor show, although it was the existing FIAT-Swallow (with its rear seats 'sunk below chassis level') that had excited *The Light Car*'s reporter the most.

The Swift-Swallow went into regular production the following March probably hardly 'overlapping' with the FIAT. In late 1930 the Swift Ten was updated slightly (acquiring a central radiator 'rib' for identification) and of course the Swift in Swallow's plumage got the same treatment. A larger fuel tank, improved cooling, and modified combustion chamber design were among the mechanical changes. *The Light Car* commented on the car early in 1931, praising the fully opening driver's-side windscreen, wide doors, usefully deep foot-wells and convenient controls (including a right-hand lever for the four-speed gearbox—a normal Swift feature). They found the car pleasant to drive, with good handling and performance

It was a great pity, therefore, that in April 1931, Swift of Coventry were put in the receiver's hands. The service department was kept going, and the assets purchased by Colliers of Birmingham in November—Colliers being professional acquirers of defunct car makes!

Unfortunately, no Swift-Swallow production figure has come to light, but it would probably be nearer one hundred than two. One fine example exists, and has been nicely-maintained for many years by Forfar tree-grower, Bill Duff.

VI.   The Standard-Swallow

One of the most appealing features of all the Swallow Cars' was the constant use of aluminium coachwork. They never 'went Weymann', as so many car and body manufacturers did.

An interesting announcement in the summer of 1929 was the introduction of a £235 metal-panelled six-light saloon based on Standard's usually-fabric 9 hp 'Teignmouth' model. Swallow obtained a similar chassis in time to put a body on it for the 1929 Olympia show but, as mentioned earlier, the radiator looked so antediluvian that Swallow's own design of cowl was fabricated and the Standard-Swallow was 'reannounced' early in 1930.

Future links were already being hinted at when, on February 7 1930, *The Autocar* said:

'For a considerable time now the special bodies made by the Swallow Sidecar and Coachbuilding Co., of Coventry, for Austin Seven and FIAT Nine chassis have had quite a vogue, the production of these bodies having steadily risen until it is now in the neighbourhood of 100 per week. The latest addition to the range of Swallow coachwork is just making its appearance on the Standard Nine chassis, and this special model has a very distinctive radiator and is known as the Standard Swallow.

'The chassis is specially prepared by the Standard Motor Co., Ltd., for the Swallow Company, and the complete car is marketed by the latter concern. In addition to the very attractive appearance of the car, it is interesting also by reason of its price, £245. This figure, moreover, includes very complete equipment, while the finish of the body is well up to the excellent reputation which the coachbuilders have achieved for their other models.

'While the lines of the body follow closely those of previous Swallow bodies, the radiator is distinctly new, and there is something of Continental line about it, as it is given a slight V front and is raked slightly towards the rear, the shell, which is chromium plated, being continued down the apex of the V to form a bar. All external bright parts are, of course, chromium plated, and regarding the windscreen an interesting point is that the driver's panel opens completely; but yet is watertight and draughtproof when closed, being secured by two clips on to a rubber strip. A suction-operated screen wiper is fitted to the lower part of the opening panel.

'A louvred tray between the dumb irons undoubtedly neatens the front view, while the front wings and their valances are formed in one piece and sweep gracefully down to short aluminium-covered running boards. Both front and rear wings fit closely to the wheels, and the back edge of the rear wings is turned slightly outwards. As the spare wheel is carried at the rear, it does not spoil the lines of the car in side view.'

The 9 hp Standard-Swallow nevertheless still looked slightly unbalanced, and for 1931 its bonnet-line was improved yet again—*and* it gained bumper bars front and rear. Then, in May 1931, the biggest of all the Swallow saloons made its début—the '15 hp' Standard Ensign-Swallow. It was Swallow's first six-cylinder saloon, and it might have made quite an impact if the new SS had not been announced so soon afterwards. At least one of these rare cars exists, and still appears at West Country events. Like the Austin-Swallows, the Standard-Swallows 'overlapped' with the SSs well into 1932.

★   ★   ★

As records have been found only from mid-1931 (the beginning of the 1932 model year in effect), there is no factory evidence relating to the Swallow-bodied Morris, FIAT and Swift models, but the last year of the Standard-Swallow—overlapping with the first SS season—is interesting. Forty-nine 1,287 cc four-cylinder Standard 'Big Nine' Swallows were made as 1932 models, but the final number was taken up to 53 by four more, made and sold (but as far as I know never advertised) as 1933 '9 hp' models:

Chassis Number	Despatched	Notes
137190	June 1932	Last 1932 model
186084	September 1932	These were the only 1933 models, with chassis and engine numbers from a new Standard Motor Co sequence
185919	October 1932	
188251	April 1933	
188254	April 1933	

All the above were delivered to the London area, except 186084 which went to Grantham.

The list of 2,054 cc six-cylinder Standard 'Ensign' Swallows *does* seem to be complete. It appears that only 56 were made in all, from the early summer of 1931, 15 of the total being made in that model year. The other 41 were 1932 models, the last one being chassis number 119872, despatched to a London customer in August 1932.

VII.   The Wolseley-Swallow

The first six-cylinder Swallows of all were the Wolseley Hornets, for which two unique Swallow bodies were produced. In January 1931 came the very smart Wolseley Hornet-Swallow two-seater, with a cunning mould line which helped make the bonnet look lower than it was in reality. A four-seater followed in the autumn. Although the Morris Minor-based Wolseley Hornet provided Cecil Kimber with more MG possibilities, Swallow's new offering filled a niche and was made in quite large numbers from the 1930-31 winter well into 1933, for it was complementary to the early SS range, too.

Not many proprietary coachbuilders were able to obtain the 1931 single carburettor Hornet chassis apart from Swallow, but in April 1932 Wolseley came out with the Hornet Special in chassis-only form for £175—twin SU carburettors and four-speed gearbox were among the appealing new features.

Wolseley's London distributor, Eustace Watkins, was early in the field, of course, and so the January 1931 announcement that Watkins had 'secured the monopoly for supplying Swallow coachwork on the Wolseley Hornet chassis in London and within 25 miles of Charing Cross' seems an anachronism—as Henlys were as usual in on the advertising of the Hornet-Swallow from the outset. Later Hornet-Swallows had the double bumpers and daft-looking 'ship-type' scuttle ventilators popularised by some Swallow saloons. Colour schemes were as bright as ever, and there was a choice of Rudge-Whitworth wire wheels—centre-lock or 'Magna'.

1932-3 Wolseley Hornet Special, with two-seater Swallow coachwork. The neat tail is shown in a picture earlier in the book. Note the skilful way the bonnet height is apparently reduced by the 'two-level' waistline. The centre-lock wire wheels add to the sportiness (The Autocar).

The Hornet-Swallow Special or 'Speed Model' cost £255 (£260 for the four-seater)—£30 more than the original Wolseley Hornet-Swallow which it did not totally replace. These little Wolseleys were popular, and only the arrival of the SS tourer made them redundant. To the Wolseley Hornet-Swallow goes the honour of being the last of the 'special-bodied Swallows' to be produced. Within five years of arriving in Coventry, the small firm had switched completely to its very own make of car—the SS.

The Wolseley Hornet

Price comparisons (Swallow and other coachbuilders)

Wolseley	Fabric saloon	£175	(April 1930)
Wolseley	Coachbuilt saloon	£185	(April 1930)
Boyd-Carpenter	Two-seater	£232 10s	(Nov 1930)
Boyd-Carpenter	Coupé	£250	(Nov 1930)
Swallow	*Two-seater*	*£220*	*(Jan 1931)*
Swallow	*Two- and four-seaters*	*£225*	*(1931-2)*
Abbey	Four-seater (open)	£235	(1931-2)
Eustace Watkins	Four-seater (open)	£220	(1931-2)
Eustace Watkins	E.W. Tickford (coupé)	£245	(1931-2)

Wolseley Hornet Special

Price comparisons (April 1932)

Wolseley	Chassis only	£175
Abbey	Four-seater (open)	£275
Swallow	*Two- and four-seaters*	*£255*
Kevill-Davies & March	Two/four-seater (open)	£289
Maltby	Four-seater (open)	£259
Maltby	Coupé	£269
Patrick	Four-seater (open)	£250
Jensen	Coupé (fixed head)	£275
Eustace Watkins	'Ariel' Tickford (fixed head)	£285
Eustace Watkins	Daytona two/four-seater	£275

For the final (1933) season, the Swallow Hornet 'Special' prices were: two-seater £255; four-seater £260. As these were the only types of 'Swallow' body to be made in any quantity as 1933 models, the Jaguar records are quite helpful, but there is no indication of what was made in the early part of 1931.

Wolseley Swallow	Wolseley Hornet		Wolseley Hornet Special	
	Two-seater	**Four-seater**	**Two-seater**	**Four-seater**
1932-3 models	100	224	21	185

These figures can be split up in three ways: 121 two-seaters + 409 four-seaters = 530; *or* 324 standard models + 206 'Specials' = 530; *or* (approx) 380 1932 models + 150 1933 models = 530.

As the four-seater was not introduced until autumn 1931 the figure of 409 is probably an absolute total for that model. By the same token, it is *certain* that no 'Special' chassis Hornet Swallows are 'missing'. Here is a small selection of individual cars:

Car Number	Despatched	Body	Notes
105004	Oct 1931	Two-seater	London Show (Nile blue)
105220	Nov 1931	Four-seater	Henly's demo (carnation)
105147	Nov 1931	Two-seater	Glasgow show (carnation & cream)
120506	Oct 1932	'Special' four-seater	London show (carnation)
121623	July 1933	'Special' two-seater	Last two-seater delivery (Exported)
121636	Aug 1933	'Special' four-seater	Last delivery (apple green; to Manchester area)

VIII.   The SS1

Lyons clashed with Walmsley over the styling of the first SS1 coupé, which was prepared so hurriedly for the 1931 London motor show. It was restyled to Lyons' liking the following year, with a longer wheelbase and the chassis frame underslung at the rear. Announced as a 'Sixteen' (2,054 cc), the SS1 was also available from the outset as a less-publicised 'Twenty' (2,552 cc). In both cases the engine was Standard's six cylinder side-valve. The first tourers with these engines were 1933 models.

Late 1933 saw further tidying of the now-established SS shape, and the coupé and tourer were joined by a saloon. Engine capacities went up to 2,143 and 2,663 cc for the 16 hp and 20 hp models respectively, and there were chassis improvements too. An addition at the 1934 motor show was the 'Airline' saloon which Lyons actively disliked, yet produced none-the-less. As well as the more obvious body changes, the windscreen was rather further forward than other SS1s', and the wing shape was altered to hide the spare wheel wells. It was the last new model to be introduced before William Walmsley left the company.

In the spring of 1935 came the last of the SS1s, the drophead coupé, which was very attractive. Because its arrival was so late in SS development, not many were made. Even rarer was the SS90, which followed Walmsley's own special two-seaters, and was really the SS Jaguar 100's predecessor. The SS90 was included in the SS1 chassis numbering sequence. All SS90s had the 20 hp (2,663 cc) engine which was still side-valve but much improved by help from Harry Weslake. The SS1 range continued for the 1936 model year, with only the standard and 'Airline' saloons listed, although the coupé, tourer, and drophead did not disappear totally.

The original SS1, with helmet wings and radiator tie-bar.

SS1—models and prices

Model Year	Model	Price	Quantity
1932	Fixed head coupé	£310	502
1933	Fixed head coupé	£325	1099
	Tourer	£325	150
1934 and 1935	Fixed head coupé	£335	200
	Saloon	£340	1,100
	Tourer	£335	365
1935	'Airline' saloon	£360	573
	Drophead coupé	£380	94
	'90' two-seater	£395	23
1936	Fixed head coupé	All	9
	Saloon	prices	44
	Tourer	reduced	36
	'Airline' saloon	by about	51
	Drophead coupé	£20	6
	'90' two-seater		1
		Chassis*	1
		Total	4,254

These quantities have been compiled from considerable study of the sales and delivery records. There seems to have been some confusion in recording the identities of 1934 and 1935 fixed head coupés and saloons; the two models were, after all, very similar to *look* at! The respective figures of 200 and 1,100 are probable, but not definite. The overall figure of 4,254 may be very slightly low. These general comments also apply to SS2 1934 and 1935 coupés and saloons. Prices shown are for 16 hp models. In 1932 and 1933, a 20 hp engine added £10 to the price; after that, the difference was only £5.

*This refers to the SS1 chassis fitted, very experimentally, with a Studebaker Straight-Eight engine. It is not certain if it was the same chassis (illustrated on page 92) that later had a supercharged engine. Other examples of 'chassis only' may be found in the following lists.

Some of the original 500 SS1s were given (by Henlys) a larger-than-standard trunk, into which a double-dickey seat was fitted. The effect was strange, to say the least (G.G. Haigh).

Here are some of the cars that have caught my eye while studying the sales records:

Original 1932-model SS1 Coupé

Car No	First destination	Notes
135001	Southampton (Jan 1932)	16 hp for C.B. Ives of White's Yacht Building and Engineering Co, Itchen. (First SS1 chassis number.)
135002	Scotland (Jan 1932)	16 hp for G.D. Stewart of Edinburgh.
135003	Scotland (Jan 1932	20 hp for Captain G.A. Moxon of Prestwick, Ayrshire.
135004	Ireland (Jan 1932)	20 ph for Eileen Gregory of Dublin.
135043	Coventry (Feb 1932)	20 hp for Captain J.P. Black of the Standard Motor Company.
135063	1931 Glasgow show	20 hp sold afterwards to F. Stuart of Glasgow.
135102	1931 Olympia show	20 hp in Apple Green/black (presumably Henlys' first demo car?)
135103	London (Feb 1932)	16 hp for A.G. Douglas Clease of *The Autocar*; 'steering column to be raised 1½ inches'.
135106	Austria (Feb 1932)	16 hp for G.H. Koch, for Vienna show.
135110	London (Feb 1932)	16 hp for Kathleen, Countess of Drogheda (White/Carnation, Reg No G.W. 6439).
135114	Manchester (Feb 1932)	16 hp for C.S. Shorrock (well-known motor engineer).
135171	Lichtenstein (March 1932)	16 hp ordered via Emil Frey of Switzerland with metric instrumentation.
135183	Nottingham (March 1932)	16 hp for George Brough, motor-cycle manufacturer.
135226	London (April 1932)	16 hp for James Mollison, aviator (husband of Amy Johnson).
135489	London (Aug 1932)	16 hp for E.W.W. Pacey, notable Brooklands driver.
135500	Austria (Aug 1932)	16 hp last but two in first SS1 chassis series; dickey seat fitted.
135501	Sussex (July 1932)	16 hp last but one of first SS1 chassis series; for Miss Withington of Crawley.
135502	London (?) (Aug 1932)	16 hp last in first SS1 chassis series, for a Henly customer.

Selection from 1933-model SS1 records

Car No	First destination	Notes
135503	1932 London Show	16 hp coupé, sold afterwards to E. Hayward of Cobham.
135541	Netherlands (Nov 1932)	16 hp coupé, shipped to Rotterdam (first item on works list of 1933 model orders received).
135619	Dorset (Dec 1932)	20 hp coupé for V.A.P. Budge of Parkstone, 1933 Monte Carlo Rally entrant.
135671	Works car (Jan 1933)	16 hp coupé with special instruction ('preselective gear') which does not appear to have been followed.
135677	Works car (?)	16 hp coupé, probably used by Douglas Clease for 1933 RAC Rally.
135934	Southampton (Feb 1933)	16 hp coupé for C.B. Ives (see 135001).
135980	Coventry (March 1933)	16 hp coupé for William Walmsley (beige paintwork).
135988	Coventry (March 1933)	20 hp tourer, for Captain J.P. Black (first of the new tourers).
136138	Scotland (March 1933)	16 hp coupé, for R.D. Hunnam of Edinburgh (regular rally competitor).
136235	London (May 1933)	20 hp tourer, for W.H. Charnock, 'the motoring bard' who found it a 'lot of fun'.
136240	(1933 FH coupé)	On permanent loan by Jaguar to Coventry Transport Museum.
136248	Coventry (May 1933)	20 hp tourer for Captain Black (although no indication as to why he had two.)
136386	Coventry (May 1933)	20 hp tourer, for William Lyons (his first SS it seems), in black.
136405	Works car (?)	20 hp tourer, probably the red Alpine Trial car (fate unknown).

The four-seater SS1 tourer, photographed in Swallow Road, a youthful Lyndon Smith at the wheel. Pleasantly non-dating, this style was carried through to the SS Jaguar range for a couple of seasons. The tourer first appeared in the spring of 1933 (L. Smith).

Car No	First destination	Notes
136416	Works prepared for Austria.	20 hp tourer, (KV5523) for Douglas Clease (1933 Scottish Rally), then G.H. Koch (for Alpine Trial).
136438	Coventry (May 1933)	20 hp tourer, for William Walmsley, again in his favourite beige.
136620	Works car	20 hp tourer, blue Alpine Trial car, later sold through Parkers of Bolton.
136625	Works car	20 hp tourer, white Alpine Trial car, later sold through Henlys, Manchester.
136627	Australia (July 1933)	20 hp chassis, 'with wings fitted' (first such case, apparently).
136683	London (July 1933)	20 hp coupé (KV5916) for F. Gordon Crosby, motoring artist.
136715	Spain (Aug 1933)	20 hp chassis 'with wings fitted', sent to Barcelona.
136742	London (Sept 1933)	16 hp coupé for Bud Flanagan, actor and comedian.
136751	Preston (Sept 1933)	16 hp coupé (last 1933-series chassis number).

Selection from 1934 to 1936 SS1 chassis series

Car No	First destination	Notes
247001	Surrey (Dec 1933)	20 hp tourer for Sydney Light of Hook; Monte Carlo Rally & Alpine Trial car.
247002	Hertfordshire (Nov 1933)	16 hp coupé for Mrs A. Connell, Bishops Stortford.
247003	1933 London Show (?)	16 hp saloon, to Henlys (first saloon demo car?)
247004	1933 Glasgow Show	16 hp saloon, later sold to R. Dunlop, Glasgow.
247005	1933 Glasgow Show	16 hp saloon, later sold to B.R. Whittaker, Edinburgh.
247337	(Exported Feb 1934)	20 hp chassis ('chassis only, open type') destination unknown.
247379	Coventry (Feb 1934)	20 hp saloon for William Walmsley, in olive green.
247471	Manchester (March 1934)	20 hp tourer (AND477) in grey for Charles Needham, rally driver.
247486	London (March 1934)	20 hp tourer for T. Leather, who raced it at Brooklands (best lap = 79.05 mph.)
247564	Coventry (March 1934)	20 hp special open *two-seater* for William Walmsley in olive green.
247653	Coventry (March 1934)	20 hp saloon for William Lyons, in black.
247716	Coventry (April 1934)	20 hp tourer for Captain J.P. Black of Standard Motor Co.
248015	Manchester (?) (June 1934)	20 hp special open *two-seater* (like 247564) in birch grey, sold through Henlys Manchester.
248123	London (July 1934)	20 hp tourer for W.G.V. Vaughan of Esher; keen rally driver.
248267	Coventry (Oct 1934)	20 hp saloon for H.N. Gillitt (Swallow-SS director).
248270	(Late 1934 saloon)	In Jaguar's own historic collection.
248291	London (Oct 1934)	20 hp 'Airline' saloon (first of this type to be despatched.)
248424	Coventry (Dec 1934)	20 hp 'Airline' saloon for T.W. Daffern (Swallow-SS director).
248436	Works car (Dec 1934)	Prototype SS90 *(see separate '90' list).*
248475	Berkshire (Dec 1934)	20 hp 'Airline' saloon for Major Sir A. Hickman, Wokingham, rallyist.
248559	Works car (?) (Jan 1935)	20 hp drophead coupé probably the prototype; later sold second-hand in Shropshire.

Car No	First destination	Notes
248750	Coventry (Nov 1934)	20 hp 'Airline' saloon for William Lyons (his least-favourite model) in lavender!
248615	Oxford (Feb 1935)	20 hp saloon, for S.W.B. Hailwood, father of Mike Hailwood, champion motorcyclist.
248669	Coventry (Jan 1935)	16 hp 'Airline' saloon, for Howard R. Davies, Swallow sidecar sales manager.
249175	India (Aug 1935)	20 hp 'Airline' saloon for 'Mr. Nehru, c/o Government of India, New Delhi'.
249205	London (April 1935)	16 hp drophead coupé (first of this type to be despatched).
249500	London (July 1936)	20 hp 'Airline' saloon (last SS1 chassis number, and last to be delivered).

The following is a complete list of SS90 chassis numbers:

Number	First UK Owner *or* Agent *or* Destination
248436*	'90, special two-seater, shortened, experimental'. (ARW395, later sprinted and rallied by B. Lewis).
249476*	Works car, AVC 477 production model, used by A.G.D. Clease and W. Lyons.
249477*	Eric Boyd, Rhu, Scotland.
249478‡	Captain J.P. Black, Standard Motor Co.
249479‡	(France).
249480	A.C. Wright, Cardiff.
249481	D.M. Naughton, W. Hartlepool (second-hand, so possibly a works car until 1937?).
249482‡	(Unknown Sussex customer.)
249483	Jack Salem, Manchester.
249484	(Netherlands.)
249485‡	A.L. Dyer, Hale Barns, Cheshire.
249486	(Parkers' of Bolton.)
249487	Mrs P. Oxenden, Jersey.
249488‡	(Henlys.)
249489‡	W. Humble, Kingston-upon-Hull.
249490*‡	O. Ormrod, Slough.

(continued on page 207)

1935 SS1 Airline prototype, photographed in Swallow Road, with the main office block beyond. At this stage, a spare wheel was countersunk into the standard SS wing. Production Airlines had skirted wings.

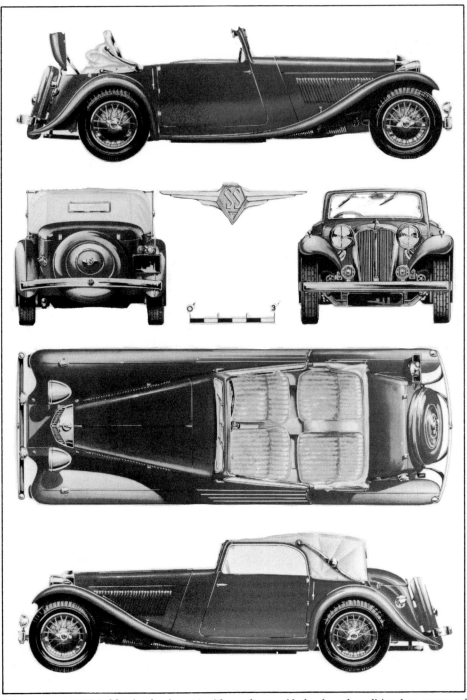

The very rare 1935-6 SS1 drophead coupé with neatly-stowable hood, and traditional rear-mounted spare wheel—a fine-looking car, drawn by former Jaguar apprentice and technical illustrator, Tim Loakes.

Number	First UK Owner *or* Agent *or* Destination
249491	R. Taylor, Leicester.
249492‡	T.E.S. Norris, London.
249493‡	B.H. Little (c/o Australian Bank, London), exported.
249494	(Henlys.)
249495	Surrey customer.
249496	H. Winstanley, Southport.
249497‡	W. Roberts, Teignmouth.
249498	(Netherlands.)

* *These cars were certainly used for competition work.*
‡ *These cars (out of 24 built) were listed by the Classic Jaguar Association in 1979.*

IX.   The SS2

The SS2 was *not* the 'second series' that its name implies. It was the smaller, four-cylinder model, whereas the SS1 was always the 'big six'. The first SS2 coupé made its debút simultaneously with the SS1 at the 1931 Olympia Show. It was really small. It was also very neat and well proportioned, and because of this it stayed in production longer than the SS1 in its original 'helmet wing' style. Based on the 'Little Nine' Standard chassis, it was offered as a coupé only, until the autumn of 1933 when it underwent a big transformation.

The original version had the 60.25 mm × 88 mm 1,006 cc engine for the two seasons it was available (as opposed to the 1,052 cc capacity usually ascribed to it). Like the 'standard' Standard Little Nine, it did acquire a four-speed gearbox after its first season, however. In autumn 1933, the Standard Little Nine chassis did get a longer-stroke (1,052 cc) engine, but the SS2 grew up even more. Swallow abandoned the Little Nine chassis for their own adaption of the new ten (1,343 cc) and 12 (1,608 cc) horsepower Standards. At that motor show, the SS2 became a full four-seater with fixed-head coupé and saloon alternatives as well as the choice of engines. In 1934 a tourer joined the range and that autumn the coupé disappeared from the catalogue. There were never 'Airline' or drophead coupé styles for the SS2. As with the SS1, only saloon models were listed for the final, 1936, season.

The SS2 coupé, as it was for the 1932 and 1933 season, based on the Standard Little Nine chassis. Like the SS1, it later gained a spare wheel cover (The Light Car and Cyclecar).

SS2 Models and prices

Model Year	Model	Price	Quantity
1932	F H Coupé	£210	274
1933	F H Coupé	£210	275
1934 and 1935	F H Coupé	£260	150
	Saloon	£265	820
	Tourer	£260	186
1935	Van	—	2
1936	F H Coupé ⎫	All prices	4
	Saloon ⎬	reduced by	85
	Tourer ⎭	about £30	—
		Total SS2	1,796

As with the SS1, the SS2 1934-5 coupé and saloon figures do not quite 'tie-up' with the apparent chassis number allocation. The total numbers for SS1 and SS2 (as listed here) do, however, tally with the *delivery* records. Regarding prices, from 1934 the SS2 had an 'underslung' chassis and a choice of engines, the prices shown here being for the 10 hp cars. A 12 hp model cost £5 extra.

The following notes relate to individual vehicles:

1932 and 1933 9 hp SS2 coupé

Car No	First destination	Notes
135959	London (?)	Probably the 1931 Olympia Show car; sold to A. Pogson of Sheffield.
126268	Birmingham (Jan 1933)	First SS2 order on Factory sales records.
150186	1932 London show	Later sold in London to Y. Molyneux Lungen.
158965	Suffolk (Sept 1933)	For N.A. Holden, Bury St Edmunds. (Last 'helmet-winged' SS2 to be delivered.)

Note: 1932 and 1933 SS2 coupés did not have consecutive chassis numbers. They must have shared Standard's own numbering system.

1934 to 1936 10/12 hp SS2

Car No	First destination	Notes
300001	1933 Glasgow Show	10 hp coupé sold via S.H. Newsome (March 1934) to A.C. Wickman (Wickman Tools).
300002	Leicestershire (Jan 1934)	10 hp saloon for P. Chamley of Leicester.
300032	London (Jan 1934)	12 hp saloon, for M.F. Maskall (first 12 hp saloon chassis number).
300041	Coventry (Jan 1934)	12 hp coupé for Dr. M. Sandoz, Holbrook Lane works doctor (first 12 hp coupé chassis number).
300379	Coventry (March 1934)	12 hp saloon, for Mrs Greta Lyons in dark blue.
300389	London (April 1934)	12 hp tourer (first SS2 tourer to be despatched).
300960	Coventry (May 1935)	10 hp special works van in olive green.
300966	Coventry (May 1935)	10 hp special works van in olive green (never photographed, it seems).
301250	Coventry (Sept 1935)	12 hp saloon for E.F. Huckvale, company secretary (last SS2 chassis number allocated).

From 1934 (a year behind the SS1) the SS2 was given the 'underslung' look. Based on 10 or 12 hp chassis, the SS2 could be had as a saloon, tourer, or coupé (as seen here).

X. The SS Jaguar

All 'Jaguar' models before the 1939-45 war were still SSs in *marque* terms. There was only one side-valve model, the first SS Jaguar 1½-litre saloon, which had the old Standard Twelve 1,608 cc four-cylinder engine. The other SS Jaguars all had the exclusive Weslake overhead-valve conversion of the 2663.7 cc Standard 20 hp six-cylinder engine, and were launched at the 1935 motor show. The saloon was the 'star', and it was supplemented by two open models of more familiar appearance. One was the SS Jaguar 100, with bodywork continuing on from the production model SS90; the other was the SS Jaguar four-seater tourer. The latter effectively used up the last hundred-odd SS1 tourer bodies and was thus a rarity, even then; but it was a useful gap-bridger until the first SS Jaguar drophead coupé appeared in 1937.

Several SS Jaguar 2½-litre chassis were sent abroad. Notable exponents of special bodywork in the late 1930s and 40s were the two Swiss importers, although Emil Frey of Zürich was more active in this field than Marcel Fleury of Geneva. Between them, however, they must have had bodies built for SS Jaguars by most of the better Swiss coachbuilders, and at the 1937 Geneva show there was a fine drophead coupé (with spare wheel hidden somewhere inside the body) that anticipated the factory's own convertible by six months.

Early coachbuilt SS Jaguars at the 1937 SS Car Club meeting at Donington. Nearest the camera is W. McGowan Gradon's side-valve '1½'; next is Lady Mary Grosvenor's '2½'. The early '1½' looked good, apart from the protruding spare wheel which would not go further into the wing.

Resumé of all SS deliveries (indicating Swallow 'overlap')

Model year	Austin Seven Swallow	Wolseley Hornet Swallow	Standard 9 & 16 Swallow	SS1 (inc '90')	SS2	SS Jaguar 1,608 cc	SS Jaguar 1,776 cc	SS Jaguar 2,664 cc	SS Jaguar 3,485 cc	Total for year
1932	108	380	90	502	274	—	—	—	—	1,354
1933	1	150	4	1,249	275	—	—	—	—	1,679
1934	—	—	—	1,166	627	—	—	—	—	1,793
1935	—	—	—	1,189	531	—	—	—	—	1,720
1936	—	—	—	148	89	700	—	1,532	—	2,469
1937	—	—	—	—	—	1,453	642	2,101	—	3,554
1938	—	—	—	—	—	55	3,748	801	711	2,209
1939	—	—	—	—	—	—	687	992	638	5,378
1940	—	—	—	—	—	—	—	141	71	899
Total (Type)	109	530	94	4,254	1,796	2,208	5,077	5,567	1,420	21,055

Deliveries in above period represent: 735 Swallow, 6,050 SS 1/2 and 14,272 SS 'Jaguar'.

SS Jaguar Home & Export Delivers (*Export figures in italics*)

Model year	1,608 cc (side-valve) saloon	1,776 cc saloon	1,776 cc drop-head coupé	2,664 cc coach-built saloon	2,664 cc tourer	2,664 cc pressed steel saloon	2,664 cc drop-head coupé	2,664 cc '100'	3,485 cc saloon	3,485 cc drop-head coupé	3,485 cc '100'	Total for year
1936	680 *20*	—	—	1,366 *82*	36 *17*	—	—	26 *5*	—	—	—	2,232
1937	1,401 *52*	—	—	1,805 *160*	27 *18*	—	—	78 *13*	—	—	—	3,554
1938	55	541 *32*	64 *5*	—	—	585 *73*	76 *12*	48 *7*	498 *40*	98 *6*	56 *13*	2,209
1939 & 1940	—	3,708 *121*	584 *22*	—	—	832 *87*	158 *35*	16 *5*	484 *43*	120 *15*	41 *6*	6,277
Home	2,136	4,249	648	3,171	63	1,417	234	168	982	218	97	(13,383)
Export	*72*	*153*	*27*	*242*	*35*	*160*	*47*	*30*	*83*	*21*	*19*	*(889)*
Totals	2,208	4,402	675	3,413	98	1,577	281	198	1,065	239	116	14,272

Although several occurred in 1936, the most obvious changes to the SS Jaguars happened for the autumn of 1937. The '1½' had a new ohv version of the Standard 14 engine; the '2½'-engine remained much the same; and there was a new '3½', to make the SS Jaguar 100 two-seater the company's first genuine 100 mile-an-hour production motor car. This was when the new steel body construction came in for the saloons, and for the new drophead which replaced the old tourer 'on paper' although it was a totally different animal.

A few special bodies were made by British coachbuilders. Memorable convertibles were made by Maltby of Folkestone and by New Avon of Warwick, two of the latter being constructed on '100' chassis to the order of Coventry's SS distributor, 'Sammy' Newsome. He might have arranged for more to be made, had it not been for the war. The design didn't hold a candle to Lyons' own one-off '100' coupé at Olympia in 1938.

The first-ever Jaguar limousine was probably the 3½-litre model bodied by Mulliner of Birmingham to the specification of Standard chief, Captain John Black. It was well-proportioned, but quite un-Jaguar-like, and had razor-edge styling; Standard's post-war Triumph Renown had a lot of 'Mulliner' in it, too!

The '100' was the first of Lyons' real rally winners. Harrop's performance in the 1939 'Monte' with a 3½-litre saloon was an outstanding but almost isolated case of an 'ordinary' SS doing well in serious competition.

*   *   *

The pre-war 'Jaguars' all had right-hand drive. As with the SS1s, I have decided to include more details of these models than some of the later ones, mainly because so little has been published on these models previously—and, of course, because they were *the* first cars to bear the famous name 'Jaguar'. The most famous of them all are the SS 100s, of which there are a number of bogus examples masquerading as the real thing. With these cars being so highly valued, *caveat emptor* applies more than ever!

Slightly broader in the beam, the all-ohv pressed-steel models from 1938 dispensed with external spare wheel mounting. This, again is a '1½', although its actual capacity was 1,776 cc. This picture was taken at the works, outside the engineering department.

Above *In 'Jaguar' guise, the tourer is quickly recognisable by its larger brake drums. Records vary slightly, but (to within five) just 100 of these ohv tourers were made, 35—including this one—being exported.* **Below** *The definitive Jaguar of the immediate pre-war era—the 3½-litre saloon. Bertie Henly and colleagues set off on a selling mission (R. Huckvale).*

SS Jaguar Chassis number list

Model	Chassis sequences	Type	UK price	Suggested total
1936/7	10001 to 13445	2½-litre saloon	£385	3,445
1936/7	18001 to 18126	2½-litre '100'	£395	126
1936/7	19001 to 19105	2½-litre Tourer	£375	105
1936/7	20001 to 22250	1½-litre (sv) saloon	£295	2,250
1938/9	30001 to 31003	3½-litre saloon	£445	1,003
1938/9	36001 to 36238	3½-litre drophead coupé	£465	238
1938/9	39001 to 39118	3½-litre '100'	£445	118
1938/9	40001 to 41445	2½-litre saloon	£395	1,445
1938/9	46001 to 46273	2½-litre drophead coupé	£415	273
1938/9	49001 to 49065	2½-litre '100'	£395	65
1938/9	50001 to 53754	1½-litre saloon	£298	3,754
1938/9	56001 to 56660	1½-litre drophead coupé	£318	600
1940	70001 to 70688	1½-litre saloon/drophead coupé	★	688
1940	80001 to 80135	2½-litre saloon/drophead coupé	★	135
1940	90001 to 90068	3½-litre saloon/drophead coupé	★	68
			Suggested grand total	14,313

★ *The 1939 3½-litre SS 100 fixed head coupé, listed at £595, remained a prototype. By 1940, prices were: 1½-litre saloon = £325; 2½-litre SS 100 and saloon = £435; and 3½-litre SS 100 and saloon = £490. Note: Drophead coupé bodies were built on 43 of the 1940 chassis, as follows '1½' = 34; '2½' = 6; '3½' = 3. (The new, 1940, numbering system was a product of the 'phoney war'.)*

Chassis for coachbuilders

(included in chassis sequences, above)

10000 series:	13	to Emil Frey, Zürich.
	2	to Marcel Fleury, Geneva.
	1	to Henlys.
30000 series:	3	to Fleury, Geneva.
	1	to Anglocars, Bucharest.
	4	to Emil Frey, Zürich.
	4	to UK (inc 2 via Henlys).
40000 series:	2	to Fleury, Geneva.
	4	to UK (via Henlys).
Total	34	(*excluding* SS 100 chassis—see notes overleaf.)

Selected chassis numbers from SS Jaguar sales records

10001	Completed Oct 18 1935, AKV 779 (demo '2½' saloon).
10003	(See 19001 overleaf).
10015	Henlys (demo).
10123	Captain Black (Standard Motor Co).
10198	F. Gordon Crosby (artist).
10409	H.N. Gillitt (director).
10443	D.S. Hand (class winner in 1936 Welsh Rally).
10695	Lady Mary Grosvenor (racing driver).
12306	One-off works-built prototype drophead coupé (bought Dec 1937) by Rex Carter, (via Henlys).
12462	2½-litre saloon, CDU 700, Mrs Lyons' car (preserved at works).
18001	Works to N. Pyman (BHP 800) after use in 1936 RAC Rally.
18002	London & Glasgow show car.
18003	P. Marx (see pages 104 and 105).

18007   F.J. McEvoy, class-winner 1936 Marne GP.
18008   Works car (see note below).
18015   Captain J.P. Black.
18026   C. de Oliveira (Portugal—see page 102).
18046   E.H. Jacob (ATM 700)—1937 Welsh Rally winner.
18050   J. Harrop—1937 RAC Rally winner.
18065   L. Kirk-Greene; later to James Leasor, writer.
18086   V.M. Hetherington (CRW 7), later to John Owen.
18105   C.E. Truett (specially altered).
19001   First Jaguar tourer (actually using saloon chassis 10003).
20001   1936 1½-litre side-valve saloon—1935 London show (BDU 983).
20006   1936 1½-litre side-valve saloon—T.W. Daffern (director).
22193 ⎫
22194 ⎭ 1937 models—supplied 'unassembled' to Frank Cavey, Dublin, importer for Ireland.
30001   Experimental department (dismantled), first '3½' saloon.
30002   Earls Court show car, 1937 (first 'non-Olympia' year).
30003   Earls Court show car, 1937
30004   Henlys (demo).
30797   Works car (DKV 101); best British performance, 1939 Monte Carlo Rally (J. Harrop).
36020   Drophead coupé for Captain Black.
39001   For Prince Michael of Roumania (CKV 250).
39035   H.E. Bradley (car prepared at Brooklands by W.T.F. Hassan).
39053   Works rally/press car (DHP 734), raced by W. Lyons (see page 108).
39054   Works car (DHP 735).
39055   Works car (DHP 736); winner, 1938 RAC Rally, driver J. Harrop.
39110   Works car (EHP 201); runner-up, 1939 RAC Rally, driver S.H. Newsome.
39118   Last 3½-litre '100' chassis number.
49001   First 1938-model 2½-litre '100'.
49010   Works car (see note below).
49065   Last 2½-litre '100' chassis number.
50001   First ohv '1½' saloon, for Digby Paul (SS service manager).
50346   For Mr Lee of Coventry Climax Engines.

SS Jaguar 100 notes

Special bodies: Two chassis (39109 and 39115) were supplied to S.H. Newsome in 1939, and given drophead coupé bodies by the New Avon company of Warwick. Two more (39092 and 39113) ordered by Emil Frey were given Swiss convertible coachwork; one made by Willy Bernath—inspired, apparently, by a jelly-mould. The post-war delivery to Belgium (49064) resulted in a curvy French-style shape by Van den Plas, displayed at the Brussels show. The best-looking special body was SS's own 1938 Earls Court Show stunner, the one-off fixed-head coupé (39088) of which Gordon March became the lucky first owner. He is at the wheel in the picture on page 109.

Engine changes: Several SS 100s have had engine changes, usually from 2½ to 3½ litres. The most famous cases are probably 18008 (BWK77)—the works/Wisdom/Newsome rally and sprint car which the company did not sell until after the war, when it was acquired by George Matthews—and 49010 (LNW 100) which was kept at William Lyons' home during the war, and then sold to Ian Appleyard who drove it with great success (with 3½-litre engine) in the 1948 Alpine and 1949 Tulip rallies.

XI.   War-time production

When the phoney war became a real one, and after initial worries about what would happen to SS Cars Ltd and Swallow Coachbuilding (1935) Ltd, a variety of contracts began to arrive. At first there was chaos, but then a system for separating all the different contract sources was devised, people got used to war-time conditions, and an impressive amount of work was done, as can be seen from the production records below.

A shoe factory near Leicester was commandeered for the company, and this provided its basis for entry into the world of machining and full-scale manufacture later on—although, of course, the shoe factory itself was vacated when war work ended. Motor vehicle manufacture was limited to the VA and VB lightweight prototypes. The sidecar shop was very productive, of course. No civilian sidecars were made, however, before these interests were sold-off as hostilities drew to a close.

Cancellation of the 'Manchester' bomber had made the new factory buildings at Swallow Road seem superfluous, but—once the contract work had begun to flow—they were to become essential. For a company which had only recently progressed beyond the role of coachbuilder, the following list indicates how successfully it rose to the occasion:

Service work

134	Whitley Bomber aircraft repaired & flight tested
339	Whitley Bomber aircraft broken down & part salvaged
857	Cheetah auxilliary drive units reconditioned & tested
80 sets	Whitley wings modified to carry heavier bombs
18	Whitley tail planes modified
333	Whitley fuel tanks repaired
(?)	Wellington mainplanes
(?)	Stirling elevators

Whitley Bomber parts

1,399	Cockpit roofs
100 prs	Bomb doors
200 sets	Landing gear doors
50	Tail planes
150 sets	Spar panels
1,100	Bomb door fenders
570	Bomb beams
1,223	Fuel tanks fireproofed
1,280	Cage formers
1,604	Former 'B'
1,150	Formers 'A' & 'C'
1,150	Formers 'D' 'E' & 'F'

Meteor III aircraft parts

98	Complete centre sections

Short's Stirling parts

1,181	Trailing edge in way of aileron
1,039	Trailing edge in way of flap
575	Leading edge outer portion
490	Leading edge between nacelles
140 sets	Trailing edge ribs
483	Dinghy stowage covers

Mosquito parts

19,562	Fuel tanks fireproof covered
500	Oil tanks fireproof covered

Spitfire parts

294 prs	Wing tips
1,586	Oil tanks
1,150	30-gallon Jettison tanks
550	170-gallon Jettison tanks

'Lancaster' parts

503	Bomb doors

'Cheetah' engine parts

3,066	Auxiliary drive casings
13,361	Front covers
8,105	Diaphragm plates
8,640	Auxiliary drive units

Aircraft gun control parts

6,998	Four gun control sets
23,954	Relay boxes
5,749	Ammunition box frames
24,309	Cartridge link chutes
18,644	Ammunition boxes
750	Oxygen bottle cradles
4,461	Ammunition boxes

Miscellaneous

5,097	Aircraft de-icing tanks
1,220	Oxford airspeed tanks fireproofed

WD Vehicles

30,052	10-cwt amphibious trailers
15,595	Airborne trailers (Special)
136	Special light scout trucks
1,640	10-cwt trailers (wood)
1,730	Mule carts
208	6-ton fuselage trailers
335	Special RAF camera carrying sidecars
3,751	WD sidecars
1,295	Box sidecars
3,927	Passenger sidecars
4,002	Canopy sets for lorries
1	VA prototype rear-engined
1	VB prototype front-engined

Above *Swallow Road in war-time, and part of the large order for sidecars negotiated by Howard Davies, the former TT rider and motorcycle manufacturer.*

Left *A 'mock-up' of the little JAP-engined prototype, complete with dummy weapons. The power unit was to be mounted in the rear, to the offside. The vehicle was called the 'VA'.*

Below *The Ford-engined VB lightweight prototype, made by SS. The straked rear tyre, on test here, was discarded for military trials (W.T.F. Hassan).*

Spring 1949, and the last of the 'pre-Mark Five' Jaguars is handed over to dealer Nick Haines by (left to right) Alec Blythe, Sam Hird, 'Sarge' Mapley, Eric Warren (sales manager), and Frank Bradley of the despatch department.

XII.   The post-war range

With certain changes, mostly caused by material shortages and other privations, the saloon range returned in 1945 as the product of the new company—Jaguar Cars Ltd, so they were the first pure Jaguars as opposed to SSs in *marque* terms. They were also the first of the company's products to have the option of driving controls on the left! The two six-cylinder engines were now made at the much enlarged Jaguar works at the top of Swallow Road which, as mentioned earlier, was an unadopted estate road off Holbrook Lane in the Coventry postal district of Foleshill. (Thus, this site has been variously described over the years as 'Foleshill', 'Holbrook Lane' and 'Swallow Road'— leading to occasional confusion.)

The four-cylinder engine continued to be made at Standard's Canley works, however, and soon it was not exclusive to Jaguar, who still called their car the '1½'. The first John Black-inspired Triumphs—the Roadster and the 'pre-Renown' saloon—were called the '1800' models. That terminology was not only more modern; it was more accurate, too, since the capacity was 1,776 cc.

In 1945 *The Motor* wrote: 'For the moment closed bodies only are available and the "100" series of open sports cars is temporarily out of production'. In fact, no SS 100s were made post-war although their occasional success in competition—thanks mainly to Ian Appleyard—helped them to seem 'current'. Eventually, however, Jaguar responded to demand and re-introduced the drophead for the 1948 season and into early 1949.

As in the 1930s, Switzerland was the main customer for 'chassis only', particularly before the factory's own convertible reappeared.

1946 to 1949 Jaguar resumé: Saloon and drophead coupé deliveries (combined total of 1½-, 2½-, and 3½-litre models)

Home 7,786, Export 4,166; Total 11,952. This *includes* 31 2½-litre drophead (Export), 73 2½-litre drophead (UK), 376 3½-litre drophead (Export), 184 3½-litre drophead (UK).

Chassis for coachbuilders (included on previous page)
2½-litre: one for Emil Frey, Zürich, one for Marcel Fleury, Geneva, one for Joska Bourgeois, Brussels. 3½-litre: nine for Frey, one for Fleury, one for Bourgeois. Total of 14 chassis.

A batch of 'Standard-engined' (four-cylinder, 1,776 cc) 1949 saloons was supplied to senior Jaguar staff, presumably in the knowledge that these would be the last 'small' Jaguars! The final chassis number (415450) was allocated to Bernard Hartshorn.

XIII.   The Mark Five

Jaguar's turning-point from not-so-ancient to distinctly modern happened via the Mark Five. At a time when there were some weird styles, and 'taste' (for want of a better word) was re-establishing itself, William Lyons shrewdly avoided doing anything too dramatic to his bread-and-butter range too soon after the war and the Mark Five was subtle rather than sensational.

The same two six-cylinder engines as before were now, in autumn 1948, available in a new chassis—Jaguar's first to have independent front suspension. (Following pre-war experiments, a torsion bar system had been chosen.) There were saloons and dropheads.

The Mark Five was not offered as a '1½', and the last of the old four-cylinder saloons were produced in the spring of 1949. (Standard-Triumph brought in their new Vanguard four-cylinder engine and soon the Triumphs were fitted with them. As the 1,776 cc engine was dropped altogether, so was the 20-year connection between Lyons' company and Black's.)

The 2½ and 3½-litre Jaguar Mark Five lasted for virtually three seasons, providing a useful overlap with the Mark Seven in 1951. Although it might not look suitable for such activities, the Mark Five did quite well in rallying. Two superb results were achieved by Cecil Vard in the Monte Carlo Rally—third in 1951 and fifth in 1953, by which time the Mark Five was well and truly obsolete.

The Jaguar Mark Five, although an interim model, had a special appeal. It was the first Jaguar production model to have independent front suspension. In the hands of Cecil Vard in particular, it did surprisingly well in rallies. This one, driven enterprisingly in the 1952 Swedish Midnight Sun Rally, by Evald Hagstrom, had cloth on the radiator cowl and blankets on the wings to protect the bodywork, on the loose-surfaced Swedish forest roads (R. Palm/J. Stenback).

Mark Five 1949-51: Saloon and drophead coupé deliveries

	UK	Export	Total (model)
3½-litre saloon	3,124	4,690	7,814
2½-litre saloon	1,114	533	1,647
			9,461
3½-litre drophead coupé	137	840	977
2½-litre drophead coupé	1	27	28
			1,005
Total (UK and Export)	4,376	6,090	10,466

Notes: Jaguar's own historic collection includes a MK V saloon, chassis number 620143.
Post-war prices are shown in one of the general tables elsewhere.

XIV.   The XK 120/140/150

While the Mark Five captured conservative imaginations, the XK 120 provided the biggest headlines that accompanied the first post-war London motor show, in October 1948. The first catalogue indicated that there would be two twin-ohc models—the XK 100 and the XK 120, their names suggesting their speed capabilities. The four-cylinder XK 100 would have had a capacity of 1,995 cc (80.5 mm bore by 98 mm stroke) and preparations for its manufacture were well advanced when it was decided to stick to the 'six'.

The 3,442 cc Jaguar XK 120 was not perfect—no motor vehicle *could* ever be called perfect—but it will go down in history as one of the great car designs of all time. Its beautiful styling and its fine engine are part of the story. The prestige and the foreign currency (mostly dollars) that it brought—directly and indirectly through subsequent Jaguar models—make the XK 120 shine through the greyness of Britain in the 1940s.

None of its successors ever looked quite as 'pure' as the original roadster, although I have a particular liking for the 1951 fixed-head coupé with its good proportions and thoughtful neatness of its 'frameless' rear window. The third body style was the convertible of 1953. All but the first 240 roadsters were built with steel main body structure. Later in its life, there were 'special equipment' models, known in North America as the 'XK 120M'.

Ron Sutton with Bill Heynes (right) and Wally Hassan at the works in 1949, shortly before taking HKV 500 to Belgium for its demonstration to the press. (See photo on page 137.)

Above *This XK 120 coupé, still owned by Jaguar, made fame by averaging over 100 mph for a whole week in 1952. Birmingham Post motoring correspondent Jack Hay (in cap) chats to Colonel Norman Steeley (right) and Stanley Rodway—joint managing directors of P.J. Evans Ltd, the Birmingham distributors—after a test run and prior to the car going on display in their showrooms. By the driver's door is rally and trials driver Ken Rawlings (Birmingham Post & Mail).* **Below** *Best looking of the XK 150 range was the roadster. This one is an XK 150S which had a triple-carburettor engine and 'mechanical' overdrive control as standard.*

The XK 140 maintained the fine styling, although the fixed-head model had a bigger 'cab', with room for very small children behind the seats. In retrospect the bumpers, which were more practical than the original ones, do not seem so clumsy as they did when they first appeared. The example on the dust jacket is one of very few XK 140 roadsters to have been sold in Britain. The XK 140 had rack-and-pinion steering, and later models featured over-drive and automatic transmission as options; but drum brakes were still standard. The 'special equipment' model had what was called a 'C' type cylinder head (confusing, because of the car of that name), and it was described in the USA as the 'XK 140 MC'.

The XK 150 was podgier, but its slightly 'dating' style was outweighed by its greatest feature—four-wheel disc braking. There was an XK 150 'S' model with three SU carburet-tors. Late models could be ordered with a 3.8-litre engine. Most sporting and attractive was the 3.8-litre XK 150 'S' roadster which had a good overdrive control; when you disengaged direct-top gear a simple linkage disengaged overdrive, too, so that you had to select overdrive yourself every time you wanted to use it.

The XK 120 was a great competition car, highlights being Stirling Moss' win in the 1950 Tourist Trophy race, Johnny Claes' 1951 *Marathon de la Route* victory, and Ian Appleyard's rallying achievements, including two RAC Rally wins and four Alpine Cups. Other XK 120 Alpine Cup winners, but only once each, were Gatsonides, Gendebien, Habisreutinger and the husband and wife team of Reg and Joan Mansbridge, the Jaguar agents for Lincoln. Leslie Johnson led several record-breaking attempts, including one in which a prototype XK 120 fixed-head coupé averaged more than 100 mph for a whole week.

Other cars were becoming more 'modern' by the time the XK 140 appeared, but it took several good 'places'—including Appleyard's second in the 1956 RAC Rally and fourth place in the 1958 Acropolis Rally by Nicky Papamichail (who had *won* outright five years before, in an XK 120). Most consistent Britisher was George ('Bobby') Parkes who did well in British Rallies with his XK 140 coupé and won the British Trials and Rally Driver's association 'Silver Star' for his 1958 performances. David Hobbs was racing his 'Mechamatic' automatic XK 140 drophead coupé successfully as recently as 1960. Walter Hansgen won a race or two in America with an XK 150 'S' roadster, while Eric Haddon and Charles Vivian won their class in the 1960 Tulip Rally with a similar car.

Never were the XK 140 and XK 150 developed for serious competition, although they were still in a class of their own among road cars. Production details of the different XKs—and indeed all SS and Jaguar cars—are included in this book. The XK 150 continued in production until the winter of 1960-61. No special body on the XK chassis was ever quite such a distinctive work of art as a Swallow Road or Browns Lane 'original'.

There have been many famous XK 120 sports cars and here is a selection, by chassis number:

660001	First RHD car, raced by Bira at Silverstone 1949 (HKV 455); then to experimental.
660002	Sent to Brysons, Australia, July 1949.
660003	Sent to Hoffman, New York, January 1950.
660022	J.L. van Dieten, Dutch racing driver, January 1950.
660040	Works-prepared, allocated to Leslie Johnson (JWK 651).
660041	Works-prepared, allocated to 'Nick' Haines.
660042	Works-prepared, allocated to Peter Walker (JWK 977).
660043	Works-prepared, allocated to Clemente Biondetti (JWK 650).
660044	Works-prepared, allocated to Ian Appleyard (NUB 120).
660057	Works-prepared, allocated to Tom Wisdom (JWK 988).
660058	Last RHD alloy body (F 1218) exported to Singapore.
660066	Oscar Swahn, Swedish racing driver.
660075	Lieutenant Colonel A.T.G. ('Goldie') Gardner (first UK delivery of 'steel' car).

660696	Used by William Lyons' son, John (KRW 923).
660731	Sold by Emil Frey to Ruef Habisreutinger (Alpine Cup Winner).
660742	(to 660747) = batch assembled by Frank Cavey in Dublin.
660748*	Fitted with Body No LT 2. (LT 3 was fitted to 660741; see note).*
660886	John Manussis, East Africa, racing driver.
660971	Experimental department, fitted with rack and pinion steering.
661071	Second Appleyard XK 120 rally car, converted to drophead body (RUB 120).
661140	Late RHD roadster, now in Jaguar Cars' own collection.
669002	Fixed head coupé (LWK 707) in Jaguar Cars' own collection.
670001	Originally white, later red (for 1949 race) then sent to Hoffman, USA.
670002	Second LHD car, HKV 500, converted to RHD, Silverstone and Liège winner.
670003	Early Western USA delivery (Hornburg, September 1949).
670004	First Canadian delivery (August 1949).
670005	First Eastern USA delivery (Hoffman, August 1949).
670138	Taken from factory (where he had been trained) to California by Philip T. Hill.
670184	Last LHD alloy body (F 1240), exported to Holland.

Three special bodies were made for Le Mans in 1951, in case the C-type was not ready. LT2 and LT3 were raced under Hornburg's aegis in America, where they were called the 'Silverstone' models. LT1 was bought by Bob Berry and raced successfully in the British Isles, fitted to his own XK 120 chassis (MWK 120).

XK resumé

	XK 120	XK 140	XK 150		XK 150S	
			(3.4)	(3.8)	(3.4)	(3.8)
Open	7,631	3,347	1,297	42	888	36
Fixed head coupé	2,678	2,797	3,445	656	199	150
Drophead coupé	1,769	2,740	1,903	586	104	89
Totals	12,078	8,884	6,645	1,284	1,191	275

Transmission options (included above)

NB: All XK 120 and XK 140 models had manual transmission *except* 385 XK 140 DHCs plus 396 XK 140 FHCs which had automatic transmission *and* the following quantities of XK 150:

	(3.4)		(3.8)	
Open	71	(Auto)	1	(All XK 150 S
	489	(O/D)	30	models
Fixed head coupé	674	(Auto)	197	had
	1,651	(O/D)	334	overdrive.)
Drophead coupé	440	(Auto)	209	
	789	(O/D)	264	

Grand totals (1949/54)	XK 120	12,078
(1954/57)	XK 140	8,884
(1957/60)	XK 150	7,929
(1958/60)	XK 150 S	1,466
		30,357

XV.   The large XK-engined saloons

For 20 years, from 1950 to 1970, Jaguar capitalised on the market for a large, fast and in-dividual saloon car—large, that is, to a European but not to an American. First came the Mark Seven—at Earls Court in October 1950, and shortly afterwards at a special show in New York. As with the XK 120, I prefer its styling to that of its successors, the Marks Eight and Nine. The Mark Seven was the car that emerged from the pile of ideas remaining after the Mark Five had been plucked from it to appear two years earlier. It looked longer and wider than it really was. The chassis was similar to the Mark Five's, but it had the great new XK engine, already well-established in the XK 120 sports car.

After a few years, automatic transmission became one of several updating options. A more powerful Mark Seven (the M-type) was introduced late in 1954. Two years later came the Mark Eight—two-tone colour schemes, one piece windscreen, and different in many ways; this was very much a 'face-lift' model. Big mechanical improvements were put into this package to create a Mark Nine for the 1958 London show. The main ones were disc brakes and the new 3.8-litre variation of the XK power unit which was having its tenth birthday already!

By 1961 a new large-scale saloon was needed in the Jaguar range, and late that year the integral Mark Ten was launched, featuring all-independent suspension, and the 3.8-litre engine with three carburettors. It was big and bulbous, but its fittings were superb, and it could be driven on the road as no big Jaguar could ever be driven before; what is more, it developed into a truly great car. There was the 4.2-litre model (late 1964) followed by a third series (re-named the '420G') two years later. A nice 420G feature, once you got used to it, was the varying-ratio steering.

Now that they are growing old, this range is becoming more and more difficult to replace by the company boss who cannot find as big a British 'personal' car that is also as comfortable or refined. The XJ is big enough for most, fortunately—but while preparing this book I have seen the occasional 420G still being chauffeur-driven, although it must have been 15 years old at least! (Indeed, late models were available as limousines, with division.) The 420G 'overlapped' with the XJ6 for nearly two years, the last of the really big Jaguar saloons being made in 1970.

Of all the larger Jaguars, only the Mark Seven was ever found suitable for racing in contemporary conditions. It won the Silverstone touring car races annually from 1952 to 1956, in which year it also won the Monte Carlo Rally having nearly done so several times before.

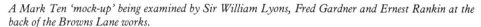

A Mark Ten 'mock-up' being examined by Sir William Lyons, Fred Gardner and Ernest Rankin at the back of the Browns Lane works.

Above *Stirling Moss takes the Mark Seven Jaguar to the first of its five successive Silverstone touring car race wins (1952-56).* **Below** *Jaguar Mark Tens for export in the early 1960s. (The Browns Lane offices underwent a major rebuild in the winter of 1984-85.)* **Right** *Based on the Mark Ten/420G structure, the Daimler limousine with 4.2-litre XK engine has been in production since 1968. Originally assembled at the Vanden Plas works in London, it was being produced at the Jaguar works in the 1980s.*

Deliveries

		Home	Export	Total
1951-5	MK VII (3.4)	7,930	12,978	
1955-7	MK VIIM (3.4)	6,243	3,818	30,969
1957-9	MK VIII (3.4)	3,764	2,448	6,212
1959-61	MK IX (3.8)	5,362	4,647	10,009
1962-4	MK X (3.8)	7,607	5,775	13,382
1965-6	MK X (4.2)	2,828	2,291	
	MK X limousine	15	3	5,137
1967-70	420G	3,435	2,304	
	420G limousine	14	10	5,763
	Total	37,198	34,274	71,472

Daimler*

1968 (to Jan 1 1985)	MKX-based Daimler			
	Limousine (DS 420)	2,681	455	3,136
	'Drive-away' DS 420 chassis	666	2	668
	Total	3,347	457	3,804

Note: Two of these XK-engined limousines were made as landaulettes by Vanden Plas and exported in 1974/5. (The limousine's predecessor, the Majestic 'Major', had been offered as a 4½-litre V8 saloon, limousine, or chassis. In its last three model years—1966 to 1968—a total of 535 had been delivered.)

A selection from the records

710001	First RHD MK VII number, Experimental; then chassis to service school.
710002	Experimental dept.
710003	First show-car (London & New York), Twilight Blue, sold to Henlys.
710004	Frequently used as 'tender car' for races/rallies (KRW 76).
710005	Exported to Hong Kong.
710006	Experimental dept fitted light alloy body; bought by R. Berry 1958.

710060   Belgium, for 'Monsieur Frère' (father of Paul Frère).
727554   1955 MK VII (updated to MK IX spec); formerly owned by the Queen Mother, now
          in Jaguar collection.
730001   First LHD chassis number, Exported to California (Dec 1950).
735556   Used by Jo Eerdmans (Jaguar Cars, New York) (1953).
750001   MK VII drophead coupé, prototype (1953); scrapped; one of two with power operated
          top.
300001   First experimental MK X.
300005   Demonstration car (6100 RW).
300006/7 1961 London Show stand.
300050   Endurance test car; crashed, 1961, (5437 RW) dismantled.
300051   Endurance test car; completed French programme (5438 RW).
351854   Experimental tests (Badalini transmission).
ID 50002/3/4 MK X 4.2-litre models, all fitted with development V12 engines.
ID 51762 Sir William Lyons' MK X limousine (FRW 169C).
ID 52494 Registered GUY I for Arthur Jones, Guy Motors.
GID 55943 Sir William Lyons' 420 G limousine (MKV 77G).

XVI.   The C-type and D-type

In the great racing years of Jaguar, to win Le Mans was the company's prime aim. Jaguars might win hundreds of other races but, after the potential shown by the XK 120 in 1950, France's world-famous 24-hour *Grand Prix d'Endurance* became the number one target for Coventry.

The XK 120C (or C-type) sports-racing car had the XK engine and many other components of the XK 120, but was lighter by virtue of its rigid tubular frame. It even had to *look* like the XK 120, at William Lyons' insistence, although the close affinity is immediately obvious only if the cars are viewed from certain angles—such was the subtlety of Malcolm Sayer's work. The three 1951 cars, one of which won at Le Mans, had twin 1¾-inch SU carburettors. 'Production' models, made in 1952 and 1953, had two two-inch SU

The big one! Jaguar's first of five Le Mans victories. Peter Whitehead (at the wheel) and Peter Walker return 'the wrong way' down the circuit with the C-type after winning at record speed. Architect of victory, Lofty England, walks behind.

The first two C-types in America, 1952. Jock Reid—Jaguar appointed service chief for the USA—changes plugs at Elkhart Lake. Nearest camera is Max Hoffman's car (XKC 009) with George Weaver at the wheel. The darker car is Chuck Hornburg's (XKC 007) with which Phil Hill gave the 'C' its first Transatlantic win. Exactly 30 years later, the US-built Jaguar V12-powered XJR-5 would make its impressive debut here, on the newer 'Road America' circuit.

carburettors. The 1953 works cars, which swept the board at Le Mans, had lighter bodies, disc brakes, and more powerful engines fitted with triple Weber carburettors. They also had better rear axle location.

If the C-type looked beautiful when it was standing still, the D-type was at its most glorious when seen approaching through a long, smooth fast bend and droning away into the distance. The D-type's multi-curved shape was the E-type's direct ancestor and Sayer's masterpiece. Its structure—with *monocoque* centre section and engine mounted within a tubular frame in front of it—was the principle upon which the E-type was based. Three wins in a row at Le Mans established the D-type as one of the most successful purpose-built sports-racing cars of all time.

D-types had dry-sump lubrication, and production models stuck to triple Weber carburation. 'Mechanical' fuel injection was first used by Jaguar at Sebring on a factory-entered 'long-nose' car in 1956, and—following action by the Momo Corporation on Briggs Cunningham's behalf, plus the factory's subsequent development work—3.8 litres *and* petrol injection were used on the factory-prepared *Ecurie Ecosse*-entered 1957 Le Mans-winner.

The regulations for Le Mans made it clear that three litres would be the top limit from 1958, and this no doubt helped influence Jaguar in deciding not to develop the D-type from then on—although private owners were given assistance (especially for the French classic) from time to time. Three litre conversions for the D-type were not a success, although Duncan Hamilton's car might have been runner-up in 1958 if Britain's toughest *ancien pilote* had not had the mother and father of all accidents when the end was in sight.

The C-type and D-type gave Jaguar that 'edge' which, historically, puts the Coventry firm's achievements among the proudest of British industry. The D-type was even made on a production line, and the 'left overs' made into XK SSs.

Resumé of C-type, D-type and XK SS production

XKC 001 to 003	1951 works team cars.
XKC 004 to 050	1952/3 'production' cars, including several raced by the works.
XKC 051 to 053	1953 works team cars.

Total: 53 C-types

XKD 401 to 406	1954 batch, including works team.
XKD 501 and 502	1955 Ecurie Ecosse cars.
XKD 503	1955 Belgian Le Mans car.
XKD 504 to 508	1955 works and Cunningham 'long-nose' cars.
XKD 509 to 575	1955/6 'production' D-types (less 16 cars, for which see 'XKSS' below).
XKD 601 to 606	Final (1956) batch of works 'long-nose' cars.

Total: 87 D-types

XKSS 701	This was the first of a series of 16 non-consecutive numbers to identify 16 'road-going' versions of the D-type from early 1957. These cars were, in fact, converted from existing D-types. Another way of counting is to say: 71 D-types plus 16 XKSS.

Notes

C-type: The 1953 'works' cars were considerably lighter and more powerful than their predecessors, and had disc brakes.

D-type: At least two D-types were converted to 'XK SS' specification after sale. On the other hand, several XK SSs have been re-converted more-or-less to D-type again!

XK SS: Chassis numbering was not done in sequence, but XKSS 701 was in fact the New York 'demonstrator'. The XKSS was never a major race winner, for it did not fit into any serious category. XKSS 757 was the most successful, winning the Macau Grand Prix in two successive years.

Engines: As well as serving its own and its customer's needs, Jaguar has from time to time prepared and supplied power units for other competitive activities—for example to successful constructors such as Cooper, HWM, Lister, and Tojeiro. The first recorded sale of such an engine was an XK unit for hydroplane recordman Norman Buckley in the spring of 1950. Another early XK engine delivery was in 1951, for Frank Le Gallais of Jersey to put in the rear of his hill-climb 'special'.

XVII. The compact saloons

The D-type may be regarded as the first monocoque Jaguar, but the 2.4 saloon of September 1955 was the original fully-integral Jaguar for volume production. As William Lyons did not smoke, the ashtray was an afterthought from Norman Dewis who did! It was hidden in a wooden fillet which you pulled out. If you had a dangling keyring, the ash would go everywhere.

The 2.4 had a tapering body, and the front wheels were more than four inches further apart than the rear ones. It had a short-stroke engine; initially Solex carburettors were used, and the mounting of them permitted the chassis-body structure to be lowered over the complete unit 'on the track' at Browns Lane. A later move to customary SU breathing apparatus meant that the carburettors had to be removed and the ports taped up while car and engine came together! The engine was a short-stroke version of the famous XK 'six', the idea of using a 'four' having been shelved earlier. Unusual features were the cantilever rear leaf springing and a Panhard rod, the mountings of which were among the most important points to reinforce for competitive motoring. The significance of the 2.4 was the genuine gap it filled in

1956 works Le Mans long-nose D-type, with its compulsory full-width screen, and some of the Jaguar racing team stalwarts: (from left) Len Hayden, Bob Penney, Peter Jones, Phil Weaver, Bob Blake, Frank Rainbow, Joe Sutton and Ted Brookes.

the market—a gap that undoubtedly exists today for people who want to 'buy British'. Not only did it have a more compact engine, but the car itself was neatly-sized too—yet 'Jaguar' right through.

Jaguar's widening market grew still further when, in the aftermath of the factory fire of February 1957, the 3.4 was announced. What a combination—the bigger XK engine in a medium-sized touring car. Overnight, Jaguar had introduced an 'everyday' 120 mph saloon! It would have been to its advantage, however, if disc brakes and a Thornton Powr-Lok differential had been offered at the beginning.

Most critics of the 3.4's looks and behaviour were silenced in October 1959, when the Mark Two 2.4, 3.4, and 3.8 litre saloons appeared. Gone were the severe rear-end taper and the smallish glass area; it was a rare case—like the original SS1 but quite *un*like the Mk VII and XK 120—where the 'second edition' was more acceptable than the first. The Mark Two Jaguars were to be the staple product of Jaguar's continued ascent of the business charts throughout the 1960s. The model stayed in production for ten years in various updated forms. Its final version, the 240, lived on into the XJ era when the value was tremendous but the design's age was showing.

Variations on the theme, which led to the XJ in terms of general size and concept, were the longer and more modern-handling 3.4S and 3.8S (or S-type) saloons. The slightly unbalanced appearance was caused by investment in new rear body press-tools but not in new front ones. If that *had* to be done, it *was* done the right way round, so to speak, for the fitting of Jaguar's now-familiar independent rear suspension (with its in-board brake discs) called for more boot and rear leg-room to compensate for its encroachment. The 'second half' of the process was completed very attractively in the 420, which was given Jaguar's biggest engine (albeit in two-carburettor form) and the 'Varamatic' power steering system.

A batch of early 2.4 Jaguars at Browns Lane, 1955. This aspect of the front offices had changed considerably by 1985.

It was at this stage—late 1966—that two years of quite difficult trading began, for the XJ6 was already a well-founded rumour and yet here was Jaguar with a regular mish-mash of saloon models. In this period, which was also one of financial restraint in Britain, Jaguar people were probably too pre-occupied to be thinking about the fundamental changes that were beginning to happen rapidly in the organisation of Britain's motor industry!

In the competition field, the 2.4 would have become better-known if it had had more than one season to prove itself. It was beaten by the Mark Seven at Silverstone in its first year (1956), but Paul Frère scored a good victory with one at his home circuit, Spa-Francorchamps in Belgium. That year's RAC Rally saw Bill Bleakley take an excellent fourth place in what was the 2.4's first international event of any kind. From 1957, the 3.4 naturally took over the role of Jaguar's 'racing tourer'; as did the 3.8-litre Mark Two in 1960. These cars dominated saloon car racing until 1963, after which the combined onslaught of the American V8s and Ford's Lotus-Cortina took command. Zenith of the Mark Two's racing career was victory by Peter Nöcker in the first-ever European touring car race championship, although 3.8s went on winning endurance races right up to 1966.

In rallying, the Morley brothers and 'Nano' da Silva Ramos gave the 3.4 its greatest wins in the 'Tulip' and *Tour de France* respectively. That year, 1959, saw three 3.4s take the Monte Carlo Rally team prize. The 3.8 Mark Two gave the consistent Bernard Consten four wins in a row in the *Tour de France* (1960 to 1963), and two similar cars won Alpine Cups in 1960, driven by José Béhra and 'Bobby' Parkes. The records taken by a 3.8 at Monza—up to 10,000 miles at over 106 mph—were a worthwhile prelude to the 1963 Geneva Motor Show to which the car was taken, straight after this demonstration (which had been led by the great motorcyclist Geoff Duke), and put on display.

The first Jaguar-engineered 'Daimler' was the 2½-litre V8 saloon of 1962. It had Edward Turner's V8 engine and Jaguar Mark Two structure. It was re-named the Daimler V8-250 at a 1967 facelift that affected the Mark Two Jaguars similarly, and lived on through 1969. In 1966 the Jaguar 420 was 'badge-engineered' into the first Daimler Sovereign, announced simultaneously. The Sovereign stayed in production for a year longer, though.

Close approximations based on delivery information

Jaguar

1956-9	2.4-litre	19,400
1957-9	3.4-litre	17,340
1960-7	2.4 (Mk 2)	25,070
1960-7	3.4 (Mk 2)	28,660
1960-7	3.8 (Mk 2)	30,070
1968-9	240	4,210
1968	340	2,630
	Total	127,380

Daimler

1962-7	2½-litre V8	11,370
1968-9	V8-250	6,250
	sub total	17,620
	Grand Total	145,000

of this total—

'2.4/3.4 shape'		36,740
'Mk 2 shape' { Jaguar		90,640
{ Daimler		17,620
		145,000

Jaguar

1964-8	3.4 'S'	9,830
1964-8	3.8 'S'	15,070
1967-8	420	9,600
	Total	32,500

Daimler

1967-9	Sovereign	
	('420' type)	5,700
	Grand Total	40,200

of this total—

'modified tail'	24,900
'modified nose'	15,300
Total	40,200

Grand total 'compact' saloons   **185,200**

Notes: Approximately 2,050 Mk 2s, 850 3.8Ss, and 850 420s were assembled abroad. 760 Daimler V8-250s were fitted with manual transmission (including 700 with overdrive).

In its element—the 3.8-litre Jaguar Mark Two saloon of brilliant French driver-tactician Bernard Consten leads a two-hour race at Le Mans, just one of many individual contests that made up the Tour de France Automobile. *This was 1963—his fourth victory for Jaguar in the* Tour.

Selection from the records

900001 ⎫
to 900005 ⎭ 2.4 saloons, built in experimental dept.

900006   2.4 works car, RVC 591.
900007   2.4 works car, RVC 592 (won at Silverstone 1957, as 3.4).
912995   2.4 E.W. Rankin (Jaguar publicity chief) WKV 41.
990320   3.4 on loan to Jaguar collection by P. Frère (his father's old car).
100003   2.4 Mk 2, first demo car YHP 788.
200001   3.8 Mk 2, first demo car YHP 790.
202313   3.8 Mk 2, 'destruction test' car, 1628 VC (sold and raced successfully).
207515   3.8 Mk 2, 'County' (one-off estate car), autumn 1962, 3672 VC.
208829   3.8 Mk 2, IRS development car, becoming 3.8 'S', IB 50029.
236215   3.8 Mk 2, used for Monza record run, 1963; 7116 VC.

XVIII.   The E-type

This car's arrival upon the motoring world has often been compared with that of the XK 120 more than 12 years earlier. Like its ancestor, it was a road car that looked like a racer—and indeed it did prove its worth on the circuits. It looked more like its direct forebear, the D-type, but it had independent rear suspension—the first production Jaguar to do so—and the 3.8 litre 'gold top' XK engine, as used in the most powerful XK 150 'S' models.

The roadster and the more dramatic fixed-head coupé—Jaguar's first 'fast-back' since their SS1 Airline!—were shown at the 1961 Geneva *salon*. With racing tyres the new car could reach the magic 150 mph but, having achieved this figure, it was difficult for subsequent models—heavier and less 'slippery'—to emulate it. For similar reasons, the early car's excellent fuel consumption was never bettered by later E-types. Indeed the only real 'niggles' were the gear change and the leg-room, both of which were soon improved. Otherwise even the most cynical motorists treated the new Jaguar with reverence because, as usual, it beat the opposition flat on price alone. Whether US journalist Henry Manney's lasting tag for it—'The Greatest Crumpet-Catcher Known to Man'—was a bonus for the E-type's image or not was always a moot point! When the 4.2-litre engine and all-synchromesh gear-box were ready, the E-type got them. A third body style, the 2 + 2, appeared in the spring of 1966, and with it came the option of automatic transmission for the first time on a Jaguar sports/GT model since 1960.

The prototype (E2A) at 1960 Le Mans practice day. It is now in a private collection.

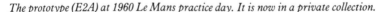

After the September announcement of the XJ6, a surprise of the 1968 London show was the last-minute appearance on the Jaguar stand of a Series Two E-type. Some of the changes on this model were a result of American 'safety' laws. Jaguar's export performance was dependent upon the E-type, for none of the 'old' saloons were being sold in the USA by this time. Finally, in March 1971, came the new Jaguar V12 engine in the Series Three E-type. The (long-wheelbase) structure was retained for the 2+2 and for an elongated open model. These cars kept the E-type magic alive although the last of them, built in 1974, were being sold well into 1975. In Britain, as the effects of inflation and the first fuel scare took hold, E-type prices were pegged while XJ6 prices began to move with the times. The E-type's price, new, never reached £4,000! The reader's attention to today's prices is commended, if only out of interest.

Competition

An unnamed Jaguar prototype (chassis E2A), was raced by the Cunningham team unsuccessfully at Le Mans in 1960. This car then ran several times in America. Its one win before being returned to the Coventry factory was by Walter Hansgen at Bridgehampton.

The true E-type, in standard guise, ran away from the opposition first time out at Oulton Park in April 1961, driven by Graham Hill, but was never a serious contender in international racing or rallying and was not promoted as such. The factory did modify an E-type considerably for John Coombs, however, and this car—usually driven by Graham Hill—led to several special E-types (with extensive use of alloys in the engine, chassis and body) being built. These are all listed overleaf. Hill had four convincing E-type wins in 1963 with Salvadori's similar machine always close but out of luck, although the latter did manage a good third place in that year's Tourist Trophy race behind two Ferraris.

In later years the E-type proved an excellent 'clubman's racer' in six-cylinder form, but it was the V12 which gained most fame when raced by Bob Tullius and Lee Mueller, with British Leyland support, in the USA between 1974 and 1976. The V12 E-type's best UK success was in 1974 when Peter Taylor (1985's UK Service Manager at Jaguar) won the production sports car championship in his own '2+2' coupé. Much faster, but not often a winner, was the V12 '2+2' with Tecalemit petrol injection and a host of other alterations, which Guy Beddington drove in 'modsports' races.

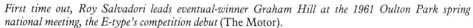

First time out, Roy Salvadori leads eventual-winner Graham Hill at the 1961 Oulton Park spring national meeting, the E-type's competition debut (The Motor).

Selection from E-type records

XK 101	1957/8, 2.4-litre alloy two-seater (pastel green body No E1A).
—	1959/60, 3 (and 3.8) litre alloy competition prototype (E2A).
850001	Production prototype (Cotswold blue, roadster body R 1001).
850002	Production prototype (Carmen red, R 1002; tried with Corvette gearbox).
850003	First demo car, 77 RW.
850004	F.R.W. England, director, 1600 RW.
850005	T.E.B. Sopwith ECD 400 (Oulton Park race winner, April 1961, G. Hill).
850006	J. Coombs, 'BUY I', then 4 WPD (developed into 'lightweight').
850007	Coombs's demo car, 9 VPD.
850008	Sir Gawaine Baillie.
850009	Peter Sargent (later given non-works fastback coupé body; fifth at Le Mans 1962).
850658	J. Coombs/works (LW conversion from 850006).
850659	Briggs Cunningham (LW = 'lightweight').
850660	Kjell Qvale, USA (LW).
850661	C.T. Atkins, 86 PJ (raced by R. Salvadori) (LW).
EC 1001	Works (semi-LW) special fastback coupé sold to E.R. Protheroe.
850662	P. Lindner (LW) 4868 WK later given works fastback coupé similar to above.
850663	P. Lumsden (LW) shared with P. Sargent; 49 FXN later fitted with non-works fastback coupé body.
850664	B. Cunningham, USA (LW).
850665	B. Cunningham, USA (LW).
850666	P. Sutcliffe, YVH 210 (LW).
850667	R. Jane, Australia (LW).
850668	R. Wilkins (LW).
850669	P. Scragg (LW).
850671	(to 850675) not used.
875001	Production prototype, LHD (roadster body 1003).
875002	(and 875003) 1961 New York show.
860001	First RHD fixed head coupé, 1VHP.
860004	For E.R. Protheroe, modified, CUT 7.
860009	For Innes Ireland.
860010	Works demo, 6162 RW.
860022	Brigadier M.W.H. Head.
860025	Hon Max Aitken.
860031	Billy Cotton.
885001	Production prototype LHD fixed head coupé.
885002	LHD 1961 Geneva demo coupé 9600 HP.
885003	(and 885004) 1961 New York show.
885005	1961 Geneva show.
885006	1961 Paris show.
(IE)16167	1968 USA-spec. 4.2 litre LHD roadster, displayed on RMS Queen Elizabeth, still virtually new, in works collection.
(IE)50001	1966 4.2 litre 2+2 demo, FVC 581D.
(IS)50001	1971 5.3 litre 2+2 demo WHP 200J.
(IS)70002	1971 5.3 litre 2+2 (LHD 'catalogue' car) TRW 920J.
EX-100	Prototype 2+2 ('Series Three') engineered to take XK engine; later sold as V12 to P. Taylor for racing (SWK 581H).
(IS)50106	Similar to above, used as six-cylinder by G. Pindar, service director, CHP 678K.
(IS)50010	1971 5.3 litre 2+2, WHP 205J (in BL collection).
(IS)2821	1975 model 5.3 roadster, Gold Medal winner Earls Court 1974, now in Coventry Transport Museum.
(IS)2823	(to 2870) Last RHD E-types built; all-black V12 roadsters.
(IS)2872	The last E-type (black roadster) HDU 555N; works collection.

Hamish Orr-Ewing with the Series Two E-type which he has owned since 1968. This great motoring enthusiast is a Jaguar plc Board member, having acted as interim Chairman during 1984-85.

E-type resumé

		Open two-seater	Fixed head coupé	2 + 2
1961-4	3.8-litre	7,820 (760)	7,670 (1,560)	—
1965-8	4.2-litre	9,550 (1,050)	7,770 (1,700)	5,600 (1,220)
1969-70	Series Two (4.2)	8,630 (690)	4,860 (910)	5,330 (870)
1971-5	Series Three (5.3)	7,990 (1,740)	—	7,300 (1,830)
	Total	33,990 (4,240)	20,300 (4,170)	18,230 (3,920)

Grand Total of E-types 72,520 (including 12,330 UK).
Note: Figures in brackets are inclusive UK ones. All on this table are to nearest ten.

XIX.   The Jaguar XJ

Today's Jaguars continue the story of motoring refinement. The XJ6 and XJ12 won the major international 'car of the year' awards, in 1969 and 1972 respectively. The first series of saloons was announced in September 1968, the second in 1973, and the third in 1979—and of course there have been many interim developments, too. The two-door models were made as Series Two only. A new saloon, code-named 'XJ40', was expected by 1987.

Jaguar's XJ-S GT model was not styled like a sports car and, when the supply of four-speed gearboxes ran-out in 1979, became the first 'sporting' Jaguar to be available only with automatic transmission. The only manual transmission saloons after 1978 were the XK-engined 3.4 and 4.2 litre Series Threes, with a fifth speed replacing the traditional bolt-on overdrive unit. An XJ-SC (cabriolet) was announced late in 1983. Its 3.6-litre, 6-cylinder engine was offered in the coupé version too. These models *did* have manual gearboxes.

Competition

For 1976 and 1977, Leyland Cars boss, Derek Whittaker, approved a scheme—dreamed-up by tuning king, Ralph Broad, and previously turned-down at Jaguar—to go motor racing with the XJ. It was intended to boost British Leyland's sales and anything else that might have needed boosting. The Group Two European Touring Car Race Championship permitted many modifications—a 'Broadspeed' speciality. Unfortunately, the weight

Above *The XJ6 and the team that created it—1968. Sir William Lyons and William Heynes stand by the car.* **Below** *John Egan, the man who led Jaguar back to self-determination, photographed at the Browns Lane offices in 1984, shortly before a major rebuild of the Coventry headquarters, completed in 1985* (Coventry Evening Telegraph).

penalty of the two-door XJ12 brought a new problem for each one that seemed solved, and the team's record was disastrous. The car that had been meant to walk over the BMW CSLs for two whole seasons, started in eight races (one in 1976 and seven in 1977), led each time (usually with two cars running), and came out of the programme with a second and a fourth place for the record books. It was a wildly costly operation, even at a time when Jaguar 'value for money' seemed to be going out of fashion. When it was clear that the money was gone for ever, and the cars were still not winners, Whittaker ordered a retreat.

In the late 1970s and early 1980s (prior to the XJR-5 project referred to in Chapter 16) Bob Tullius' Group 44 campaigned the XJ-S with great success in the USA. It was not until 1982 that the opportunity came to race Jaguars at international level in Europe, with the introduction of 'Group A' for four-seaters. The European Touring Car Championship series looked like remaining a BMW monopoly, despite the new formula which allowed fewer modifications than Group 2. Then racing driver and businessman Tom Walkinshaw made a study of the XJ-S, and the result was greeted favourably by John Egan and his technical chief Jim Randle.

The TWR-Motul XJ-S won four major races in 1982, including the Nürburgring 6-hour. This led to official works backing for a two-car team in 1983, during which the opposition was stronger; this time the Jaguars scored five ETC victories, and only niggling problems and mistakes prevented Walkinshaw from taking the championship. In 1984 with a three-car team, he took the title, having led the points table from start to finish of the twelve-race series. Highlight of the season was the victory by Walkinshaw, Win Percy, and Hans Heyer of Germany—a former 'ETC' champion—at Spa-Francorchamps in July 1984. This was the first win for Jaguar in a major 24-hour race for 27 years, and it happened in the very week that Jaguar shares went on sale once again. What a week *that* was . . . in a new record year.

Jaguar XJ-S and BMW 635CSi—rivals on the race track, as in the showroom. Here, Chuck Nicholson, Tom Walkinshaw's co-driver in 1983, leads their greatest rival, Helmut Kelleners, at Vallelunga.

Deliveries of XJ-type four-door models

Fiscal Year	Jaguar 6-cyl	Daimler 6-cyl	Jaguar 12-cyl	Daimler 12-cyl
1969	8,085	6	–	–
1970	17,525	2,695	–	–
1971	23,546	5,158	–	–
1972	14,885	4,074	326	70
1973	14,850	3,206	2,894	809
	(Series Two) 1,656	(Series Two) 291	(Series Two) 168	(Series Two) 21
1974	18,270	4,282	4,744	1,560
1975	14,229	3,800	2,239	665
1976*	15,440	3,843	3,283	579
1977	10,956	3,393	1,913	404
1978	15,422	4,178	3,284	908
1979	1,528	288	429	155
	(Series Three) 6,146	(Series Three) 2,260	(Series Three) 937	(Series Three) 522
1980	9,836	2,747	814	604
1981	10,216	1,294	457	415
1982	14,422	2,654	518	835
1983	17,412	3,206	341	1,668
1984	19,578	4,579	1,509	1,005
'Series one'	78,891	15,139	3,220	879
Series Two	77,501	20,075	16,060	4,292
Series Three	77,410	16,740	4,576	5,049
Totals (at 1/1/85)	233,802	51,954	23,856	10,220

Deliveries of XJ-type two-door models

Fiscal Year	Jaguar XJ6 C	Daimler Sovereign	Jaguar XJ12 C	Daimler Double-six	Jaguar XJ-S 5.3 (manual)	XJ-S 5.3 (automatic)	XJ-S 3.6 (manual) Coupé	XJ-S 3.6 (manual) Cabriolet
1974	6	–	9	–	–	–		
1975	1,968	367	493	48	4	213		
1976*	2,659	663	979	159	130	3,890		
1977	1,835	638	339	175	143	3,718		
1978	73	8	42	26	63	3,154		
1979	–	–	–	–	12	2,402		
1980	–	–	–	–	–	1,131		
1981	–	–	–	–	–	1,252		
1982	–	–	–	–	–	3,348		
1983	–	–	–	–	–	4,457	80	11
1984	–	–	–	–	–	5,813	474	178
Totals	6,541	1,676	1,862	408	352	29,378	554	189

XJ resumé to January 1 1985 (Jaguar and Daimler)

Four-door 6-cylinder	285,756
Two-door 6-cylinder (complete)	8,217
Four-door 12-cylinder	34,076
Two-door 12-cylinder (complete)	2,270
XJ-S coupé 12-cylinder	29,730
XJ-S/XJ-SC 6-cylinder	743

Note: All engine-size, wheelbase, and 'Vanden Plas' variations are included above.

**1976 was a 'long' year, from October 1 1975 to December 31 1976. Since then, the financial year has become the calendar year.*

Above *Avon Coachwork of Warwick and Lynx Engineering of Sussex are two British firms to have offered drophead coupés and estate cars based on Jaguar XJ models. Here Jaguar's President and founder takes an interest in an XJ12C conversion by Avon.*

Below *Announced in the autumn of 1983, the 3.6-litre XJ-SC was the first Jaguar to be offered from the works with a soft top since the E-type's demise in early 1975.*

American-built XJR-5 competition prototype, seen winning the 1984 Miami Grand Prix.

Selection from 'XJ' records

(IL) 1001	4.2-litre XJ6 production prototype (automatic) MVC 202G.
(IL) 1006	4.2-litre XJ6 production prototype (overdrive) MWK 22G.
(IL) 1370	Sir William Lyons' regular car PHP 42G; in works collection.
(IL) 2079	Tested with 3,565 cc Jaguar V8 engine; PKV 666G.
(IL) 2927	Tested with 5,343 cc Jaguar V12 engine, RHP 133H, later supplied to Silverstone as fire-tender.
(IL) 3777	Tested with 3,565 cc Jaguar V8 engine, RRW 513H.
(IL) 4449	Another XJ6 fitted with V12 engine in 1969, for Sir William Lyons.
(IL) 5866	2.8-litre XJ6 for H. Mundy, RKV 799H (3.4 engine and five-speed gearbox).
(IP) 1001	First production XJ12, RHD, BWK 418K.
(2J) 1855	1975 XJ 4.2C, used by P. Craig, later in works collection.
(2R) 3757	1975 XJ 12L used by H. Mundy (6.4-litre engine and Jaguar five-speed gearbox) HRW 75N.
(2W) 1017	1975 XJ-S kept by Jaguar in works collection.
(2S) 11348	1978 Sovereign saloon kept at Radford works as example of modern Daimler (Series Two).
(2G) 1604	1978 XJ 5.3C, last 'coupé' built, kept in 'Heritage' collection.

XX.   Home and export table

These figures show the total quantities of SS and Jaguar delivered, as at January 1985. They include 'Jaguar' Daimlers from their introduction in 1962. 'Traditional' Daimlers (ie: SP 250s and Majestics) are not included, except for the last few Majestic Majors (1965 to 1968), final assembly of which took place at Browns Lane rather than the Radford works.

At two points, asterisked, changes in the financial year should be noted, as they resulted in two artificially-long 'years'. Sir William Lyons, Jaguar's founder, retired in 1972 after two record-breaking years. The new record figures, for 1984, do not include 105 prototypes which were completed that year.

Deliveries

Year ending	Home	Export	Total	Notes on passenger car business
1932 (July 31)	736	40	776 ⎫	SS cars only (ie, Swallow
1933 (July 31)	1,394	131	1,525 ⎬	bodies and sidecars
1934 (July 31)	1,574	219	1,793 ⎭	*not* included).
1935 (July 31)	1,507	213	1,720	SS cars only.
1936 (July 31)	2,283	186	2,469	SS and SS Jaguar cars.
1937 (July 31)	3,311	243	3,554	SS Jaguar cars only.
1938 (July 31)	2,021	188	2,209	Major change in manufacture.
1939 (July 31)	5,126	252	5,378	Production problems overcome.
1940 (July 31)	817	82	899	The 'Phoney War'.

(War-time activities detailed separately on page 215.)

Year ending	Home	Export	Total	Notes on passenger car business
1946 (July 31)	816	316	1,132	Less than 12 months' output.
1947 (July 31)	3,393	949	4,342	LHD introduced.
1948 (July 31)	2,013	2,173	4,186	Exports exceed UK deliveries.
1949 (July 31)	2,089	1,224	3,313	New model range introduced.
1950 (July 31)	2,721	3,926	6,647	XK 120 production begins.
1951 (July 31)	1,532	4,273	5,805	Mark Seven introduced.
1952 (July 31)	1,001	7,978	8,979	Move to new factory.
1953 (July 31)	2,471	7,643	10,114	Continuation of export drive.
1954 (July 31)	4,796	5,335	10,131	⎫ Strengthening of
1955 (July 31)	4,462	5,438	9,900	⎭ home market.
1956 (July 31)	5,305	6,847	12,152	2.4 saloon introduced.
1957 (July 31)	6,338	6,614	12,952	⎫ Expansion facilities
1958 (July 31)	8,375	9,177	17,552	⎭ following 1957 fire.
1959 (July 31)	10,400	10,476	20,876	
1960 (July 31)	9,664	9,677	19,341	Mark Two saloons introduced.
1961 (July 31)	13,844	10,174	24,018	E-type introduced.
1962 (July 31)	10,895	11,135	22,030	Mark Ten introduced.
1963 (July 31)	12,754	12,235	24,989	First 'Jaguar' Daimlers introduced.
1964 (July 31)	14,142	10,206	24,348	S-type saloons introduced.
1965 (July 31)	15,041	9,560	24,601	('Majestics' included from 1965.)
1966 (July 31)	13,838	12,098	25,936	Last year of full independence.
1967 (July 31)	10,624	12,026	22,650	'BMH Year'.
1968 (July 31)	14,515	9,800	24,315	BL's formation.
1969 (Sept 30)	12,239	14,970	27,209★	(Aug 1 1968 to Sept 30 1969.)
1970 (Sept 30)	12,001	18,422	30,423	XJ6 in full swing.
1971 (Sept 30)	14,183	18,406	32,589	*Record year for old company.*
1972 (Sept 30)	11,814	11,174	22,988	Strike (ending of piecework.)
1973 (Sept 30)	12,932	16,883	29,815	'England Year'.
1974 (Sept 30)	15,925	16,640	32,565	'Robinson Year'.
1975 (Sept 30)	11,984	12,311	24,295	'Ryder Year'.
1976 (Dec 31)	12,441	19,462	31,903★	(Oct 1 1975 to Dec 31 1976.)
1977 (Dec 31)	10,564	13,124	23,688	(Calendar year from now on.)
1978 (Dec 31)	13,020	14,326	27,346	⎫ 'JRT Years'.
1979 (Dec 31)	7,668	7,193	14,861	⎭
1980 (Dec 31)	5,890	9,372	15,262	Appointment of John Egan.
1981 (Dec 31)	5,006	8,806	13,812	Quality before quantity.
1982 (Dec 31)	6,822	15,112	21,934	⎫ Full Jaguar management
1983 (Dec 31)	6,560	20,771	27,331	⎭ team operational.
1984 (Dec 31)	7,557	25,798	33,355	*Record year for new company.*
	356,404	413,604	770,008	Total SS/Jaguar deliveries, as at January 1 1985.

XXI. Jaguar—value and achievement

August 1 to July 31	Typical UK car prices (inc tax) (Model Year)	Major Competition wins (calendar year)	New cars delivered	Profit after Tax
1945	(Jaguar Cars Ltd, formed; sidecar business sold.)		NIL	1,413
1946	Saloons '1½' £684, '2½' £889, '3½' £991	—	1,132	£22,852
1947	Saloons '1½' £787, '2½' £991, '3½' £1,099	—	4,342	£113,446
1948	Saloons '1½' £865, '2½' £1,089, '3½' £1,199	Alpine Cup (Appleyard, SS 100)	4,186	£136,261
1949	Mk V saloon or drophead '2½' £1,189, '3½' £1,263	First Silverstone Production car Race (Johnson, XK120)	3,313	£63,469
1950	Mk V Saloon or drophead '2½' £1,247, '3½' £1,263	Alpine Cup (Appleyard, XK); Tourist Trophy (Moss, XK)	6,647	£159,198
1951	Mk VII £1,276; XK 120 £1,263	Two Alpine Cups (Appleyard, Habisreutinger, XKs); RAC & Tulip Rallies (Appleyard, XK); Liège-Rome-Liège Rally (Claes, XK); Le Mans 24-hr Race (Walker/ Whitehead, C); TT (Moss, C)	5,805	£149,505
1952	Mk VII £1,694; XK 120 open £1,678, fixed head £1,694	Two Alpine Cups (Gatsonides, Appleyard, XK); Reims Sports Car GP (Moss, C.); Jersey Road Race (Stewart. C.)	8,979	£156,016
1953	Mk VII £1,775; XK 120 open £1,759, fixed head £1,775	Three Alpine Cups (Appleyard, Gatsonides, Mansbridge, XKs); Le Mans (Hamilton/Rolt, C); Reims 12 hr Race (Moss/ Whitehead, C); Acropolis Rally (Papamichail, XK); RAC Rally (Appleyard, XK)	10,114	£190,364
1954	Mk VII £1,616; XK 120 open £1,601, fixed head £1,644, drophead £1,660	Reims 12-hr Race (Wharton/Whitehead, D)	10,131	£217,085
1955	Mk VII M £1,616; XK 140 open £1,598, fixed head £1,616, drophead £1,644	Sebring 12-hr Race (Hawthorn/ Walters, D); Le Mans (Hawthorn/ Bueb, D); Watkins Glen GP (Johnston, D)	9,900	£260,343
1956	Mk VII M £1,711, 2.4 £1,344; XK 140 open £1,692, fixed head £1,711, drophead £1,741	Monte Carlo Rally (Adams/Bigger /Johnston, Mk VII); Le Mans (Flockhart/Sanderson, D); Reims 12-hr Race (Hamilton/Bueb, D); Watkins Glen GP (Constantine, D)	12,152	£326,676
1957	Mk VIII £1,830, 2.4 £1,431, 3.4 £1,672; XK 150 fixed head £1,940, drophead £1,970	Le Mans (Flockhart/Bueb,D); Watkins Glen GP (Hansgen, D)	12,952	£315,321
1958	Mk VIII £1,830, 2.4 £1,495, 3.4 £1,672; XK 150 fixed head £1,940, drophead £1,970	Tenth annual Silverstone success— two saloon race winners (Hawthorn, Hansgen, 3.4s)	17,552	£624,337

August 1 to July 31	Typical UK car prices (inc tax) (Model Year)	Major Competition wins (calendar year)	August 1 to July 31	
			New cars delivered	Profit after Tax
1959	Mk IX £1,995, 2.4 £1,495, 3.4 £1,672; XK 150 open & fixed head £1,940; XK 150S £2,187	Tour de France Automobile (Ramos, 3.4); Tulip Rally (Morley, 3.4)	20,876	£1,385,059
1960	Mk IX £1,884; Mk 2 £1,534 (2.4), £1,669 (3.4), £1,779 (3.8); XK 150S (3.8) drophead £2,204	Two Alpine Cups (Béhra, Parkes, 3.8s); Tour de France (Consten, 3.8)	19,341	£1,022,043
1961	Mk IX £1,884; E-type open £2,098, fixed head £2,197	Nürburgring 6-hr Race (Lindner/ Nöcker, 3.4); Tour de France (Consten, 3.8)	24,018	£1,144,541
1962	Mk X £2,256; Mk 2 £1,489 (2.4), £1,619 (3.4), £1,727 (3.8); E-type open £2,036, fixed head £2,132	Nürburgring 6-hr (Lindner/ Nöcker, 3.8) & 12 hr Races (Lindner/Walter, 3.8); Tour de France (Consten, 3.8); Nöcker wins ETC title.	22,030	£1,334,652
1963	Mk X £2,022; Mk 2 £1,348 (2.4), £1,557 (3.8); E-type open £1,829, fixed head £1,913	Nürburgring 6 & 12-hr Races (Lindner/Nöcker, 3.8); New Zealand 6-hr Race (Archibald/ Shelly, 3.8); Tour de France (Consten, 3.8)	24,989	£1,235,075
1964	S-type saloon £1,669 (3.4); S-type saloon £1,759 (3.8)	Coupe de Paris GT Race (P. Sutcliffe E)	24,348	£1,458,171
1965	Mk X (4.2) £2,199; E-type (4.2) open £1,934, fixed head £2,033	New Zealand 6-hr Race (Ward/ Coppins, 3.8)	24,601	£1,663,180
1966	Mk X limousine £2,393; E-type '2 + 2' £2,245	New Zealand 6-hr Race (Archibald/Shelly, 3.8)	25,936	£1,517,492
1967	420G £2,238; 420 £1,930	(*NB: This was the first year of British Motor Holdings, and the final year of Jaguar's annual report.*)	22,650	£1,151,035

Note: Daimler car (but not Daimler or Guy commercial vehicle) deliveries are included from 1962. Apparent price fluctuations, indicated in the 1950s, and 1960s, were usually caused by changes in car tax.

Footnote: The BL years

1968 to 1980	XJ6 (1969) 4.2 £2,254; XJ6L (1972) 4.2 £3,415; XJ12 (1972) 5.3 £3,672; XJ12L (1972) 5.3 £3,994; V12E-type open (1971) £3,319, (1975) £3,743; XJ-S (1976) £8,900.	Several North American championships and many races won by E-type and XJ-S; Bob Tullius most successful driver in the 1970s.	See page 241	No profit and loss figures issued

The freedom years

From 1980 to date	XK (1985) 4.2 £16,595; XJ (1985) 5.3HE £21,995; XJ-S (1985) 5.3HE £23,385; XJ-SC (1985) 3.6 £20,756.	Further success by Tullius and his Group 44 team; Walkinshaw (XJ-S) wins 1984 ETC title.	See page 241	For latest financial information see Chapter 16

The racing programme helped maintain Jaguar's charisma in the US during the 1970s, when there were problems in the UK. Here Bob Tullius drives his group 44 team's first Jaguar, a V12 E-type, on a celebratory lap after one of its many victories, culminating in Tullius becoming US National Champion for 1975 in his SCCA class, defeating hordes of Corvette drivers. Beside him is his chief engineer (still a consultant to Group 44) Brian Fuerstenau, and on the left is Michael Dale, Vice-President of Jaguar Cars Inc today. Making the roadster a '3 + 2' are Ernest Speck and (behind Dale) Jim McCrocklin.

XXII.   Exports in the 1980s

In five years between the first and second editions of this book, Jaguar was rescued from British Leyland (in whose custody it had never been allowed to develop) to become a proud, independent British business again. Between 1980 and 1985 the scale of Jaguar's problems, related to quality and productivity, was reduced radically. The story of this return to independence and prosperity is told in Chapter 16 of the main text, in which the main trading progress is also recorded (see page 184). The purpose of this final section of the new edition is to highlight the market successes. The simplest indication of the sharp rise in output can be found on page 241.

Progress in the establishment of a reduced number of caring companies to handle the Jaguar and Daimler franchises has been rapid. The home and overseas markets are covered on pages 179 and 180. Here, however, it may be added that a return to specialist representation was, by 1985, helping to restore the Continental market as a major contributor to Jaguar exports. As Director of European Operations, seasoned campaigner John Morgan (who had spent his later BL days in Japan) smoothed the path in many countries where interest in the marque had waned. Examples of renewed links with pre-BL and Jaguar friends occurred in Italy, where Bepi Koelliker in the north and Fattori & Montani in the south resumed direct trading with Coventry—as did Carlos Salamanca for Spain, soon to be admitted to EEC membership. Likewise Jacques de Clippel of Antwerp, who had kept close ties with Jaguar ever since the early export boom days, became the new importer for the independent new Jaguar company in Belgium. In addition to Germany (mentioned in Chapter 16), new Dutch and French importers carried the Jaguar name; moreover, the headquarters of Jaguar France were (for the first time in many years) well situated in the heart of Paris. 'Streag' of Switzerland was associated with the company founded more than 60 years earlier by Emil Frey—William Lyons' original overseas Swallow agent.

In the Middle East, the Far East and in Australasia, the Jaguar name had been making great strides; but it was in North America that the most dramatic progress was made.

North America

Over the years there have been several occasions when the very existence of Jaguar depended upon the receptiveness of the United States for its motor cars. The stories of the abortive attempt to sell SSs there in the 1930s and of the later successes have been covered in the main text. On an adjacent page is a year by year record of Jaguar's North American achievements, including deliveries of cars to Canada. Some of the 'dips' are more easily explicable than others. (Reference to the Part One text, and to the table on page 241, should help.)

The extraordinary recent achievement in the USA began when John Egan opened his heart to the American dealers. Their response in 1981 led Egan to concentrate the Jaguar revival effort upon their territory, and the result was dramatic.

Graham Whitehead, his deputy Michael Dale, and John Mackie in Canada (all expatriate Britons)—and their staffs—put all their experience into co-ordinating that effort, while the board of Jaguar Cars Ltd in Coventry organised delivery of the goods. John Egan cites the areas of manufacturing and quality, led by Michael Beasley and David Fielden respectively, for particular recognition in this recovery programme. As can be seen from the table, deliveries (that is to say: despatches from the works) to the USA exceeded 10,000 for the first time ever in 1982; and in 1983 they passed the 15,000 mark.

In 1984, as other markets were being re-developed, the North American success story was maintained. Unusually, December turned out to be a record USA sales month, in which Jaguar Cars Inc's dealers sold 2,139 cars. This represented 1,689 XJ6 saloons (previous best: 1,507 in March 1984) and 450 XJ-S 5.3-litre coupés (previous best: 378 in June 1984). A year earlier, 17,000 sales for the year had seemed to some an optimistic forecast; as it was, 18,000 units were surpassed. The position of the dollar against the pound was, of course, highly favourable—but it was equally clear that the American buyer had responded to the enthusiasm of a streamlined dealer network selling and servicing good, reliable motor cars. 'We expect 1985 to be another good year for Jaguar,' reported Graham Whitehead in his first 1985 press comuniqué. 'Our forecast for US sales is 20,000 cars.' (1984 was also a record for Canada, with the far from insignificant figure of 1,000-plus units sold.)

Back in Coventry, 1985 production was off to a good start, with Browns Lane plant director Walter Turner reporting a record 3,930 cars completed up to and including February 1 1985, but excluding January 1 and 2. Continuation of this performance could be expected to lead to further records. (37,600 units was the 1985 production target.)

Through racing the E-type and the XJ-S, Group 44 and Jaguar developed the V12 engine into a regular winner on the track. In 1982, a mid-engined V12-powered prototype was built by Group 44 to Lee Dykstra's drawings. By the end of 1984 the XJR-5 had scored five victories and numerous high placings in the highly competitive IMSA race series, and had made a tentative and impressive Le Mans debut. A return to Le Mans was anticipated in 1985.

Further news from Browns Lane in February 1985 included expectation of a transfer of limousine production from Browns Lane, where space was once again at a premium. It was thought that it would be re-assembled at Radford—better known locally (and therefore appropriately) as 'The Daimler'—under the direction of the veteran Jack Randle and the man expected to succeed him, Eynon Thomas.

The Castle Bromwich body plant, under Gerry Lawlor, continued to supply Browns Lane with top-quality goods, and there was talk of further significant improvements to come, especially in painting techniques. Thus could Jaguar be seen to be serving its customers around the world with one of the greatest of British products.

Analysis of Jaguar's three best years, in terms of output, demonstrates the significance of the North American market and how it increased dramatically.

Financial Year from:	October 1970	October 1973	January 1984
To (inclusive):	September 1971	September 1974	December 1984
Deliveries for USA/Canada:	5,717	6,996	19,425
Deliveries for all export markets:	18,406	16,640	25,798
Total deliveries:	32,589	32,565	33,355

Breakdown of the above totals, by model, is as follows:

Jaguar saloons:	**XJ (first series)**		**XJ Series Two**		**XJ Series Three**	
	2.8	4,960	2.8	169	3.4	861
	4.2	16,486	4.2	15,523	4.2	18,717
	5.3	N/A	5.3	4,753	5.3	1,509
	Sub-total:	21,446	Sub-total:	20,445	Sub-total:	21,087

Jaguar coupés/sports:		**E-type**		**E-type**	**XJ-S/XJ-SC**	
	4.2 open	348	—	—	—	—
	4.2 coupé	389	—	—	3.6 cabriolet	474
	4.2 2+2	3	—	—	3.6 coupé	178
	5.3 open	133	5.3 open	3,405	5.3 coupé	5,813
	5.3 2+2	2,691	5.3 2+2	2	—	—
	Sub-total:	3,564	Sub-total:	3,407	Sub-total:	6,465

Jaguar XJ CKD:	Sub-total:	2,100	Sub-total:	2,584	Sub-total:	NIL

Total Jaguar	**(1970-71):**	27,110	**(1973-74):**	26,436	**(1984):**	27,553

Daimler saloons:	**(First series)**		**Series Two**		**Series Three**	
(XJ types)	2.8	1,089	—	—	—	—
	4.2	4,069	4.2	4,282	4.2	4,578
	5.3	N/A	5.3	1,560	5.3	1,055
	Sub-total:	5,158	Sub-total:	5,842	Sub-total:	5,633

Daimler limousines:	4.2	265	4.2	248	4.2	135
	Chassis only	56	Chassis only	56	Chassis only	34
	Sub-total:	321	Sub-total:	304	Sub-total:	169

Total Daimler	**(1970-71):**	5,479	**(1973-74):**	6,129	**(1984):**	5,802
Grand totals for year	**(1970-71):**	32,589	**(1973-74):**	32,565	**(1984):**	33,355

Notes: The 1984 total includes 969 cars with manual transmission, of which 323 were XJ saloon types. The total does NOT include 105 sundry prototypes produced in 1984, and 'delivered' for test or legislative purposes.

1984 represents an all-time record in terms of total despatches and exports. The outstanding development of the North American market has been the key to Jaguar's remarkable recovery during the early 1980s. A separate table indicates the marque's performance in the USA/Canada.

Post-war deliveries to USA and Canada

Financial Year (to end of)	Despatched to USA	Canada
July 1947	7	0
July 1948	245	0
July 1949	135	12
July 1950	826	224
July 1951	1,552	182
July 1952	3,243	96
July 1953	5,218	275
July 1954	1,834	204
July 1955	3,239	182
July 1956	3,871	346
July 1957	3,592	347
July 1958	4,607	510
July 1959	5,596	808
July 1960	4,934	523
July 1961	3,422	609
July 1962	5,716	445
July 1963	4,113	211
July 1964	4,037	222
July 1965	3,669	237
July 1966	5,418	351
July 1967	6,702	323
July 1968	4,429	382
Sept 1969	6,833	418
Sept 1970	7,384	433
Sept 1971	5,500	217
Sept 1972	4,734	297
Sept 1973	7,652	475
Sept 1974	6,483	513
Sept 1975	5,736	400
Dec 1976	8,688	727
Dec 1977	3,503	324
Dec 1978	5,676	518
Dec 1979	2,943	242
Dec 1980	2,896	237
Dec 1981	5,192	406
Dec 1982	10,502	333
Dec 1983	15,059	495
Dec 1984	18,366	1,059

Above *Three of the first post-war exports to the USA: 1948 3½-litre Jaguar saloons on the Southampton waterfront.*
Below *Graham Wright Whitehead, President of Jaguar Cars Inc and UK Jaguar board member, with best-selling $32,000 1985 Jaguar XJ6, photographed against a Manhattan background.*

Notes: Financial Year changes meant unrealistic figures for 1969 and 1976. Jaguar Cars North America and Jaguar Cars of Eastern Canada were created in the mid-1950s. Jaguar Cars Inc was operating in 1958. 57 SSs (including ten for Canada) had gone to North America pre-war.

Index

Note: This general index has been compiled for use with the main narrative (ie, up to page 184 *only*). Many subjects are mentioned again in Part Two (from page 185 onwards), in which the separate headings are, however, considered to occur frequently enough to constitute an index in their own right.